SHAKESPEARE'S ANALOGICAL SCENE

Joan Hartwig

PARODY AS STRUCTURAL SYNTAX

Shakespeare's Analogical Scene

University of Nebraska Press

Lincoln and London

Publication of this book was
aided by a grant from
the National Endowment for
the Humanities.

Portions of the following
chapters have previously
been published in different
form: Chapter 3 as "Macbeth,
the Murderers, and the
Diminishing Parallel,"
Yearbook of English Studies 3
(1973): 39–43; Chapter 6 as
"Feste's 'Whirligig' and the
Comic Providence of *Twelfth
Night*," *ELH* 40 (1973): 501-13;
Chapter 7 as "Parodic
Polonius," *Texas Studies in
Literature and Language* 13
(1971): 215–25; and Chapter 8
as "Cloten, Autolycus, and
Caliban: Bearers of Parodic
Burdens," in *Shakespeare's
Romances Reconsidered,*
ed. Carol McGinnis Kay and
Henry E. Jacobs (Lincoln:
University of Nebraska Press,
1978), pp. 91–103, and *"The
Tempest:* Parallels and
Parodies," in *The Shakespeare
Plays: A Study Guide for the
Second Season* (University
Extension at the University
of California, San Diego,
1980 season), pp. 140–49.

Library of Congress
Cataloging in
Publication Data is
given on last page

TO MY MOTHER,

MOTLEY, MIRANDA,

MISTY, & JACK

Contents

Plates

Acknowledgments

The dramatic use of parody has intrigued me for years, and this book examines how parody as a particular kind of analogical structure increases the audience's pleasure in Shakespeare's plays. For encouraging my interest in parody, even while he urged me to find a better word, I am grateful to Lawrence J. Ross, whose teaching and direction have exercised and strengthened my ability to enjoy Shakespeare. Many others have encouraged that delight, and some have directly helped me to shape the final version of this book. Jackson I. Cope, Jeanne A. Roberts, and Thelma N. Greenfield have been generous with their time and comments on the entire manuscript, and Stanley Stewart, Mary Lynda Livingston, and John T. Shawcross have offered helpful suggestions on parts of it; for their criticism I am grateful. The experience of working in the library and with the members of the staff at the Folger Shakespeare Library, the Huntington Library, and the British Library has been exhilarating. The photography department of the Folger Library has been especially kind in reproducing the emblems from Ripa, Whitney, and Peacham that appear herein.

I would like to thank the National Endowment for the Humanities for a fellowship that allowed me to concentrate on this work initially and the University of Kentucky for a sabbatical year in which to pursue it. I also appreciate permission from the editors of *Texas Studies in Literature and Language, Yearbook of English Studies* and their publisher, MHRA, the *Journal of English Literary History,* the University of Nebraska Press, and *The*

Shakespeare Plays Telecourse of the University Extension at the University of California to include parts of essays that first appeared in their publications.

For citations throughout I have used Alfred Harbage's edition of *William Shakespeare: The Complete Works* (Baltimore, Md: Penguin Books, 1969).

SHAKESPEARE'S ANALOGICAL SCENE

Chapter 1

DIFFERENT KINDS OF ANALOGICAL SCENES

Analogy is one of the oldest as well as one of the most fascinating forms of reasoning, having always possessed a mysterious power to create a sense of wholeness in human perception of the world. Renaissance dramatists were exquisitely tuned in to their audiences' awareness of the inherent analogies between the stage and the world of everyday existence, and they energized that analogical sensibility with their parallel scenic structures.

In his use of analogical scenic structures Shakespeare is not unique, but he is exemplary. His plays clearly demonstrate what was a dramaturgical commonplace for his age: scenes tend to progress because of their analogical relationships with what precedes and what follows as much as by narrative causality. For example, when Cinna the Poet moves onto the stage in III.iii of *Julius Caesar*, there is no narrative connection with III.ii and IV.i, yet the action, phrased in recognizably comic rhetoric, has a deeply significant analogical connection with these scenes. Likewise, when Peter catechizes the Musicians in IV.v of *Romeo and Juliet*, this action has no necessary place in the narrative sequence of events, yet it functions as an alleviator of melancholy and as a parodic recapitulation of the play's dueling principle. It is often considered a barrier in facilitating the narrative pace, and usually part or all of that section of the scene is omitted.[1] When modern producers of Shakespeare's plays are puzzled by the presence of certain scenes (or think that their audience will be), they use the cutter's knife. Their deletions imply that modern audiences no longer have a pervasive operating assumption about the power of analogy.

The dictionaries of Shakespeare's contemporaries most often defined "analogy" as "proportion" and "convenience" or "correspondence."[2] Francis Bacon used the term this way in *The Advancement of Learning*: "For natural prudence, or the part operative of natural philosophy, we will divide it into three parts, experimental, philosophical, and magical: which three parts active have a *correspondence and analogy* with the three parts speculative, natural history, physic, and metaphysic."[3] Modern usage is similar, although we rarely use "convenience" to mean "to come together." Nonetheless, we still employ "analogy" in the sense of its Greek root, "*ana+logos,*" to mean things that possess a similar reason or relationship, and the idea of "correspondence" between things equivalent or parallel is central in our concept of "analogy."

Francis Fergusson, in his influential study of *Hamlet* as "The Analogy of Action," calls attention to the problem that in modern critical usage the term "analogy" has a protean and slippery application. Fergusson employs the term, which he derives from St. Thomas Aquinas, to talk about relationships between concrete elements that we perceive directly in watching and in reading a play.[4] My use of analogy, like Fergusson's, attempts to define dramatic context through its interacting parts. My chief concern is with the way particular scenes are related to others within a play not only by verbal and thematic connections but also through staging. This approach ultimately connects these scenes analogically to the play's main action, what Fergusson calls "the supreme analogue" (p. 116), but it begins with particular scenes in plays that have often proved puzzles to audiences.

For the scenes I examine in this study, part of the puzzle's explanation involves "parody." Like the concept of analogy, the concept of parody—one kind of analogy—is difficult to talk about, primarily because modern usage has blurred the distinctions between it and other similar terms. In 1965, for instance, Dean Frye called critical attention to the overuse of "parody" to suggest any "parallel" and to call for at least a reconsideration of the term's misapplication. Richard Levin quickly seconded Frye's distinction that "reduction" is not the only effect that "parody" creates. Levin's attempt to redress the imbalance imposed by "parody-hunters" was to reinstate the term "foil" for clown subplots. Both Frye and Levin seem to be arguing *for* the double function of parody—to heighten as well as to comically reduce the thing imitated—but both seem reluctant to allow the word "parody" to convey such meaning.[5] Nine years later, Leo Salingar, in *Shakespeare and the Traditions of Comedy,* still had not found a better word than parody to suggest what he wants to say about Aristophanes:

And this is more than parody. While strict parody is purely reductive, mimicking the original so as to make it seem ridiculous and confining itself within the bounds of mimicry, Aristophanes will turn the similitude round for an unexpected but searching comment on social realities, to treat it freely as a springboard for new fantasies of his own.[6]

I find no necessity to use the term so "strictly" as these critics insist. Traditionally, "parody" has a larger scope. Derived from the Greek word "paroidia," it originally meant a song placed beside or against. John Florio includes the Latin version of the word in his 1598 *A Worlde of Wordes:* "parodía, a turning of a verse by altering some wordes." In his 1611 dictionary, *Queen Anna's New World of Words,* Florio adds the term "paródo, the beginning of the Chorus his speech,"[7] which derives from another Greek word, "parodos," that designated the side entrance into the Greek theater's "orchestra" as well as the first song sung by the chorus after entering. Other dictionaries of the period seem to omit both terms until Samuel Johnson gives "parody" this definition: "A kind of writing, in which the words of an author or his thoughts are taken, and by slight change adapted to some new purpose."[8] To illustrate the term's usage, Johnson quotes Alexander Pope's comment, "I have translated, or rather *parodied,* a poem of Horace, in which I introduce you advising me." In other words, "parody" as "imitation" was not considered in the earlier usage to contain only the "stricter" sense of ridicule.[9]

Not only because of its earlier usage do I use "parody" to mean more than its modern "stricter" sense, but also because, even in modern perceptions, parodies seem to have a twofold effect. The original scene, action, gesture, or poem initially is reduced to comically disproportionate terms, often simply by maneuvering the figurative into the literal. In the next instant, however, the original is recalled through the reduced terms of its imitation, and in the process of the original's being re-seen as it was meant to be seen, it regains authority and fresh meaning. The function of parody is more complex than travesty or burlesque (with which the term is often equated) in that it not only causes us to see the "serious" action replayed in reduced terms: it also asks us to rethink both actions in light of each other's values. Most often, those values, held as absolutes at either end of a spectrum, undergo important modifications because of their parallel relationships. "Burlesque" draws in and limits meaning to its proportions, whereas "parody," after the initial reduction, leads out of itself and lends a fresh perspective on that which it imitates.[10] The parody emphasizes similarities between the original and the imitation; yet the difference in levels of enactment is so great that it activates the potentialities of meaning in the original. Because of this almost automatic re-viewing process it promotes, the parody heightens and expands, even as it qualifies, the meaning of that which it imitates.

The larger subsuming category for the scenes discussed in this study is "analogy"—used to identify scenes that are alike. Within this semblance, however, contrasts breed, especially in the parodic scene. The sense of correspondence is basic to all kinds of analogy, but parody is a special kind of parallel. Parody's distinct power is to reduce the imitated scene, action, speech, or gesture to simplistic terms before it causes the viewer to reconsider the original in a clearer though more complex way. To examine the difference between "parallel" and "parody," consider the Gloucester plot of *King Lear* and the Polonius plot of *Hamlet*. In the Gloucester plot, the audience is presented with actions that anticipate as well as recapitulate the central action much the same way that Polonius's actions do for Claudius's actions. But whereas the Gloucester plot makes physical what Lear undergoes psychologically and emotionally—sight in blindness—it does not reduce by simplistic imitation. Gloucester's resurrection, which is manipulated by Edgar, anticipates through an almost comic fiction Lear's redemption from madness by Cordelia. The "fall" at Dover's cliff places physical boundaries around the "miracle" of recovery so that the psychological awakening of Lear may be more fully apprehended. Reduction to the physical is necessary because it sets limits to that which has no boundaries: the boundless values thus become apprehensible because they are contained within analogical boundaries. In II.i, when Polonius employs Reynaldo to find out what Laertes is doing in Paris by saying that Laertes is known for "drinking, fencing, swearing, quarrelling, drabbing," the reason for his elaborate scheme seems to be primarily to satisfy a father's prying curiosity about his son. When Claudius, in the next scene, employs Rosencrantz and Guildenstern to discover the cause of his "son" Hamlet's "transformation," he has serious need to discover Hamlet's thinking. Thus Polonius reduces to a comic simplicity Claudius's serious and more urgent purposes. Gloucester's experience shapes a reduced view of what Lear is to undergo, but it is not in itself reductive as is the Polonius action."

Although ridicule or reduction to the ridiculous level is often a mark of parody, it is not the only purpose or even a requisite effect. Nor is parody always comic.[12] Parodic scenes frequently are not recognized because there are at least two basic kinds: those that involve serious consequences and those that do not. Two of Christopher Marlowe's plays illustrate the two kinds. In *Doctor Faustus,* the comic scenes involving Wagner, Robin, Dick, and eventually the Horse-courser, the Carter, and the Hostess work by juxtaposition to show reduced versions of Faustus's experiments with necromancy. But whereas Faustus's practice of black magic leads to fatal results for him, the comic conjurations seem to be without very serious consequences for those characters. The Horse-courser gets wet when the horse Faustus sold him turns to straw, the Carter loses his hay, Robin and Dick are turned into an ape and a dog, but none of these consequences approach serious suffering or create more than a temporary discomfiture (Benvolio's horned self-exile is a different case). In *The Jew of Malta*, on the other hand, the parodic actions always move toward serious, if not fatal, consequences. The Friars Barnardine and Jacomo, for example, in their battle over who shall win Barabas's soul (and therefore his money) parody the general theme of money as chief value in life, and in their forthright parody of that theme, as well as in their parody of the medieval psychomachia, they are laughable.[13] Yet when their greed leads to their destruction, the audience may feel uncomfortable at having laughed.

The three scenes of *Macbeth* discussed in chapter three also illustrate these two kinds of parody. The Porter's playing a devil-porter at the Gate of Hell has no further consequence for the Porter, and this allows us to relax momentarily within his comic literalities. The scene in which Macbeth hires the murderers to kill Banquo repeats the earlier persuasion scene with Lady Macbeth in more limited terms, but the consequence of this meeting (Banquo's murder) controls the degree to which we find this reduced parallel amusing. Likewise, Malcolm's outright simplification of evils through objective classification and his assumption of them parody Macbeth as monster. But because Malcolm is the necessary hero to defeat Macbeth, we find it awkward to recognize the operation of parody.

Distinctions within the vocabulary of comedy are difficult because categories tend to overlap and sometimes even to merge; therefore, it is important to attempt to isolate parody from its comic kinfolk. It is equally important to define the ways in which parody resembles and yet distinguishes itself from other kinds of analogy.

One kind of analogical scene that has much in common with parody is the emblematic scene. In the gardeners' scene of *Richard II*, for example, the physical activities—the binding up of the "dangling apricocks," the trimming of the "heads of too-fast-growing sprays," and the rooting away of the "noisome weeds" (III.iv.29–39)—are actions the gardener requires to keep the garden healthy. His helper draws the analogy between this literal garden and the "sea-walled garden" that is England, wondering why they should tend their little garden while "the whole land is full of weeds." His question prompts the gardener to tighten the analogy by pointing out:

> O, what pity is it
> That he [Richard II] had not so trimmed and dressed his land
> As we this garden! . . .
> Had he done so, himself had borne the crown,
> Which waste of idle hours hath quite thrown down.
> (III.iv.55–66)

At this point in the scene, for the gardeners, the analogy seems to be between the Duke of York's specific garden at Langley and the kingdom, but when the Queen comes forward from her hiding place and rebukes the gardener as "Thou old Adam's likeness . . . What Eve, what serpent, hath suggested thee/ To make a second fall of curséd man?" the specific garden realizes its symbolic potential.

For the audience the emblematic nature of the scene has been apparent from the gardener's opening speech.[14] This garden at Langley, well-tended, demonstrates "this other Eden, demi-paradise" that John of Gaunt's dying speech recalled *was* England before Richard II turned "this blessed plot" into "a tenement or pelting farm" (II.i.40–67). The Queen, however, would imbue it with the attributes of the garden after the fall because the gardener dares to suggest that her husband is deposed. Thus, while the literal garden resembles in its husbandry the prelapsarian Eden, the land under Richard II's reign with his self-encouraged deposition is emblematic of the second fall of man; subsequently, England in its fall includes the specific garden at Langley. Each garden, the literal and the figurative—Langley and England—draws the other into its scope of reference.

Another emblematic scene, more abrupt in its presentation of symbolic attributes, is Hector's discovery that the "goodly armor" he has pursued and captured is a "most putreféd core, so fair without" (*Troilus and Cressida*, V.viii.1). One of the play's major themes is the disarming of Hector, but Hector has not succumbed to any wiles, not his wife's or Helen's, to disarm. Yet almost as a digression from his main purpose in battle—to defeat with honor the Greeks who have accepted his challenge—he pursues the soldier for his armor: "I'll have thee for thy hide." He has just allowed Achilles to go free as a matter of courtesy when Achilles was at his mercy (V.vi); he has refused to continue the fight with Ajax because of their blood-relationship (IV.v); he has rejected Thersites as a possible combatant because he has no "honor" (V. iv); and yet he pursues this mannequin of knighthood without questioning its substance.[15] Only Hector can disarm himself. After Hector lays aside his armor to investigate the display of glory that has seduced him, he is set upon by Achilles' Myrmidons, killed, and led to eternal loss of honor by being dragged at Achilles' horse's tail "through the shameful field."

The goodly armor and the putrefied body that it shields resemble no realistic soldier, but insist on being examined as an emblematic moment in the play's frenzied movement toward the ultimate undermining of all the idealisms with which it began. Not only is love seen to be flirtation as ego-fulfillment (on both sides), but honor in battle is seen to be lust for exterior glory. All of the play's major themes may be seen emblematically in that theatrically fragile moment when Hector views the "putrefièd core, so fair without."

Emblematic scenes have the process of simplification in common with parodic scenes, although on the surface they seem to be quite different types of enactment. The process by which they lead the audience to enlarge its perspective, however, is similar. Both parody and emblem simplify in order to expose complexities. The parodic scene reduces metaphor to a specific concrete action, and the emblematic scene makes specifically concrete that which was abstract. Or, as Francis Bacon puts it, "emblem reduceth conceits intellectual to images sensible, which strike the memory more" (*Advancement of Learning*, II.xv.3).

Parody and emblem as two aspects of a similar presentational device may be viewed simultaneously in *Hamlet's* Gravediggers' scene. In the first segment of the scene the Gravediggers discuss the cause and consequences of Ophelia's death in terms of acci-

dent versus suicide. Their parody of legalistic/religious delibera-
tions and judgment makes a commonplace out of the poetically
heightened description of Ophelia's drowning spoken by Gertrude in the preceding scene. To create a major pause in the
performance at this point (which editorial act-division has ad-
vised) obscures the parallel between Ophelia's death with its two
commentaries and Polonius's death with Hamlet's evaluation of
it. In both cases—the deaths of Polonius and Ophelia—the audience is asked to shift its perspective suddenly from the apprehension of a living being like ourselves to the consideration of that
person's dead body as an inanimate thing capable of nothing but
objective classification. Hamlet "lug[s] the guts [Polonius] into
the neighbor room" and hides him, and Ophelia becomes the
depersonalized actor in a legal quibble:

It must be *se offendendo;* it cannot be else. For here lies the point: if I
drown myself wittingly, it argues an act, and an act hath three
branches—it is to act, to do, and to perform. Argal, she drowned herself
wittingly. (V.i.8–11)

The tautological authority of the Clown's tripartite definition
is amusing at the impersonal level of classification, but we
remain mystified about what really happened in Ophelia's
death. The report by Gertrude is twice removed from the reality, and an overwhelming ambiguity surrounds the question of
"will" in Ophelia's drowning. But with the Gravedigger's report, distinctions between acting, doing, and performing co-
alesce into one plane of possibility. For the entire play, Hamlet
(and the audience with him) has been distinguishing the meanings of an act within varying and conflicting potentialities of
role-playing: "acting" and "performing" are not "doing," as we
have witnessed Hamlet perceive. Yet here in the Gravedigger's
comic equation, we are at last released to understand the be-
fuddling distinctions that each term insists be made between
them. "Acting" with its punning significance of the theatrical
putting-on of a role other than what the person is; "doing"
with its ambivalent sexual and direct physical action implied;
and "performing" with its adjustments according to the per-

former's sense of how the audience perceives him *are* distinct values of the "act." What seems on the surface of the Clown's speech to be tautology, on reflection becomes a meaningful differentiation.

What is most significant in the process of play-viewing is that the audience is allowed only enough time to become aware that the Clown's talk is not so simplistic as it appears to be. Moments later, Hamlet leads us to a more profound, philosophical appraisal of the skull's evaluation of human intention. And, as any playgoer knows, the fuller comprehension of his experience of the play is retrospective. The needling sense of reductive simplicity coupled with enlarging apprehensions of mortality occur at the same moment while we watch this scene, and reverberations of this apprehension continue throughout the remaining actions of the play. To have Hamlet's *memento mori* without its "placement" by the Gravedigger's nonchalance over death (and Hamlet's own casual cataloguing of Polonius) in the background is to dispense with death's complexity—that complexity which *all* of the play's moments probe. Death is simultaneously awe-inspiring and ridiculous: the Ghost's apparition and Yorick's stinking skull (or Polonius's body being used to play hide-and-seek). The audience's immediate apprehension of this ambivalence is required by the series of scenes that simultaneously presents both angles of vision within a continuum that fuses both perspectives into a single focus.

One of the most intricate kinds of scenic parody is the one that precedes the action it imitates—proleptic parody. Most often this kind of scene immediately precedes that which it is related to, such as Polonius's directives to Reynaldo in II.i, which directly precede and parodically imitate Claudius's commission to Rosencrantz and Guildenstern, II.ii. On occasion, however, Shakespeare places such a scene early in the play only to return to it near the climax of the action. For example, in *Othello,* II.i, Iago playfully launches into a catalogue of women that evokes protests from both Desdemona and Emilia. In order to while away the time until Othello lands in Cyprus, Desdemona responds to Iago's comic rhetorical display:

I am not merry, but I do beguile
The thing I am by seeming otherwise.—
Come, how wouldst thou praise me?
(II.i.122–24)

In the process of describing "fair" and "foul" and "wise" and "foolish" women in shifting couplings, Iago comes finally to a description of "a deserving woman" that exactly formulates Desdemona's own virtues as later revealed in the play:

She that was ever fair, and never proud;
Had tongue at will, and yet was never loud; . . .
She that, being ang'red, her revenge being nigh,
Bade her wrong stay, and her displeasure fly.
(II.i.148–52)

Although he ends disparagingly here—"She was a wight . . . to suckle fools and chronicle small beer"—this catalogue of women's vices and virtues, established through Iago as court jester, almost certainly will be recalled during the scene in which Desdemona prepares for her final sleep. Her question to Emilia, "Dost thou in conscience think—tell me, Emilia—/That there be women do abuse their husbands/In such gross kind?" (IV.iii.58–60), sounds almost stubbornly ingenuous when compared with her witty repartee with Iago in II.i:

Well praised! How if she be black and witty? . . .
Worse and worse!
These are old fond paradoxes to make fools laugh i' th' alehouse.

Desdemona earlier, though herself innocent of the vices Iago describes in women, nonetheless apprehends their potentialities. In the scene with Emilia, her disbelief in woman's capacity to deceive, "I do not think there is any such woman," marks the retreat she has made to a young girl's innocence under the onslaught of Othello's incomprehensible accusations. Her sophisticated wittiness in the earlier scene, even there confessed to be uncomfortable, cannot be resumed when her essential nature faces desecration. The existence of the earlier scene, which in retrospect may be viewed as proleptic parody, gives credence to a

Desdemona of psychological and emotional complexity who would otherwise be missing. The reduction to primordial natures in both Desdemona and Othello—innocence and violence—has tragic value because we have seen them appear to be civilized and social beings, more sensitive than the "curlèd darlings" of Italy, yet essentially unknown to themselves. When they are bound to their Cyprean rock without the buffers of their learned natures, they become, with overwhelming surprise to each other, different and unknowable. This regression is clear enough in Othello's character, but a similar and understandable regression in Desdemona's parallels his and makes theirs a dual tragedy rather than a singular one. Each figure becomes simpler than he or she was, and because of their increasing reliance on instinct, each fails to know the other whom each came to know through society's established modes of behavior.

The situation with Desdemona is worth special notice because Shakespeare allows us to see her in her more confident moments, a lady assured in the social arts, able to engage playfully with a jester like Iago (even when her heart longs to know of Othello's safety) or with a jester like the Clown in another scene (when she seeks to mend Cassio's position and thus needs to find out where he "lies").[16] In all situations but the final ones, Desdemona is alert to society's recognition that external form should represent interior person. Her bemused observation that "Lodovico is a proper man. . . . He speaks well" is almost a farewell to those recognitions. She moves then into the willow song and her absolute innocence of woman's inconstancy.

The audience, too, has been led through iterative scenic language to a perception that would have been inconceivable, except to Brabantio, in the play's opening scenes. That we have come full circle, as Brabantio predicted Othello would, is surely one of the play's most difficult ironies. Othello's race *did* matter; Desdemona's wonder at the foreigner's great adventures *did* prove her undoing; the witchcraft so vociferously denied by Othello in Act I becomes a singularly significant value in the lost handkerchief. That all these seemingly irrational, benighted suppositions become the actual truths that obliterate the other possibilities of character present at the play's beginning must surely astound the audience as much as it does Othello.[17] The intimation that the play's action has been cyclical because Brabantio's narrow view in Act I has been validated works against larger awarenesses that the play has all along engaged. What we thought was a ridiculously limited vision in Brabantio (induced by Iago) has now proved to be the pattern for the play's larger action. Initial reduction of the forthcoming action provides both a sounding board against which we measure the larger dimensions of Othello's fall and a paradigm that warns of the inevitable outcome wrought through Iago's seduction of the imagination.

The kind of scene that I have been describing and illustrating is more than just a "mirror" for other actions in the play because it does more than reflect other action.[18] It builds accretively toward climactic revelation of what the analogues mean. It reorients and reshapes what we have seen, are seeing, and will see, often through a comic, but always through a literalizing, perspective. To eliminate these scenes because they are inessential to the narrative or because producers fear that the modern audience may not perceive their analogical relevance flattens the experience of the play. The readings that follow are a plea for reconsidering the value of such special and often puzzling scenes. That each scene has evoked some confusion about its purpose for readers throughout recent centuries may also suggest that we are still in need of reorienting our modern perspective to include what we inherently respond to—analogical modes of seeing.

Chapter 2

CINNA, BIANCA, AND ELBOW:
MINOR CHARACTERS AND
THEIR MAJOR PARODIC SCENES

I

The principle of analogical scenic structure may be observed most readily in small scenes or parts of scenes that at first glance appear to break the pace of the narrative progression. Frequently these scenes distinguish themselves by being cast in the parodic mode, and by imitating conventional comic formulae. Such a scene appears in *Julius Caesar,* a play sparse in comic moments, when Cinna the Poet wanders into a crowd that has been brutally energized by Mark Antony's funeral speech.

Critical reaction to this scene has been strong and various. Algernon de Vivier Tassin in 1916 disdained it: "chiefly it performs a decided disservice to the plot. It makes the gap of time and difference of material all the more frustrating of the continuity of interest."[1] The *Variorum* contributors were more charitable toward the idea that Shakespeare might have intended an unusual dramatic effect. Stapfer called it "the blackest action committed by the people, in all Shakespeare's Roman plays. . . . [In Plutarch] it is a very deplorable occurrence, but it is not an odious or a vile one, outraging all feeling and reason. . . . Shakespeare, a bolder and more searching anatomist of the human monster, has added a refinement of cruelty and folly to their crime." Kreyssig voiced an opinion with which I emphatically agree: "Were it not that the fate of the poet Cinna is related by Plutarch, one would like to consider this whole incident as a characteristic invention by Shakespeare."[2]

More recent critics have come closer to the heart of the structural matter, comprehending that this peculiar scene somehow encapsulates meanings crucial to the play.[3] I would like to examine *how* this scene provides a significant "imitation of an action."

Shakespeare created many individual scenes with beginnings, middles, and ends, playlets within themselves.[4] Separating this brief scene from its context, we recognize that it has three main parts: the introductory recollection of Cinna's dream, spoken in verse; the questions and answers between the Plebeians and Cinna; and the concluding action. The dream is described in Thomas North's translation of Plutarch twice, once in the "Life of Julius Caesar" and again in the "Life of Marcus Brutus."

There was one of Caesars frends called Cinna, that had a marvelous straunge and terrible dreame the night before. He dreamed that Caesar bad him to supper, and that he refused, and would not goe: then that Caesar tooke him by the hand, and led him against his will.[5]

But there was a Poet called Cinna, who had bene no partaker of the conspiracy, but was alway one of Caesars chiefest friends: he dreamed the night before, that Caesar bad him to supper with him, and that he refusing to goe, Caesar was very importunate with him, and compelled him, so that at length he led him by the hand into a great darke place, where being marvelously affrayd, he was driven to follow him in spite of his hart. This dreame put him all night into a fever.[6]

Looking at Shakespeare's version, we discover that he compresses Plutarch's detail, and in so doing alters the facts slightly.

> I dreamt to-night that I did feast with Caesar,
> And things unluckily charge my fantasy.
> I have no will to wander forth of doors,
> Yet something leads me forth. (III.iii.1–4)

Shakespeare's Cinna *did* "feast with Caesar" in his dream; Plutarch's Cinna was bidden to go forth in order to sup with Caesar. In Plutarch, Cinna's hesitation is primarily in the dream; in Shakespeare, the emphasized hesitation is the actual going "forth of doors." The details of the dream itself are minimized in Shake-

speare, although the foreboding quality of it is not. The unde-
fined "something" that leads him forth is in the actuality rather
than in the dream, whereas in Plutarch Cinna goes out because he
wishes to honor Caesar's funeral.

On the other hand, consider what Shakespeare does with the
dialogue between the Plebeians and Cinna. In Plutarch, when
Cinna learns that Caesar's body is being burned in the market-
place, he goes there.

When he came thither, one of meane sorte asked what his name was? He
was straight called by his name. The first man told it to an other, and
that other unto an other, so that it ranne straight through them all, that
he was one of them that murdered Caesar: (for in deede one of the
traitors to Caesar, was also called Cinna as him selfe) wherefore taking
him for Cinna the murderer, they fell upon him with such furie, that
they presently dispatched him in the market place.[7]

And bicause some one called him by his name, Cinna: the people thinking he had bene that Cinna, who in an oration he made had spoken very
evill of Caesar, they falling upon him in their rage, slue him outright in
the market place.[8]

Allowing for the inevitable differences between "historical" narration and dramatic depiction of the same action, it is nonetheless
clear that Shakespeare has elaborated this section of the scene.
The Plebeians catechize Cinna as they would a stranger visiting
from another land:

> What is your name?
> Whither are you going?
> Where do you dwell?

There are other instances in Shakespeare's plays of such routines.
When Coriolanus encounters Aufidius and the servingmen in
Antium, they ask, "Whence com'st thou? What wouldst thou? Thy
name?" (IV.v.54); and the outlaws examine Valentine in *The Two
Gentlemen of Verona* in a similar way: "Whither travel you? . . .
Whence came you? . . . Have you long sojourned there?"
(IV.i.16–20). Both Coriolanus and Valentine are strangers to the

places where they have come, but Cinna is a Roman citizen, an old friend of Caesar's. The events in the Forum have chaotically changed ordinary prodecures. Not only is Cinna questioned as if he were a foreigner, he is questioned by commoners. In contrast with the opening scene, the prerogative of interrogation has been inverted. There the tribunes Flavius and Marullus demand that the commoners identify themselves by their trades; here the commoners demand identification from the poet.

Their next question, "Are you a married man or a bachelor?", seems to have little to do with the situation, but considered together with Cinna's witty answer—"wisely I say, I am a bachelor"—and the Second Plebeian's jest—"That's as much as to say they are fools that marry. You'll bear me a bang for that, I fear"— it signals the kind of comic routine Shakespeare is employing here.

In discussing Feste's remarks about Olivia in *Twelfth Night*, Leo Salingar calls attention to the tradition of folly that surrounds the question of marriage.[9] Rabelais, for example, has Pantagruel advise his servant Panurge to consult a Fool and his oracles on whether to marry, even though Pantagruel assumes that Panurge would eventually be cuckolded anyway. In Erasmus's *Praise of Folly,* one of the first questions Folly asks, when describing the "powers and pleasures" derived from her, concerns marriage: "What man, I ask you, would stick his head into the halter of marriage if, following the practice of the wise, he first weighed the inconveniences of that life?"[10] And Feste says to Viola/Cesario that Olivia "will keep no fool, sir, till she be married; and fools are as like husbands as pilchers are to herrings, the husband's the bigger" (III.i.32–34).

In addition, stock situations of cuckoldry in the *Commedia dell' Arte* and the marriage debates in medieval English literature both passed into the comic tradition from which Shakespeare drew. That the question of wisdom and folly was almost inevitably associated with the question of marriage is clear, and frequently it was comic fare.[11]

Sexual fidelity or the lack of it is often the focus of bawdy jokes, and the Renaissance playwrights developed a number of euphemisms for the act of sexual intercourse.[12] One of the words that came into slang usage much later, according to Eric Partridge and the O.E.D., is "bang," although "thump" was used by Shakespeare (as in the servant's description of Autolycus's ballads in *The Winter's Tale*, IV.iv.190–99). Under the etymology of "fuck" in *A Dictionary of Slang and Unconventional English*, Partridge notes that Shakespeare used nine transitive and five intransitive synonyms for that word, and that Florio's was the earliest dictionary to record it. According to Partridge, it means literally, "to strike, hence to copulate with: cf., therefore, *bang* and *knock*."[13]

Shakespeare's only other uses of the word "bang" occur in the past tense, once in *Twelfth Night* when Fabian tells Sir Andrew how he should have "accosted" Olivia and "with some excellent jests, fire-new from the mint, banged the youth [Viola/Cesario] into dumbness" (III.ii.19–21), and in *Othello* when one of the gentlemen describes the halting of the Turkish fleet by the sea tempest (II.i.21). Both these instances and the Plebeian's comment to Cinna, "You'll bear me a bang for that, I fear," make perfect sense if the word "knock" or "beating" is substituted for "bang," and most editors explain the word in this way. Considering the sexual innuendoes preceding the Plebeian's remark, however, a sexual pun seems likely. The word "bear" frequently means bearing the weight of the man in sexual intercourse as well as the child resultant from that union: for example, in *The Taming of the Shrew*, when Petruchio remarks, "Women are made to bear, and so are you," Kate replies, "No such jade as you, if me you mean" (II.i.201–2). The idea of a bachelor who fathers children was also a jesting matter, according to Partridge, who cites *3 Henry VI*, and there are other instances.[14]

If we read the Second Plebeian's line with these sexual meanings in mind, the following is a possible paraphrase: You, Cinna, will have to substitute for me with my wife in the act of sexual intercourse, if what you say is true—that is, a married man is a fool—because I will no longer be the fool, and if my wife discovers that you advise me not to be married, she will demand that someone else provide her with sexual action.[15] The "I fear" at the end of the line may be a light threat to Cinna, but it seems also to be a recognition of the logical conclusion that follows the proverbial statement that only bachelors are wise because they do not marry.

Whether these sexual innuendoes operate here or not makes a difference only in recognizing to what degree Shakespeare intended to disorient his audience by leading them through familiar comic routines with expectations that are to be violently thwarted. To read "bang" as "to hit" or "to beat" (the more recognized aspect of the pun) suggests typical behavior in farce, especially when the servant undergoes a beating, as do the two Dromios in *A Comedy of Errors* when they are mistaken for each other. Because the Plebeians are treating Cinna as an inferior, a promise to beat him is entirely appropriate—for Roman comedy.

The rhetorical pattern followed by the central and longest part of this brief scene fits under several different categories of formal "argument."[16] It is an "anatomy" wherein Cinna's parts are divided by disjunction—first rhetorically and then physically. It is a kind of pun—"antanaclasis"—whereby in repetition "a word shifts from one of its meanings to another." It demonstrates the "fallacy of accident which results from the false assumption"; "the fallacy of ignorance of the elench" (a syllogism gathering a conclusion contrary to the assertion of the respondent); as well as the "fallacy of many questions," wherein, Sister Miriam Joseph says, "clowns are especially adept." As a matter of fact, Cinna's encounter with the Plebeians fits so many rhetorical categories that it is difficult to determine which fallacy Shakespeare was attempting to imitate. That he was trying to alert his audience to the rhetorical patterning can hardly be doubted.

The verbal pattern "directly, briefly, wisely, and truly" is repeated not just once (in Cinna's answer to the Plebeians' multiple question) but twice in their *second* interrogation of him as they pause for each of his answers. The rhetorical "climax" of this repetition comes when Cinna says, "Truly, my name is Cinna." Of all the questions and answers, this should have been the one that dispelled the ambiguities. But it only raises them. Cinna was in fact the name of a conspirator who had made himself conspicuous, both in Plutarch and in Shakespeare, by speaking against Caesar in the funeral orations at the Forum, and the crowd remembers that. Therefore the Plebeians respond, "Tear him to pieces." The truth has become not only the last factor in identification for Cinna the poet, it has become the most irrelevant factor. When he shouts that he is a poet, not a conspirator, the Plebeians cry, "Tear him for his bad verses! . . . It is no matter." This is another distinction between Shakespeare and his source in Plutarch—Shakespeare makes certain that the audience realizes that the Plebeians know the difference between Cinna the conspirator and Cinna the poet.[17] Logic, and the rhetoric that employs it, has been used on the populace in the preceding scene by Brutus and by Antony. Now the populace is using it on Cinna, to similarly disjunctive effects, providing a parody of the loftier scene.

First, Brutus has appealed to their reason abstracted from feeling; then Antony appeals to their emotions, which, when aroused sufficiently, cannot stay for reason. Contrasted with the scornful attitudes expressed by the tribunes Flavius and Marullus in the opening scene ("You blocks, you stones, you worse than senseless things!"), and Brutus's imperious approach ("hear me for my cause, and be silent, that you may hear"), Antony's affected humility and consideration of their feelings ("You are not wood, you are not stones, but men"), together with the exposed and bleeding wounds of Caesar, carry the Plebeians into an unaccustomed state of self-respect and confidence. Antony's rhetorically assumed pose as one of them, possessing no "power of speech to stir men's blood. I only speak right on," inspires their mindless revenge. The Plebeians conclude their own rhetorical game of wit with Cinna by discarding the value of the word: "I am not Cinna, the conspirator. . . . It is no matter; his name's Cinna! Pluck but his name out of his heart, and turn him going."[18]

Verbally, the Plebeians' conclusion recalls Brutus's reasoning that the conspirators must not kill anyone but Caesar:

> Let us be sacrificers, but not butchers, Caius.
> We all stand up against the spirit of Caesar,

And in the spirit of men there is no blood.
(II.i.166–68)

In bringing such an idea to its literal realization, Brutus and the conspirators have already provided a stage picture more horrible than anything Shakespeare created after *Titus Andronicus*. While believing themselves to be sacrificers, the conspirators "wash" from their hands to their elbows in Caesar's literal blood, and thus demonstrate beyond any conceptual denial that they are butchers. With the murder of Cinna, apparently also onstage, Brutus's theory of bloodless sacrifice and its literal enactment are reduced to shocking absurdity.

The entire scene seems to have been cast in the comic mode, if not so obviously as the opening banter between the tradesmen and the tribunes, at least more clearly than the later scene where the cynic poet intrudes on Brutus and Cassius as they argue in the battlefield tent.[19] Cinna is a stranger to his situation, despite the fact that he is a Roman, and walks into a built-in reaction—a hatred of his name—without a notion of his lack of context. His entrance is comic in conventional ways, like Sebastian's in *Twelfth Night* and Antipholus of Syracuse's in *The Comedy of Errors;* however, here the potentially comic situation turns into a horrible butchery, not of a Caesar, but of someone the audience has never seen before. Cinna's introductory musings about his dream and his foreboding imitate exactly what we have seen Julius Caesar consider because of Calphurnia's dream and other auguries. Decius appeals to Caesar by reinterpreting the dream as a favorable portent, by the prospect of the Senate's offering Caesar a crown, and finally by doubting Caesar's "manliness" (II.ii). Cinna's reasons for remaining at home and then for going forth are much less specific: *"things* unluckily charge my fantasy. . . . Yet *something* leads me forth." His imitation of the earlier action is nevertheless clear.

Similarities between the two scenes also point to their differences. In both, the innocent victim denies his foreboding and walks into predetermined savagery that quickly destroys him: in Caesar's case the conspirators have determined the violence, but in Cinna's case the spirit of malevolence has been spurred by Antony. Before reading the will, Antony warns the crowd that hearing it "will inflame you, it will make you mad," and after he unleashes their fury, Antony backs away with a remarkably irresponsible malediction:

> Now let it work. Mischief, thou art afoot,
> Take thou what course thou wilt. (III.ii.260–61)

We watch almost spellbound as his malediction moves upon the ignorant and innocent poet Cinna. Then the shock hits—greater because Cinna has seemed to be a comic figure out of a familiar routine.

When we see Cinna the Poet being torn apart for his name or for his bad verses, we see through and behind this scene into the preceding assassination of Julius Caesar. Cinna's disintegration is the imitation of significant action on an impersonal scale, and it is dramatically necessary in order to inform the audience of what the earlier, more personally evaluated action means. Cinna is both an irrelevant and an appropriate victim. Julius Caesar might have seemed to us to be potentially capable of tyranny, and thus the object of "justifiable" political annihilation—this at least is Brutus's view.[20] But there is an ambivalence in the depiction of the conspirators' attitudes toward Julius Caesar that is not resolved until this seemingly irrelevant murder of Cinna, when it becomes clear to the audience that possible threats of would-be emperors may or may not become actual threats, but that the erasure of potential tyrants (or conspirators or poets) results in indiscriminate destruction and chaos. In the very next scene, we see Antony, Octavius, and Lepidus pricking names on their own arbitrary roll of candidates for eradication; and two scenes later we witness the enmity that results from the conspirators' deed affecting them as well. Brutus and Cassius, whose participation in the assassination bound them together, now experience between themselves the divisive and destructive forces that their deed released. As it makes commonplace by reduced imitation the more significant assassination of Julius Caesar, the Cinna-the-Poet scene also becomes emblematic of the chaos born out of such a murder.

Other analogical scenes forward the plot more directly, and the minor characters who appear in them seem more relevant to the narrative than does Cinna. In *Othello* (III.iv) Bianca takes the magically endowed handkerchief from Cassio and in the following scene (IV.i) returns it to him in view of a concealed Othello. Her first appearance comes at the end of one of Shakespeare's most fascinating scenes of analogical structure. Each of its five sections shows characters engaged in the act of "lying."[21]

The first segment functions like a comic prologue to the scene, with the Clown refusing to tell Desdemona where Cassio lies (that is, lodges), because he does not know. His verbal fencing with her question "Do you know, sirrah, where Lieutenant Cassio lies?" focuses on the word "lie" and its triple meanings: to speak falsely, to lie down (to lodge), and to have sexual intercourse. Desdemona is hardly in the mood for such dalliance with words, but the Clown's quibbling with variations of the word's value forces her to less ambiguous language: "Can you enquire him out, and be edified by report?" Ambivalent language is pointedly connected to what happens in the next part of the scene, where her communication with Othello through words breaks down.[22]

After the Clown leaves to "catechize the world" to find Cassio, Emilia and Desdemona discuss the handkerchief's loss. In answer to Desdemona's question "Where should I lose that handkerchief, Emilia?" Emilia lies: "I know not, madam." Not only is this a direct lie on her part, throughout the segment in which Othello's fiercely reiterative questioning of Desdemona causes Desdemona to lie, Emilia's silence is an act of lying.

Othello, as he enters, admits in an aside that he "dissembles" since Iago has already informed him that Cassio has the handkerchief. Unlike her usually forthright self, Desdemona lies by denying the handkerchief is lost—"It is not lost. . . . I say it is not lost"—and, in order to shift the subject from Othello's uncomfortable preoccupation to more "important" matters, every time

thereafter that Othello calls for the handkerchief, she speaks of
Cassio, indelibly linking the two in Othello's mind.

Iago has begun welding Cassio and the handkerchief in
Othello's imagination with lies about Cassio's dream in the preceding scene:

> I lay with Cassio lately,
> And being troubled with a raging tooth,
> I could not sleep. . . .
> In [his] sleep I heard him say, 'Sweet Desdemona,
> Let us be wary, let us hide our loves!'
> And then, sir, would he gripe and wring my hand,
> Cry, 'O sweet creature!' and then kiss me hard,
> As if he plucked up kisses by the roots
> That grew upon my lips; then laid his leg
> Over my thigh, and sighed, and kissed, and then
> Cried 'Cursèd fate that gave thee to the Moor!'
> (III.iii.413–26)

E. A. M. Colman calls this "a doubly bawdy piece of fiction . . .
since it combines indefinite suggestions of sodomy with the most
precise description of a coital act in the whole of Shakespeare."[23]
This poison is followed by the lie that Iago saw Cassio "wipe his
beard" with the precious handkerchief. No wonder that Othello
nears madness when Desdemona insists on talking of Cassio's
"sufficiencies" instead of confessing that she no longer has the
handkerchief.

When Othello leaves, confounded by his wife's mendacity, he
has neared speechlessness in his fury. Desdemona at last perceives that he may be capable of feeling jealousy and that the
handkerchief may possess "some wonder" in it. To this troubled
situation Cassio enters with Iago and more or less demands that
Desdemona pursue his cause with Othello: "I would not be de-
layed." Desdemona, still shaken by her husband's gruffness, tells
Cassio that "My advocation is not now in tune. . . . You must a
while be patient." Iago, of course, picks up her perception that
Othello is angry and goes off to see for himself what his machina-
tions have wrought. Berating herself for having judged Othello

hastily, Desdemona promises Cassio that she will try to find her husband and move Cassio's suit.

Left alone onstage, Cassio waits for Othello, and Bianca enters. Their first exchanges, until he gives her the handkerchief, are courteous and apparently loving, as Cassio tactfully lies: "I'faith, sweet love, I was coming to your house." Bianca's concern over his long absence is delivered with exaggeration of detail:

> And I was going to your lodging, Cassio.
> What, keep a week away? seven days and nights?
> Eightscore eight hours? and lovers' absent hours,
> More tedious than the dial eightscore times?
> O weary reck'ning! (III.iv.172–76)

With a hint of a nagging tongue, Bianca's speech accomplishes a variety of dramatic effects. First, she establishes her almost obsessively focused feeling for Cassio, what Iago describes in the next scene's soliloquy as "the strumpet's plague/ To beguile many and be beguiled by one." Second, she elongates the time period of the Cyprus action.

A complex critical debate has been waged over the "double-time" scheme in *Othello*,[24] but whatever theoretical position is taken, Bianca's speech is clearly major in making the Venetian troups' stay in Cyprus seem long enough in the audience's perception to render Othello's suspicions possible rather than simply ludicrous. That Shakespeare should use a love-inspired courtesan to promote the idea of expanded duration is ironically appropriate. For a possessive lover, the absence of the loved one seems interminable; when jealousy is aroused, that time period becomes torturous. What we have been witnessing happen to Othello in more gradual terms is now being summarized by Bianca.[25]

The moment that Cassio hands Bianca the handkerchief, he arouses her jealousy. The swift change from loving phrases and courteous treatment of each other that follows in her accusation, "This is some token from a newer friend," and his remonstration, "Go to, woman!", exactly parody the breakdown of Othello's love because of his aroused jealousy. The suddenness of Bianca's jealousy, over the same "ocular proof" that is to convince Othello, imitates Othello's psychological reaction within a reduced range, and, as it does so, reminds us that he was not so easily suspicious. In neither case is their jealousy justified by the existence of a rival lover, but in both cases this fact alters nothing.

That Cassio would ask Bianca to copy the handkerchief is itself a parody—an imitation on a reductive scale. Compare his comments about the handkerchief with Othello's:

> I like the work well: ere it be demanded,
> As like enough it will, I'd have it copied.
> (III.iv.189–90)

> There's magic in the web of it.
> A sibyl that had numb'red in the world
> The sun to course two hundred compasses,
> In her prophetic fury sewed the work;
> The worms were hallowed that did breed the silk;
> And it was dyed in mummy which the skillful
> Conserved of maiden's hearts. (III.iv. 69–75)

By the juxtaposition of these two segments of the scene, we are being asked to consider Bianca's taking out a copy of the handkerchief with the awesome sibyl sewing in prophetic fury. The two images collide in polarity. Even so, Shakespeare allows Bianca her own kind of fury when she returns it to Cassio, uncopied: "There! Give it your hobby-horse. Wheresoever you had it, I'll take no work on't" (IV.i.152–53).

Cassio's denial to Bianca that he has another mistress is true, but when he asks her to leave so that Othello will not see him "womaned," he dissembles, as do most of the other characters in the scene. His hypocrisy is of lesser consequence perhaps than the lies of Emilia, Iago, Desdemona, and Othello, but he nonetheless contributes to the ambience of partial truths and outright lies that allows Iago's villainy to flourish. As we discover in the next scene, when Iago leads Cassio to laugh scornfully over her infatuation, Cassio is also lying in his affirmations of love for Bianca. Thus Cassio, as well as Bianca, presents a parody of Othello, but his dissembling is less complex than Othello's, whose very nature is torn apart by love and jealousy, unable to do away with one or the other as he intended (III.iii.191). Cassio feels neither love nor jealousy, but concern only for his reputation.

With additional structural irony, the final segment of III.iv answers both literally and figuratively the question Desdemona asks the Clown at the scene's beginning: "Do you know, sirrah, where Lieutenant Cassio lies?" Cassio lies with Bianca in all three senses of the word. Both beginning and ending segments follow established comic routines—the clown's word-play and Bianca's jealousy (with the suggestion of shrewishness)—and they enclose the most serious preliminary confrontation of Desdemona and Othello before he determines to kill her for her infidelity. The focus on the word "lie" anticipates Othello's agonized turning of the word just before he falls into a senseless fit in the next scene.

Lie with her? lie on her?—We say lie on her when they belie her.—Lie with her! Zounds, that's fulsome.—Handkerchief—confessions—handkerchief! . . . It is not words that shakes me thus. (IV.i.35–42)

After Othello revives from this fall, he is ready to believe the substitution of Bianca—the whore—for Desdemona, which is what Iago leads him to see from his hiding place.

Because it is the character of Bianca that Iago discusses with Cassio in IV.i while Othello mistakes it for a discussion of Desdemona, Bianca literally is being used as a stand-in for Desdemona. In theatrical terms, Iago is not only casting, directing, and controlling the responses of his actors but is also manipulating the reactions of the hidden audience to whom he presents his pantomime. Othello's exclamations in the early part of his furtive witnessing indicate that he sees but does not hear what is being said:

—Look how he laughs already!
—Now he denies it faintly, and laughs it out.
—   Now he importunes him
    To tell it o'er. Go to! Well said, well said!
—Do you triumph, Roman? Do you triumph?

—So, so, so, so! They laugh that win!
—Have you scored me? Well.
—Iago beckons me; now he begins the story.

Othello is "as good as a chorus," and if it were not for the surrounding context of tragic potentiality, we might mistake this scene as something out of Roman comedy. The stage picture is certainly comic, and the routines that Iago leads Cassio and Othello through show them both to be dupes of his method. Bianca's return, with her jealous anger fully expressive now, is like that of the shrewish wife in Roman comedy—a strange working out of conventional formulae.[26]

Seeing the handkerchief in the hands of Bianca and then of Cassio pushes Othello beyond the edge of reason, and he is now ready for murder, of both Cassio and Desdemona. The audience has seen what Othello has seen, but we have understood more. Bianca's jealousy and Cassio's helplessness to appease it as he follows after her—"she'll rail in the street else"—parodically imitate the confrontations between Othello and Desdemona that immediately precede and follow this inversion. To superimpose the reduced image on the tragically heightened one partially dispels the ludicrous from the major action at the same time it points to that action as a commonplace. Othello is both Everyman and uniquely himself. As Iago says, "There's millions now alive/ That nightly lie in those unproper beds/ Which they dare swear peculiar." Othello is a figure who, because of his own narrowed perception of what is outside himself, causes irretrievable catastrophe. Ordinary men and women, like Cassio and Bianca, effect no such consequences.

Bianca performs a surrogate role for Desdemona in Othello's eyes, and for the audience she performs a parody of Othello. She also participates in a triad of female images that progressively descends from the ideal: from Desdemona to Emilia to Bianca. Iago's catalogue of women in the opening scene on Cyprus (II.i)—"There's none so foul, and foolish thereunto,/ But does foul pranks which fair and wise ones do"—is remembered in the appearance of Bianca and in the questioning of Emilia by Desde-

mona as they prepare the wedding sheets for her unsuspected
martyrdom:

> Dost thou in conscience think—tell me, Emilia—
> That there be women do abuse their husbands
> In such gross kind? (IV.iii.59–61)

The pain intensifies because Desdemona's question is not a rhetorical one. She cannot understand what other women do rather
readily—as Emilia tactfully points out, "the world's a huge
thing" for which to be unfaithful to one's husband. Desdemona
cannot even apprehend that *other* women *would* commit such
gross violations of fidelity—that such an accusation should be
directed at her hardly enters her comprehensive range. The audience knows, as do Emilia and Iago, and Cassio and Bianca, that
this is the ordinary occurrence, the reason why cuckoldry is such
a common joke. But neither Desdemona nor Othello can believe
such an action possible to a husband and wife who married for
love despite opposition from family and state. Othello and Desdemona share an idealism that is only postulated by the people
around them. Because they cannot imagine a ground between the
ideal, which they have known, and the corrupt, which they cannot tolerate, Othello moves toward preternatural violence and
Desdemona moves toward virginal innocence. They are precisely
paired in the absolute idealism they apply to each other, and
Cassio and Bianca are exactly paired in their lack of capacity for
that ideal.

Just as Bianca participates in a parodic variation on the nature
of women through which Desdemona's idealism is revealed, the
men in the play provide a similar imitation of Othello. First
Brabantio, then Roderigo, then Cassio falls to Iago's manipulations. Each is a suitor for Desdemona's loyalty in one form or
another, and each feels betrayed by her continuing concentration
of fidelity on Othello. Only Othello, however, believes that she
has found a focus elsewhere. Yet Othello is like the others in
doubting Desdemona's reliability, and he, like the others, substitutes Iago's word for hers. Roderigo provides the most obvious
parody of Othello, but he is simply at the lower point of a scaled

parallelism that others share, as is Bianca when seen in the external light of appearances. That both Roderigo and Bianca parody Othello rather than Desdemona in their actions suggests that Othello's lack of reason is more subject to ridicule than Desdemona's ignorance of emotional and sexual casualness.

III

In another play that explores sexual promiscuity with similar intensity (probably written the same year as *Othello*, 1604), Shakespeare also employs characterization in diminishing parallels. In *Measure for Measure*, the major pattern is the abdication of responsibility rather than Iago's ability to manipulate the insecure. This pattern of abdication includes the working out of substitutions.

In the first scene, Duke Vincentio prepares both Escalus and the audience for his transference of authority to the virtuous Angelo. He asks Escalus,

> What figure of us, think you, he will bear?
> For you must know, we have with special soul
> Elected him our absence to supply.

The words are sacramentally reverberative; only later do we understand how Angelo makes their active meaning sanctimonious. To Angelo himself in the opening scene, the Duke gives his commission: "In our remove, be thou at full ourself." Angelo's first action as he substitutes for the Duke is to condemn Claudio to death for his premarital union with Juliet. As Lucio says later, "Would the Duke that is absent have done this?" Nonetheless, in committing his position and person to Angelo, the Duke has created a situation with the potential to transform more than Angelo's identity.[27]

The scene in which Shakespeare brings this thematic concern into parodic focus is II.i. Like the common participation in the "lie" scene of *Othello*, this scene has several parts. The prologue in this instance is serious rather than comic and, together with the ending segment, is preoccupied with the imminent death of Claudio. The serious prologue and epilogue encase comic business that defeats the skill of the judicious to decipher—exactly opposite to the scene in *Othello,* where comic beginning and ending enclose an enlarging tragic action.

Angelo begins his debate with Escalus on the question of justice by comparing the law to a scarecrow that must always be changing its shape in order to frighten the birds of prey. Escalus picks up the gardening metaphor and speaks as a husbandman, suggesting that it is better to prune a little than to fell the plant or tree altogether:

> Let us be keen and rather cut a little,
> Than fall and bruise to death.[28]

Escalus then points out Claudio's noble lineage and argues by analogy that the same thing could have happened to Angelo, "Whom I believe to be most strait in virtue," had time and place coincided with his wishing. Escalus unwittingly anticipates the situation that develops between Isabella and Angelo, in which Angelo not only is tempted beyond any former experience of passion but falls with much less excuse of honorable intent than Claudio. At the moment, however, ignorant of his capacity for lust, Angelo refuses the analogy. To his credit, he does not weight his defense on his lack of a common flaw but on the absoluteness of the law. In recognizing the proverbial truth that those who judge are not always innocent of the crime they condemn in others, he inadvertently brings up the notion of a jury:

> I not deny
> The jury passing on the prisoner's life
> May in the sworn twelve have a thief, or two,
> Guiltier than him they try.

In Claudio's case, however, Angelo has not employed a trial by jury—his judgment is absolute and his sentence summary: "See that Claudio/ Be executed by nine tomorrow morning."

Escalus's rhymed couplets mark the end of the scene's first segment:

> Well, heaven forgive him; and forgive us all.
> Some rise by sin, and some by virtue fall.

34

> Some run from brakes of ice and answer none,
> And some condemned for a fault alone.

As they voice sententiae,[29] these lines sound a note of inevitability about Angelo's judgment and Claudio's fate. But, as Hilda Hulme points out, Escalus's paradox concerning the rise and fall of vice and virtue, which was excluded by Thomas Bowdler in his *Family Shakespeare* (1818), "seems still to be understood as having some crude sexual reference."[30] To recognize the doubleness of Escalus's language in these formulations of sententiae allows us to see how they ease a transition from the formal debate on the relation of justice and sexual activity to the free-for-all debate over the same question introduced by Elbow and his offenders.

Doubleness of language, puns, and malapropisms characterize Elbow's accusations and Pompey's defense. Elbow's first hypothesis, "If these be good people in a commonweal that do nothing but use their abuses in common houses, I know no law," employs several sexual double entendres. "Commonweal" and "common houses," "use" and "abuses," all refer to general sexual activity, and "nothing" is a notorious euphemism for sex and/or sexual organs.[31] Elbow is not necessarily aware of how loaded his diction is, but then, neither is he aware of his words' usual meanings or of the law he professes to know. The comedy of the scene, in fact, turns on his failure to understand words and the law. Whereas we have just heard Angelo argue for exact observance of the law's letter, we now witness one of the law's officers garble not only its letters but its meaning.

The switch from verse to prose marks the change of mode, as does the insistence on "humoural" names for each of the comic characters. Elbow defines himself, "I do lean upon justice, sir," and Pompey adds, "he's out at elbow." Master Froth is both "drawn in" to the taphouse and "drawn by" the tapster, his name an obvious reference to the foam-head of draft beer. Pompey Bum works for Mistress Overdone, who has had nine husbands, "overdone by the last," and his own name provides Escalus with two notable jests:

Troth, and your bum is the greatest thing about you, so that, in the beastliest sense, you are Pompey the Great. . . . I advise you, let me not find you before me again upon any complaint whatsoever; no, not for dwelling where you do. If I do, Pompey, I shall beat you to your tent, and prove a shrewd Caesar to you. (II.i.205–7; 231–36)

These low-life characters seem to have been named so that these particular jokes can be made about them in this scene, a farcical technique that many critics have found objectionable. Escalus's participation at the level of Pompey's bawdy wit also causes problems for those who would prefer to see him as beyond this sort of crude comedy. Sir Philip Sidney's well-known criticism of "mongrell Tragicomedie," which mixes modes as well as types of characters, sets a respectable precedent for such objections.[32] Nevertheless, the mixture seems inherent in the development of English drama, and it became ever more attractive to Shakespeare as he developed his dramaturgical ease within the more accepted modes of tragedy and comedy.

Sidney Musgrove's comment that Escalus's joke about Pompey's "bum" is "unworthy of him" shares a perspective with Ernest Schanzer, who says:

It is Escalus who in this play illustrates the *via media* between the two excesses in the administration of justice. He possesses the proper mixture of severity and mercy which marks the ideal judge. . . . The Elbow-Pompey-Froth scene, excellent comedy though it is, seems to have been introduced mainly to show the ideal judge at work. Escalus is full of patience, humanity, and tolerance, in sharp contrast to Angelo, who leaves half way through the hearing.[33]

Yet this "ideal judge" releases both of Elbow's accused, exacting only a promise that they will reform, a promise that Pompey, at least, makes clear he has no intention of fulfilling: "The valiant heart's not whipt out of his trade." At the end of the scene Escalus himself censures the actions he has taken within it:

Mercy is not itself, that oft looks so;
Pardon is still the nurse of second woe.

Whether Escalus is conscious of evaluating himself here is not important—Shakespeare has him speak the moral in a rhymed couplet so that the audience cannot miss its ironic application to his pardons of Froth and Pompey.[34]

A major function of the scene is to show us Angelo, the Duke's substitute, in action as a judge. Heretofore we have only heard about his arrest of Claudio for violating the somnolent law against fornication in Vienna. Now we hear him debate that question with Escalus, but, more important, we witness the unevenness of his justice in practice. When Elbow hopelessly muddles his accusations through his inversions of language and Pompey digresses at almost every word of his defense, Angelo grows impatient and gives over his authority to Escalus, "Hoping you'll find good cause to whip them all."

Curiously enough, Angelo's abrupt departure from the scene has been viewed from opposite positions. Josephine Waters Bennett, in agreement with most commentators, calls it "his first failure as a ruler,"[35] but J. W. Lever, in the Arden edition, asserts that "Angelo does not show neglect of duty or marked severity," because he needs to be elsewhere at the "hearing of a cause" (II.ii), and "whipping was a normal punishment for bawds."[36] Viewed as an imitative action, however, Angelo's abdication parallels that of the Duke's giving over his governing responsibilities in Act I. Neither Angelo nor the Duke demonstrates the sturdiness required of a perfect ruler, the Duke because he would avoid appearing tyrannical by enforcing the law, and Angelo because he has little interest in judging unimportant criminals (and probably because he lacks a sense of humor).

Rosalind Miles, in a brief summary of this scene's "dramatic parallelism," points out several instances in which "lowly protagonists are unconsciously acting out the drama of the play's principal characters."

The dealings of Escalus with Froth, Pompey, and Elbow, pattern out the involvement of Claudio, Isabella, and Angelo with the Duke as their final judge. As in the main plot, there is at the centre of this hearing a confused young man, Froth, who like Claudio is brought to account for a crime which he is hardly aware of having committed. His advocate, Pompey, is reminiscent of Isabella as he employs all his verbal resources in a deliberate attempt to cloud the issue and to exculpate Froth. Like

Isabella again, Pompey is, despite his eloquence, often in danger of making things worse for the object of his attentions. The accuser, Elbow, is incapable of recognising the distinctive features of the offence, but echoes Angelo in his determination that the offender must be punished.[37]

Miles primarily notes instances in which this scene anticipates with "proleptic irony" dramatic patterns soon to be repeated by the principal actors; but it is also important to recognize that the scene repeats without confusion the essential pattern of abdication/substitution with which the play begins. It acts as a fulcrum, as do the "lie" scene in *Othello* and the Cinna-the-Poet scene in *Julius Caesar*, balancing the dramatic action on either side of it and drawing into its comic focus central themes that expand through the process of reduction.

One aspect that Shakespeare distills in this scene through the device of punning is the sexual hunger universal in humankind. Elsewhere in the play, it is made specific enough (as in Claudio's remarks to Lucio explaining Juliet's pregnancy, I.ii.148–50, and in Angelo's proposition to Isabella, II.iv.158–64), but here it becomes the denominator of all the language. Not even Elbow's "respected" wife escapes suspicion. Escalus himself is drawn in by Pompey's bawdy quibble when he insists, "Come me to what was done to her." Pompey says, "Sir, your honor cannot come to that yet," and Escalus indicates that he catches the ribald sense in which his command was misconstrued: "No, sir, nor I mean it not." The "precise" accusation and its punishment may become clouded in this scene, but the question of sexual encounters becomes increasingly clear as one examines the puns.

Following Escalus's paradoxical line, "Some rise by sin, and some by virtue fall," which Hilda Hulme suggests may be "another joke" for "those who enjoy the bawdy realism of *Measure for Measure*" and which, she says, "would serve as an apt commentary on what all the play's pother is about,"[38] the language of the entire scene wittily emphasizes sexual activity. "Common house . . . hot-house . . . ill house . . . bawd's house . . . naughty house . . . stewed prunes . . . china dishes . . . pin . . . point . . . eaten . . . cracking the stones . . . the thing you

wot of . . . come . . . open . . . done . . . Overdone . . . draw"—
all these words refer in some way, usually punningly, to sexual
intercourse and the aftermaths thereof, and these are only the
more obvious references.

Could he negotiate the language, Elbow would like to lodge an
accusation against Pompey for leading Elbow's wife into the
brothel and against Froth for accepting her favors there—were
she a "woman cardinally given." One of the few critics to pay
Elbow's garbled language detailed notice as anything but diver-
sionary is Gordon Ross Smith, who finds that Elbow's "malapropisms are invested with heavy satire":

Within a political interpretation of the play these malapropisms are
understandable as reflections upon the nature of authority: people in
authority in Renaissance Europe affected a facade of virtue, behind
which they behaved in Machiavellian fashion, or what is worse, asserted
a Christian moral sanction for patterns of behavior which violated Christian ethics but which helped to keep those persons of authority in
power.[39]

This heavy extrapolation may be too tidy a wrapping up of the
scene's loose ends, but inadvertent sense does seem to cohere
within the confusion of Elbow's wild accusations and their di-
gressive rejoinders. That coherence implies that everyone is susceptible to sexual appetite—even Elbow's wife, who becomes the
object of Pompey's joke in his answer to Escalus's "what was
done to Elbow's wife, once more?" Punning on the word "done"
to mean "sexual copulation,"[40] Pompey jests, "Once, sir? There
was nothing done to her once," insinuating that whatever happened, happened more than once. Elbow himself, misinterpret-
ing "respected" to mean "suspected," seems to protest too much
about his premarital innocence.

POMPEY By this hand, sir, his wife is a more respected person than any
of us all.
ELBOW Varlet, thou liest; thou liest, wicked varlet. The time is yet to
come that she was ever respected with man, woman, or child.
POMPEY Sir, she was respected with him before he married with her.
ESCALUS Which is the wiser here, Justice or Iniquity? Is this true?

39

ELBOW O thou caitiff, O thou varlet, O thou wicked Hannibal! I respected with her before I was married to her? If ever I was respected with her, or she with me, let not your worship think me the poor Duke's officer. (II.i.156–68)

In his protestations of sexual abstinence before marriage, he parodies Angelo's response earlier in the scene: " 'Tis one thing to be tempted, Escalus,/ Another thing to fall." Nor have we lost the sound of the Duke's estimate that

> Lord Angelo is precise,
> Stands at a guard with envy; scarce confesses
> That his blood flows, or that his appetite
> Is more to bread than stone. (I.iii.50–52)

Only Angelo, it seems, is exempt from humanity's common flaw, and that exception alters in the next scene when he discovers his own susceptibility through desire of Isabella: "Ever till now,/ When men were fond, I smiled and wondered how" (II.ii.186–87).

Within this comic trial scene two essential questions are under consideration: what is the relationship of sexual gratification to justice, and how effectively and justly can substitutes govern? The weight of the language as well as of the situation puts "justice" in the center with "sex" and "substitution" as factors on either side of an equation. To paraphrase an old geometric theorem, things "associated" with the same thing are associated with each other. Thus, the preliminary ground for an issue that becomes crucial later in the play—the bed-trick—is set down in this scene.

The obvious substitutions that occur are Angelo for the Duke in the beginning of the scene; after Angelo's departure, Escalus's replacement of him as a judge; and, at the end of the scene, Elbow's having "continued" overlong in his office as the "poor Duke's constable."[41] Elbow's comic transposition of the adjective meant to characterize his humility as a "poor constable of the Duke's," like so many of his misplacings, turns out to be an accurate assessment. With officers like these carrying out his laws, the Duke is in fact a "poor Duke." Elbow's lengthy term in office, seven-and-a-half years, a more than full apprenticeship period, has taught him nothing except the availability of bribes. Under Escalus's examination, Elbow freely admits that he substitutes for the annually elected constables "for some piece of money." Escalus, hardly pleased by this information, orders him to bring in other names, "the most sufficient of your parish," setting in motion a reconstitution of justice. One wonders, however, if this motion will be any more successful than Escalus's reprimands to Froth—"Master Froth, I would not have you acquainted with tapsters. . . . Get you gone, and let me hear no more of you"—or to Pompey—"let me not find you before me again upon any complaint whatsoever . . . fare you well." The fact that Pompey does eventually end up in prison, escorted there by Elbow (III.ii), points up both the inappropriateness of Escalus's mercy wasted on those hardened to repentance and of Angelo's harsh withholding of such mercy from Claudio, who has confessed and repented and is willing to mend his ways.

Both positions held by Angelo and Escalus at this scene's opening are parodied by the comic action that elaborates on their initial debate. Angelo also creates self-parody with his impatient exit, considering his opening argument in defense of his merciless judgment on Claudio:

> 'Tis very pregnant
> The jewel that we find, we stoop and tak't
> Because we see it; but what we do not see
> We tread upon, and never think of it.
> (II.i.23–26)

Applied to Angelo's own actions, Claudio is the "jewel" he has found to exemplify his stand on fulfilling the letter of the law, and Elbow, Froth, and Pompey are the unseen jewels he chooses "to tread upon, and never think of." But the audience, as well as Escalus and the silent Justice on stage throughout this scene, do see and think of these comic figures, and our reflections almost certainly find Angelo's rationale too limited for human nature. Escalus's counterbalancing view, likewise, if not entirely debunked within the scene, emerges as futile. That both positions are parodied in this early scene prepares the audience to watch for a measure, such as the disguised Duke's, that binds itself neither to Angelo's purist expressions nor Escalus's tendencies toward the laissez-faire, but to an emerging formulation that mixes both ends and finds the middle. Substitutions may be necessary in order for the Duke to discover that neither extreme works satisfactorily in active human affairs, but the working out of the substitution motif in II.i makes it clear that balance and an encompassing vision of all factors that operate in society require a complexly *virtu*ous ruler.[42]

Chapter 3

PARODIC SCENES IN *MACBETH:*

THE PORTER, THE MURDERERS, AND MALCOLM

I

Macbeth is both one of Shakespeare's shortest plays and one of his most structurally controlled. In that respect, form imitates content because it is a play about control, or at least about the attempt to control forces that have ambiguous, possibly undefinable valences. Somewhat paradoxically, many arguments have been advanced to demonstrate (or to assert) that the play in the First Folio is a "cut" version with certain "interpolated" scenes.[1] For example, John Dover Wilson, whose penchant for interpolation is often ingenious, speculates that several scenes are missing from the first acts of the play.[2] Given the principle of analogical structure, however, each scene can be understood in terms of its immediate context without recourse to such speculations. Thomas De Quincey rescued the Porter's scene from Coleridge's criticism that it was a spurious aberration, and much significant study of that scene's symbolic value has followed.[3] As these studies have shown, there is a tighter interconnection between what the Porter says and the focal concerns of what precedes and follows his remarks than merely topical reference indicates. For instance, the generally held assumption that the Porter's speech alludes to Father Garnet's famous trial, in which he used equivocation to escape punishment for his alleged participation in the Gunpowder Plot of 1605, encourages us to ignore the point that it comments, in parodic terms, on themes central to the play.[4]

Equivocations, of course, pervade the play, and, in his dialogue with Macduff, the Porter defines the concept bluntly:

Much drink may be said to be an equivocator with lechery: it makes him, and it mars him; it sets him on, and it takes him off; it persuades him, and disheartens him; makes him stand to, and not stand to; in conclusion, equivocates him in a sleep, and giving him the lie, leaves him. (II.iii.28–32)

Nonetheless, other connections between this scene and the rest of the play are my major concern.

The physical sound of the knocking has begun in the preceding scene shortly after the murder of Duncan, and there has been a steady crescendo until the Porter bursts the tension with his wry remark that "Here's a knocking indeed!" The sensory continuation of the knocking that brings the dread of discovery to the Macbeths integrates the Porter's scene with the preceding action at the same time his comic perspective creates a peculiar ambiguity for the audience—we are encouraged to perceive the situation both emotionally with felt horror and intellectually with critical distance. Damnation evokes surprise only in that it is so general—it touches everyone: "If a man were porter of hell gate, he should have old turning the key. . . . I had thought to have let in some of all professions that go the primrose way to th' everlasting bonfire."

The knocking continues throughout the Porter's soliloquy, alternating the anticipation of dreadful discovery with the Porter's observations that make of Hell an ordinary place. The farmer, having stored his grain hoping for a poor crop only to find that a plentiful crop is anticipated, hangs himself. Aside from being an old joke in a proverbial sense, it refers to a familiar world where the political economics of marginal speculation occur daily. Shakespeare also may have meant to allude to the current low price of wheat, which would make the remark contact the world of the ordinary even more pertinently for his audience.[5]

As the Porter welcomes others who have "come in time," he advises them to "have napkins enow about you; here you'll sweat for't." Sweating is one of the familiar cures for venereal disease,[6] and this line may connect with the ones about the English tailor who steals out of a French hose. Hilda Hulme suggests that "tailor" may be a euphemism for "penis,"[7] and, if so, all four words—sweat, tailor, French hose, goose[8]—have a common referent in the lechery that drink equivocates. The Porter's depiction of Hell's tormented as suffering from sexual disease that results from lechery thus draws a thematic analogue for the diseased world created by the perverse desire of Macbeth and his lady.

Other events retrospectively link the Porter's comment about the farmer to the play's larger context. Macbeth's recognition that "To be thus is nothing but to be safely thus" (III.i.48) and Lady Macbeth's echo in the following scene, "Naught's had, all's spent" (III.ii.4), recall that they had killed Duncan in the expectation of enjoying the crown. For Macbeth, however, the prospect of Banquo's children inheriting that crown makes his own reign empty; and for Lady Macbeth, dwelling in "doubtful joy" eventually leads her to self-destruction, just as the farmer's hoarding against the future ends in suicide. In reciting the farmer's case, the Porter voices proverbial wisdom. As we witness the Macbeths' discontent and insecurity move them further into self-destructive actions, we see the proverb taking on particular demonstration.[9]

The Porter's address to the equivocator, whether it be an allusion to Father Garnet or not, reflects Macbeth's moral plight exactly as he recognized it in his earlier soliloquy (I.vii). Neither the anonymous traitor nor Macbeth can "equivocate to heaven," where the truth is known. With the continuous knocking the Porter grows weary in his role: "Never at quiet! . . . I'll devil-porter it no further." At this point the ironic parallel is most revealing. The Porter can assume that his castle's gate is Hell-Gate and that he is a devil-porter, but for him this is a metaphorical game. When he tires of playing it, he can resume his literal identity as a porter of Inverness Castle, mindful of the emoluments his job may bring. Opening the gate to Macduff and Lennox, he asks for money, "I pray you remember the porter," and casts off the symbolic portentousness of his role, at least as far as *he* is concerned (*we* cannot help but recall the coin that Charon requires before allowing newcomers to cross his river into Hell).

The ease with which he sheds his role contrasts with Macbeth's inability to drop his role-playing once the gates are opened.

The Porter's conscious choice to assume a role imitates not only Macbeth but also Lady Macbeth: the difference between the Porter and the two principal players is that he can divest himself of his role and they cannot. They have locked themselves in to their assumed identities by the very extremity of the violations they perform on themselves, a fact that they fail to recognize at first, but that becomes horribly self-evident as the play progresses. Lady Macbeth's invocation to the powers of darkness— "Make thick my blood. . . . Come to my woman's breasts/ And take my milk for gall. . . . Come, thick night"—transports her beyond the "ignorant present" and transforms her into a being without pity—what she would classify as a man. Macbeth, as he hardens his feelings to become the man she would have him be, loses boundaries as well as control: "I am in blood/ Stepped in so far that, should I wade no more,/ Returning were as tedious as go o'er" (III.iv.136–38).

Lady Macbeth's version of "manhood," which controls both her and her husband's decisions, is one that excludes softness, compassion, grief—qualities that Shakespeare elsewhere demonstrates go by the way in times of extremity. For example, as Mark Antony looks on his friend Julius Caesar's butchered and bleeding body, he prophesies that this resultant "curse shall light upon the limbs of men":

> Blood and destruction shall be so in use
> And dreadful objects so familiar
> That mothers shall but smile when they behold
> Their infants quartered with the hands of war,
> All pity choked with custom of fell deeds.[10]

Such is the curse that lights on Scotland after Duncan's murder and Macbeth's ascension to the throne. Ross describes it to Malcolm in the English court:

> Alas, poor country,
> Almost afraid to know itself. It cannot
> Be called our mother but our grave, where nothing

But who knows nothing is once seen to smile;
Where signs and groans, and shrieks that rent the air,
Are made, not marked. (IV.iii.164–69)

Lady Macbeth, and the motherland of which she is now queen, can no longer procreate, but can only destroy and entomb. Macbeth's questions to the doctor who has witnessed the psychological damage that Lady Macbeth's denial of her feminine role has wrought explicitly associate Lady Macbeth and Scotland in their illness.

Canst thou not minister to a mind diseased . . .
Cleanse the stuffed bosom of that perilous stuff
Which weighs upon the heart?
. . . If thou couldst, doctor, cast
The water of my land, find her disease,
And purge it to a sound and pristine health,
I would applaud thee. (V.iii.40–45, 49–52)

Lady Macbeth's disease is beyond the reach of the doctor's art: self-induced, her illness must be cured from within. The land, reflecting the heartlessness of its rulers in its sickness, can be cured only by the expulsion of that evil. Oedipal in his failure to recognize himself as the cause of Scotland's disease, Macbeth ironically wishes for his own destruction.

Both Lady Macbeth and Macbeth have chosen their roles in "manly" heartlessness, yet their natures rebel against what their conscious wills have decreed: hers in the futile, repetitive, and uncontrollable gesture of cleansing her blood-spotted hands; his in ever-increasing hollowness of response until he experiences despair. Unlike the Porter, who returns at will to his quotidian identity from his symbolic "devil-portering," the Macbeths cannot annul their inversions of their natures.

The active reversal of their natural roles begins when Lady Macbeth reads Macbeth's letter about the prognostic greeting of the three Weird Sisters. She fears that Macbeth's manliness will have too much of the milk of human kindness to take advantage of the situation that circumstances have shaped for them, so she proposes to become the man herself. Her invocation to take away her feminine nature and her motherly potentiality (I.v.38–52), to engender only force without pity, clarifies her perception of manliness, which is like the play's opening evaluation of manly valor used to describe Macbeth:

> For brave Macbeth (well he deserves that name),
> Disdaining Fortune, with his brandished steel,
> Which smoked with bloody execution,
> Like valor's minion carved out his passage
> Till he faced the slave;
> Which ne'er shook hands nor bade farewell to him
> Till he unseamed him from the nave to th' chops
> And fixed his head upon our battlements.
> (I.ii.16–23)

Lady Macbeth echoes the martial words in her realization that Duncan will soon arrive at her castle:

> The raven himself is hoarse
> That croaks the fatal entrance of Duncan
> Under my battlements. (I.v.36–38)

Almost immediately thereafter, we hear Duncan and Banquo eulogizing the "pleasant seat" and the "sweet . . . delicate air" that surround Lady Macbeth's castle. It would take more naiveté than Shakespeare could have presumed for his audience to ignore the irony of contrast that is here established: Lady Macbeth intends evil destruction for the unwitting guests who are approaching with customary anticipations of her forthcoming hospitality. A further irony of perception is implicit, however, and it is one that involves a textual crux. Is Banquo's "martlet," as Nicholas Rowe emended the First Folio's "barlet", really a house-martin, as so many generations of readers have assumed? Marvin Rosenberg, echoing A. P. Paton in the Variorum *Macbeth*, hopes that the "barlet" will eventually show up,[11] but Rowe's emendation seems secure, primarily because Shakespeare refers to the "martlet" one other time.

When the Prince of Arragon in *The Merchant of Venice* deliberates whether to choose the golden casket, he infers that the "many men" of its motto could mean

... the fool multitude that choose by show,
Not learning more than the fond eye doth teach,
Which pries not to th' interior, but like the martlet
Builds in the weather on the outward wall,
Even in the force and road of casualty.[12]

The Prince of Arragon does not think highly of the martlet's failure to perceive beyond, or at least within, exteriors, and implies that it is foolish to build its nest on the outward wall where it has no protection from natural adversities. Banquo, on the other hand, praises the symbolic appropriateness of the martlet's nesting where "the air is delicate," an expression of "heaven's breath." In both instances, the speaker creates through his evaluation a dramatically ironic situation. Despite his acuteness in perceiving a trap within the golden casket's motto, the Prince of Arragon chooses wrongly because he arrogantly refuses to "jump with the common spirits" and then chooses "as much as he deserves"—the silver casket's fool's head.[13] Banquo's appraisal of the air surrounding Macbeth's castle also fails to perceive additional possibilities of equivocal appearances. He, like the Prince of Arragon's martlet, perceives only the exterior of the building where the martlet builds,[14] not the evil within where Lady Macbeth has just invoked the spirits to "unsex" her, to take her breasts' milk for gall, determining to act the man's part if her husband should fail.

When Lady Macbeth shifts her role from female to male, her outward appearance becomes a disguise, one that deceives not only Duncan and Banquo, but even Macduff, who says,

'Tis not for you to hear what I can speak:
The repetition in a woman's ear
Would murder as it fell. (II.iii.79–81)

In comedy, the change of role from female to male is almost a donnée in the plot's formula, but, as Rosalind points out, her assumption of man's clothing changes only her external appearance: "Dost thou think, though I am caparisoned like a man, I have a doublet and hose in my disposition?"[15] Lady Macbeth, on the other hand, leaves her external appearance to signify that she is female but alters her "disposition." She imitates the comic pattern, in other words, by inversion, and she assumes a disguise not in order to discover or encourage truth, but to confound it.[16]

Lady Macbeth is wary that her husband may not meet her standards for "manliness" because he is likely to suffer a paralytic tension between ambition and morality and subsequently fail to unleash the energy of their ambition. Her vision of manliness, which she eventually persuades Macbeth to see and affirm, excludes what Duncan, Banquo, and Macduff assume to be natural components: loyalty, compassion, love. When Macbeth does in fact hesitate to proceed with Duncan's murder out of consideration for such values, she chastises him with a metaphor that becomes a literal concern in the actual carrying through of the murder. She asks him,

> Was the hope drunk
> Wherein you dressed yourself? Hath it slept since?
> And wakes it now to look so green and pale
> At what it did so freely? (I.vii.35–38)

Cleanth Brooks comments that "the metaphor may seem hopelessly mixed,"[17] but he is chiefly interested in the consistency of the clothing metaphor. As a description of a person ("hope") who has overimbibed, then slept, only to wake up with the effects of a hangover, the passage is perfectly consistent. As an image, it anticipates at least two instances in which excessive drink makes men less than men: the "surfeited grooms," who "mock their charge with snores," and the Porter, who confesses to Macduff that he and others "were carousing till the second cock" and he is now feeling several effects of drink. In addition, Lady Macbeth, having drugged the grooms' drinks, seems to have taken some drink herself—"That which hath made them drunk hath made me bold"—and her signal for Macbeth to proceed is the bell that indicates his "drink is ready." Thus, excessive drink "unmans" the grooms and the Porter, whereas a small amount encourages her in her manlike pursuits. The Porter's comic catalogue of drink's effects, moreover, stresses the same point that Lady Macbeth makes in her persuasion of Macbeth. The Porter says: "Lechery, sir, it [drink] provokes, and unprovokes: it provokes the desire, but takes away the performance." Lady Macbeth follows her description of Macbeth's "drunken hope" with the threat:

> From this time
> Such I account thy love. Art thou afeard
> To be the same in thine own act and valor
> As thou art in desire? (I.vii.38–41)

Enveloped in her taunting questions is a sexual challenge: if you cannot carry out this plan, you are not a man, nor can you perform what you desire sexually. The control so necessary to her concept of manhood she is now ironically undermining both for Macbeth and for herself. In her sleepwalking, she pathetically attempts to return to a state of procreative love-making as she reiterates, "To bed, to bed, to bed!" Once they commit themselves to the deed, however, the consequences cannot be "trammeled"—"What's done," she comes to realize, "cannot be undone."[18]

A further point of comic parallel between the Porter's remarks and the murder scene that it follows begins with Macduff's question, "Was it so late, friend, ere you went to bed,/ That you do lie so late?", and ends with the exchange that the Porter's answer leads them to:

PORTER . . . in conclusion, [drink] equivocates him in a sleep, and giving him the lie, leaves him.
MACDUFF I believe drink gave thee the lie last night.
PORTER That it did, sir, i' the very throat on me; but I requited him for his lie; and, I think, being too strong for him, though he took up my legs sometimes, yet I made a shift to cast him. (II.iii.31–37)

The key phrase on which both the Porter and Macduff play is "giving the lie," a term common in the art of fencing. Frank Kermode, in the Riverside edition, notes that "the passage puns on at least three senses of *give one the lie:* (1) call one a liar, (2) lay one out flat, (3) cause one to urinate (lie=lye, slang for 'urine')."[19]

Sonnet #138, as well as the Clown's exchange with Desdemona about where Cassio lies (discussed in the preceding chapter), attests to the fact that "lie" is one of Shakespeare's favorite words for punning: "When my love swears that she is made of truth,/ I do believe her though I know she lies." The Porter's reference to having received the lie in "the very throat on me" plays with the typical challenge—you lie in your throat—in a fashion similar to that of *Othello's* Clown: "for me to devise a lodging, and say he lies here or he lies there, were to lie in my own throat."[20] Not only is dueling (a typical test of manhood) parodied by the Porter's remarks, but also the "equivocating sleep" that gave him "the lie" reminds us of the immediately past dramatic action. Macbeth has murdered sleep in killing Duncan while the king slept. Through the Porter's parody, Macbeth becomes metaphorically like the equivocator "drink," undoing manhood in the very attempt to achieve his and Lady Macbeth's vision of manliness.

II

The Porter's scene has been recognized by critics as a scene of parody because it employs obviously comic routines and word-play,[21] but less obvious, or at least less noticed, is the parodic connection between the scene in which Macbeth hires two murderers to kill Banquo (III.i) and the scenes that precede and conclude the murder of Duncan. The curious aspect of the scene is that Macbeth's lengthy persuasion of the murderers is totally unnecessary. They are willing to perform any deed either "to spite the world" or "to mend . . . or be rid" of their lives. Although they accept Macbeth's diatribe against Banquo without question, they make quite apparent their indifference to his argument.

The dramatic pattern in Macbeth's persuasion of the murderers and in Lady Macbeth's earlier persuasion of him to murder is unmistakably parallel: Macbeth deliberates the rationale for and against murdering first Duncan and then Banquo in soliloquies that are interrupted; this is followed by a persuasion to act; this, in turn, precipitates commitment to the deed; and, finally, Macbeth ritualizes the business in fateful couplets:

Hear it [the bell] not, Duncan, for it is a knell
That summons thee to heaven, or to hell. (II.i.63–64)

It is concluded. Banquo, thy soul's flight,
If it find heaven, must find it out to-night.
(III.i.141–42)

The similarities are clear enough, but there are also major differences of an evaluative sort. First, of course, is the switch in Macbeth's position from the one persuaded to the one who persuades. He moves from actor to director. His need for motive is not so strong as it was with Duncan, and he now has one that he has not fabricated—fear of discovery. Actually, the motives multiply in his soliloquy: Banquo's nature is "royal," the temper of his mind is "dauntless," and his valor is governed by his wisdom. Banquo's goodness is a reason for his death because Macbeth has estranged himself from goodness in murdering Duncan; now, in order to maintain himself, Macbeth must destroy his opposite. Besides, Banquo shares the prophecy with Macbeth and fathers Scotland's future kings. In contrast to his lack of motive to kill Duncan, Macbeth has many reasons to kill Banquo.

The reasons he lists for the murderers are, of course, all fiction; his report of Banquo's misdeeds contradicts everything he has just admitted in his soliloquy. The move from a powerful consideration of choice in soliloquy to a simplified and even reversed explanation in dialogue clearly echoes his retreat from the truth in the earlier scene with Lady Macbeth, where the only explanation he offers for not murdering Duncan is that he would enjoy his newly bestowed honors and "golden opinions" for a while without chancing a taint. The cosmic judgment that he feared would overwhelm him he speaks of to his wife as mere reputation. In his soliloquy concerning Banquo he also is aware of incurring damnation:

For Banquo's issue have I filed my mind;
For them the gracious Duncan have I murdered;
Put rancors in the vessel of my peace
Only for them, and mine eternal jewel

Given to the common enemy of man
To make them kings. (III.i.65–70)

To the murderers he reduces his reasons to political expediency: Banquo is an irritant to his health and ease, but Banquo has friends who would regret Macbeth's sweeping him away. The logic of the shift from soliloquy to public statement is not identical, but the pattern of change from apocalyptic vision to practical image-protection is the same.

The parallel continues in its reduced way to imitate the earlier scene. When Macbeth tells his wife that they "will proceed no further in this business," she lashes out at him for his cowardice. When the hired murderers enter and seem acquiescent enough to Macbeth's plans, he lashes out at them in much the same manner. In this case, Macbeth's arguments are wasted since he has no need to persuade. Yet the reiteration of this pattern performs its dramatic duty. It makes the audience see under the reductive light of parody what we have already given some acceptance to. Whereas we were formerly embroiled in Macbeth's dilemma—how to act without true cause, knowing the dire consequences of the act—we now see the rhetorical posturing of a Macbeth who will "make love" to the tools of villainy in order to expiate his own guilt. In the distance between the two levels of action, the audience learns a critical perspective.

Macbeth's re-enactment of the pre-murder scene is not simply an attempt to place it for himself psychologically, as Lady Macbeth's sleepwalking scene apparently is, yet there is a curious insistence on "control" that suggests that Macbeth is satisfying a need that was frustrated in his murder of Duncan. The situation with the murderers is cut-and-dried, but Macbeth places excessive demands on it to become an emotionally purgative action. Even so, when the murderers at the end attempt to rise to his demands, he cuts off their imperfect response with his own conclusion:

MURDERER 2   We shall, my lord,
   Perform what you command us.

MURDERER I   Though our lives—
MACBETH Your spirits shine through you. Within this hour at most
   I will advise you. (III.i.126–29)

Macbeth is staging this scene and he wants to avoid the problems that his previous loss of control caused in the murder of Duncan. The discrepancy between Macbeth's requirements of the murderers and their own needs, however, deflates whatever victory he feels he has achieved as manipulator of actors and events. Subsequently, the murderers bungle their assignment as badly as Macbeth did his: he forgot to smear the grooms with blood, bringing the murder weapons with him from the scene of the crime, and they allow Fleance to escape.[22] On this occasion, however, Lady Macbeth cannot pick up the pieces, because Macbeth has excluded her from his design.

The most obvious point of parodic contact between the two scenes is the argument of manliness used as persuasion to murder. Surface similarities lead us to see intrinsic differences between the two arguments. Lady Macbeth accuses Macbeth of backing down on a commitment because he is afraid to act, and she buttresses that accusation by pointing out that "time" and "place . . . have made themselves" appropriate for the carrying out of his previously desired action. If you do not want to rely on your manly instincts, realize that circumstances demand accord; destiny, external design, claim this act from you. Her concluding taunt is to compare what she would do under similar circumstances and what Macbeth seems not to be doing. The moral question at the heart of Macbeth's hesitation never surfaces: the question of manliness concerns the daring to act in order to achieve one's desires.

Macbeth's argument to the murderers is that Banquo has beaten them down with all sorts of indignities and that no man should be so patient as to bear these oppressions; therefore, they should revenge themselves for wrongs done to them. When they protest in agreement, "We are men, my liege," Macbeth points out that there are many kinds of men, just as there are many kinds of dogs, but if they choose to be of the higher ranks of manhood they will kill Banquo. The moral question here is supererogatory since the murderers are willing to do anything "to spite the world," but Macbeth makes it central to his persuasion. The situation is thus simplified both in motive and reaction.

As parody, the scene not only looks backward to Lady Macbeth's persuasion of her husband to screw his "courage to the sticking-place"; it also looks forward to the disintegration of Macbeth's human identity. These murderers are machines, stripped of human response, indifferent to the world that has annihilated their feelings:

MURDERER 2   I am one, my liege,
   Whom the vile blows and buffets of the world
   Hath so incensed, that I am reckless what
   I do to spite the world.
MURDERER 1   And I another,
   So weary with disasters, tugged with fortune,
   That I would set my life on any chance,
   To mend it or be rid on 't. (III.i.108–14)

How different, as expression of a philosophy, are these statements from those Macbeth himself utters toward the end of the play?

> I have lived long enough. (V.iii.22)

> I'll fight till from my bones my flesh be hacked. (V.iii.32)

> I have supped full with horrors. (V.v.13)

> Out, out, brief candle!
> Life's but a walking shadow, a poor player
> That struts and frets his hour upon the stage
> And then is heard no more. It is a tale
> Told by an idiot, full of sound and fury,
> Signifying nothing. (V.v.23–28)

> I 'gin to be aweary of the sun,
> And wish th' estate o' th' world were now undone.
> (V.v.49–50)

Both the murderers and Macbeth reach the same state of despair in which action without purpose is the only meaning left to them. Of course, Macbeth's statements of this recognition far surpass those of the hired assassins in poetic power. Nonetheless, all speak from the same philosophical zero.

The hiring of the murderers parallels markedly two of Macbeth's most intense moments on stage. In one respect, the parody reduces Macbeth's actions to the level of absurdity, both literal and metaphysical, but, in another, the similarities of these instances insist that the difference between them in moral and dramatic scope be recognized. The audience could not care less about the murderers as people, but we care intensely about Macbeth, who is driving himself toward inevitable destruction because he violates the premises of divine order in human action. The shallowness of the murderers thus heightens the complexity of Macbeth when he finds himself in similar situations. At the same time, the narrowness of a view that permits haphazard murder as an expression of valueless existence provides a critical perspective through which we must view Macbeth's actions. He gives us another view, which is emotionally engaging; but while we are drawn by his energetic evil, we must also be made aware of how far he violates our moral perspective. The murderers accomplish this in Shakespeare's tremendously serviceable scene. They reduce by similarity and heighten by difference the major issues confronting Macbeth and the audience. Because the mirror is smaller, we see more clearly how narrow Macbeth's fictional reality is.

III

Another scene in this well-wrought play has caused both critics and directors difficulty, that is, the scene between Malcolm and Macduff in the English Court (IV.iii). It is undeniably a static scene, and directors are often at a loss to know how to make it visually dynamic. Should Malcolm loll lasciviously about the stage while he tells Macduff of his ascending order of vices? Or should the two confront each other stiff-legged and exchange passages? There are no easy solutions as to how to handle the stage "business" here, but perhaps a perception that Malcolm is imitating Macbeth in clearly parodic terms—simplification through exaggeration—might be helpful. Because of the gravity of the context, one hesitates to consider Malcolm as a parodist, but he is providing an imitation of Macbeth in his self-report of total viciousness. Resembling Lady Macbeth in her assumption of an opposite nature, Malcolm also imitates the Clown's province of switching roles at whim, as the Porter has done earlier.[23]

It is true, of course, that Shakespeare is following closely the account in Holinshed, and much of what appears to be structural parody in the play is also in the source. A comparison between the chronicle account and Shakespeare's scene will indicate what Shakespeare wanted to stress in his version. The two versions of the Malcolm-Macduff exchange are roughly the same length, over a thousand words each, even though the prose seems longer than the dramatic verse. A major difference is that, in Holinshed, Macduff already knows of the murder of his wife and children by Macbeth when he approaches Malcolm. Shakespeare makes it a significant point that Macduff is ignorant of this when Malcolm says:

> This tyrant, whose sole name blisters our tongues,
> Was once thought honest; you have loved him well;
> He hath not touched you yet. (IV.iii.12–14)

With the murder of Macduff's son onstage having immediately preceded this remark, the audience cannot help but perceive the irony of Malcolm's remark. Thus, Shakespeare makes us anticipate Macduff's discovery throughout the dialogue between him and Malcolm and then later magnifies the irony when he has Ross enter and fail to reveal the news right away.

In Holinshed and in Shakespeare, Malcolm is suspicious that Macbeth has sent Macduff to trick him, and therefore he lies about his own nature's evil to test Macduff's loyalty to Scotland. In Shakespeare, however, Malcolm explains his suspicions to Macduff before he begins the lies about himself. In this he is like the Macbeth of the hiring scene, where Macbeth reveals his need to dissemble his authorship of Banquo's murder. Both Malcolm and Macbeth are manipulating others in a Machiavellian way, but both are explaining more than they have to.

The first "temptation" Malcolm presents is his voluptuousness, "immoderate" in Holinshed, without "bottom" in Shakespeare. Macduff's response, though clearly derived from Holinshed's account, offers a subtle change in Shakespeare's version.

HOLINSHED: "Heerunto Makduffe answered: this suerly is a verie euill fault, for manie noble princes and kings haue lost both liues and kingdomes for the same; neuerthelesse there are women enow in Scotland, and therefore follow my counsell. Make thy selfe king, and I shall conueie the matter so wiselie, that thou shalt be so satisfied at thy pleasure in such secret wise, that no man shall be aware thereof."[24]

SHAKESPEARE: MACDUFF   Boundless intemperance
In nature is a tyranny. It hath been
Th' untimely emptying of the happy throne
And fall of many kings. But fear not yet
To take upon you what is yours. You may
Convey your pleasures in a spacious plenty
And yet seem cold—the time you may so hoodwink.
We have willing dames enough. There cannot be
That vulture in you to devour so many
As will to greatness dedicate themselves,
Finding it so inclined. (IV.iii.66–76)

The subtle change is in Macduff's view of his own role in helping a lascivious Malcolm to the willing dames of Scotland. The Holinshed Macduff offers to convey the matter so that no one shall be aware of Malcolm's use of Scotland's women; implicit in the statement is Macduff's willingness to act as procurer as well as public relations manager for Malcolm. Shakespeare's Macduff, on the other hand, does not so proffer his services. In addition, he suggests that the women are willing (in Holinshed they are simply plentiful), and that many, at least enough to satisfy his lust, would dedicate themselves to Malcolm's purposes in order to achieve greatness for themselves by association. The fascinating difference between the two responses is how Macduff uses the word "convey." In Holinshed, Macduff shall do the conveying: in Shakespeare, Malcolm "may convey" his own "pleasures."

The second vice Malcolm confesses is "avarice," and the account is much the same in both versions, except that Holinshed's Malcolm tells a fable of the fox who would rather have the satiated flies hover over her sore and suck her blood than be beset by new and hungrier ones, in order to stress that Scotland is better off being ruled by Macbeth than it would be under Malcolm. In both instances Macduff deplores avarice as a worse vice than lust, but he assumes that Scotland is rich enough to satisfy Malcolm's appetite this way also.

The third complex vice in Holinshed is dissimulation, deceit, and betrayal; in Shakespeare it is the will to

> Pour the sweet milk of concord into hell,
> Uproar the universal peace, confound
> All unity on earth. (IV.iii.98–100)

In neither case can Macduff tolerate Malcolm's final confession of vice, and he begins to take his leave, rejecting Malcolm as a possible ruler of Scotland. Why, one wonders, does Shakespeare make the change from dissimulator, deceiver, and betrayer to provoker of discord, disharmony, and disunity? Perhaps because Malcolm is at the moment practicing dissimulation, Shakespeare thought the proposed violation of the world's order not only a more dire offense but also more dramatically tactful. Or perhaps Shakespeare, as dramatist, was more concerned with the consequences of action, and Holinshed, as historian, was primarily interested in describing the act. For whatever reason, Shakespeare's Malcolm espouses a cosmic destruction similar to what Macbeth has understood his own actions to promote in the murders of Duncan and Banquo. Macduff's revulsion is intense, and he voices his rejection of Malcolm in similar terms in both Holinshed and Shakespeare: he feels himself to be "banished" from Scotland, a man without hope.

At this point in both accounts, Malcolm gives up his assumed viciousness and confesses to his real virtues. Worth noting is the fact that Shakespeare's Malcolm is much more elaborate than

Holinshed's, who says succinctly, "Be of good comfort Mak-duffe, for I have none of these vices before remembered." Shake-speare has Malcolm revoke each self-inflicted calumny:

> but God above
> Deal between thee and me, for even now
> I put myself to thy direction and
> Unspeak mine own detraction, here abjure
> The taints and blames I laid upon myself
> For strangers to my nature. I am yet
> Unknown to woman, never was forsworn,
> Scarcely have coveted what was mine own,
> At no time broke my faith, would not betray
> The devil to his fellow, and delight
> No less in truth than life. My first false speaking
> Was this upon myself. (IV.iii.120–31)

Paul Jorgensen suggests that perhaps Shakespeare goes too far toward making Malcolm innocent in this retraction: "At the risk of making his savior of Scotland Innocence personified rather than a real character, Shakespeare lays on the childlike qualities relentlessly."[25] Wilbur Sanders, on the other hand, sees some problems for the audience in accepting such a complete turn-about: "Duncan is the lost possibility, Malcolm the diminished necessity. Royalty of nature once slain, only the meaner virtues of circumspection and prudence can survive. . . . The very act of envisaging the corruption of his own nature has tainted him."[26] I am inclined to think that Shakespeare has Malcolm rehearse each vice as he denies them *so that* the difficulty of accepting either side of his confession is emphasized—*so that* the audience accords with Macduff's experience of the equivocation: "Such welcome and unwelcome things at once,/ 'Tis hard to recon-cile." In Holinshed there is no hesitation by Macduff as Mal-colm leaves off his explanation: "Incontinentlie heereupon they imbraced ech other, and promising to be faithfull the one to the other, they fell in consultation how they might best prouide for all their businesse, to bring the same to good effect."

Part of Shakespeare's design in this scene seems to be to show Macduff undergoing trials similar to those Macbeth has experienced earlier in order to underscore our perception that Macbeth's choices were singularly his own. After following Holinshed so closely up to the point of Macduff's expression of confusion, Shakespeare now departs from that source altogether. He introduces a "doctor" whose primary purpose is to recall, for Malcolm and his guest, the king's ability to cure "the evil" that medical art cannot cure. The setting up of an analogy between this doctor and the one that appears in Macbeth's court in the next scene is also part of the doctor's function: neither physician is able to effect a cure for the malady he witnesses. That the King of England can, as Malcolm describes it, by "a most miraculous work" express heaven's grace to his subjects recalls the lost Duncan and Macbeth's perversion of kingship. Through the inevitable comparison, Macbeth becomes a diabolical parody of the good King of England.[27]

Macduff's final trial in this scene is to experience Ross's equivocation in telling what has happened to his family. At first, Ross is evasive when Macduff asks, "How does my wife?" and answers with what only he and the audience know is a pun: "Why, well." When Macduff asks, "And all my children?" Ross also responds, "Well too." Shakespeare uses this pun in another play, when Cleopatra questions the messenger from Italy about whether Antony is alive or dead.[28] In *Antony and Cleopatra*, punning is the modus operandi, and the audience, with Cleopatra, anticipates doubleness in language; in *Macbeth*, however, despite our familiarity with equivocations by this point, Ross's puns come as a shock. We have witnessed the violence Lady Macduff and her son suffered at Fife and know that the pain Macduff will feel on discovery of the truth will be intensified by his having been led to believe that all is well. It seems almost too cruel for Ross, a kinsman, to promote such a reversal. For the Weird Sisters and their apparitions, of course, it seems less unfair to lead Macbeth down the same path of assumption:

> for none of woman born
> Shall harm Macbeth. . . .
> Macbeth shall never vanquished be, until

> Great Birnam Wood to high Dunsinane Hill
> Shall come against him. (IV.i.80–81, 92–94)

Macbeth, after all, has been a traitor in killing Duncan, and to be deceived by the Weird Sisters is appropriate punishment; but is there any sense in which Macduff deserves such deception?

When Ross visits Lady Macduff at Fife, she calls her husband a traitor: "When our actions do not,/ Our fears do make us traitors." Ross tries to argue with her that Macduff had acted out of wisdom rather than fear when he fled to England, but she can only see it from her position of being deserted. She exclaims:

> He loves us not,
> He wants the natural touch. . . .
> All is the fear and nothing is the love,
> As little is the wisdom, where the flight
> So runs against all reason. (IV.ii.8–14)

Even Malcolm finds Macduff's desertion of his family in such a time a cause to doubt him:

> Why in that rawness left you wife and child,
> Those precious motives, those strong knots of love,
> Without leave-taking? (IV.iii.26–28)

No matter that Ross excuses Macduff by pointing out the cruelty of the times, "when we are traitors/ And do not know ourselves [to be so]," Lady Macduff cannot alter her view. Macduff has deserted his family, whatever his motive, and that is a personal kind of treason as she perceives it. In addition, Macduff's intent to overthrow the legal King of Scotland technically makes him what he is called, "a traitor." Macbeth's reign has made Macduff move against his own family's safety as well as against the "established" order in trying to quell the madness that Macbeth has engendered. The peculiar dialogue between Lady Macduff and her worldly wise young son emphasizes how inverted the world order has become, at least in Scotland:

SON Was my father a traitor, mother?
WIFE Ay, that he was!
SON What is a traitor?

WIFE Why, one that swears and lies.

SON And be all traitors that do so?

WIFE Every one that does so is a traitor and must be hanged.

SON And must they all be hanged that swear and lie?

WIFE: Every one.

SON Who must hang them?

WIFE Why, the honest men.

SON Then the liars and swearers are fools, for there are liars and swearers enow to beat the honest men and hang up them.

(IV.ii.44–57)

Irony accretes when, following this dialogue, Malcolm "swears and lies" in order to test Macduff, one of the few "honest men," so that both may "hang"—or behead—the ultimate traitor, Macbeth.

Parallelisms between Malcolm and Macbeth abound in IV.iii, especially in their pragmatic disregard for truth. Malcolm's imitation of the evil king that outdoes Macbeth in fiendishness reduces to simple absolutes the complex nature of Macbeth's motives and actions with which we have become so absorbed. The simplification acts, as parody always does, to distance us from our former engagement with Macbeth's energetic deterioration so that we see him more clearly for what he has become rather than allowing what he formerly was—brave, valiant, noble—to modify our vision.

Not only Malcolm's parody of Macbeth's evil nature but also Macduff's confrontations of and responses to equivocations "place" Macbeth for us so that we more accurately perceive his moral position. Macduff's "Such welcome and unwelcome things at once/ 'Tis hard to reconcile" (IV.iii.138–39) carries echoes of Macbeth's "This supernatural soliciting/ Cannot be ill, cannot be good . . . . function/ Is smothered in surmise and nothing is/ But what is not" (I.iii.130–31; 140–42). One difference in their experiences of equivocation, of course, is that Macbeth is being manipulated by supernatural beings, and Macduff by men, and their responses reflect that. When Malcolm reveals his deception, Macduff is puzzled, cautious. When Ross tells him first that his family is well and they rest in peace, and second, that they have been "savagely slaughtered," Macduff's response is to grieve. When

Macbeth realizes that he has been duped by the prophecies of the Weird Sisters and the apparitions, he feels anger and despair:

> I 'gin to be aweary of the sun,
> And wish th' estate o' th' world were now undone.
> (V.v.49–50)

In contrast to Macduff, who "feels" grief at the death of his wife and babes, Macbeth finds himself worn out of feeling when the news of his wife's death comes: "There would have been a time for such a word."[29]

Perhaps the most emphatic connection between the two who are parallel in so many ways is the return to the question of "manliness."

> MALCOLM   Be comforted.
> Let's make us med'cines of our great revenge
> To cure this deadly grief.
> MACDUFF He has no children. All my pretty ones?
> Did you say all? O hell-kite! All?
> What, all my pretty chickens and their dam
> At one fell swoop?
> MALCOLM Dispute it like a man.
> MACDUFF   I shall do so;
> But I must also feel it as a man.
> (IV.iii.213–21)

Macduff points by contrast, as the murderers did by similarity, to the crucial elimination of what is requisite for manliness—the pity, the milk of human kindness, the capacity to feel, that distinguishes individuals in the catalogue of humanity.

Chapter 4

ROMEO AND JULIET:

THE SIGNIFICANCE OF SEQUENCE

I

Perhaps no play exhibits clearer patterned analogies than does *Romeo and Juliet*. As an early play, it reveals development from cruder experiments with scenic analogy, and yet it does not quite succeed in some of its sequences. To put it another way, the play's apparent obviousness sometimes obscures for the modern eye the subtle conceptions that probably gave rise to its "excludable" scenes.

One such scene is Romeo's encounter with the Apothecary (V.i). Its performance record is peculiar in both filmed and staged productions. If it is not omitted altogether, it is usually hurried through as a minor narrative embarrassment because the plot can certainly survive its omission.[1] One notable pair of productions—notable because they exhibit opposite extremes in the same director's concept—is Franco Zeffirelli's stage production of 1960 and his film production of 1968. According to John Russell Brown, the stage version, though successful "with the young characters in the earlier part of the play," failed "to represent the authoritative figures . . . with a comparable life-likeness"; and "important moments of grief also seemed underplayed." Brown continues,

Romeo's address to the Apothecary showed the failure to represent a more considered grief. This is a speech of peculiar difficulty, for it must manifest complex reactions. But Zeffirelli concentrated on its agitation, so that his Romeo repeatedly struck and browbeat the 'caitiff wretch.'[2]

In his later film version, Zeffirelli omitted the scene altogether, moving from his decision to depict gratuitous violence to gratuitous silence.

Shakespeare, on the other hand, seems almost inordinately concerned with *describing* the Apothecary, not once but twice. When Romeo receives news of Juliet's apparent death, he thinks immediately of the Apothecary and, as he crosses the stage following Balthasar's departure, Romeo describes both him and his shop.

> I do remember an apothecary,
> And hereabouts 'a dwells, which late I noted
> In tatt'red weeds, with overwhelming brows,
> Culling of simples. Meagre were his looks,
> Sharp misery had worn him to the bones;
> And in his needy shop a tortoise hung,
> An alligator stuffed, and other skins
> Of ill-shaped fishes; and about his shelves
> A beggarly account of empty boxes,
> Green earthen pots, bladders, and musty seeds,
> Remnants of packthread, and old cakes of roses
> Were thinly scatterèd, to make up a show.
> Noting this penury, to myself I said,
> 'An if a man did need a poison now
> Whose sale is present death in Mantua,
> Here lives a caitiff wretch would sell it him.'
> O, this same thought did but forerun my need,
> And this same needy man must sell it me.
> As I remember, this should be the house.
> Being holiday, the beggar's shop is shut.
> What, ho! apothecary! (V.i.37–57)

When the Apothecary enters, he has only a few lines of hesitant response to Romeo's request for poison, yet Romeo takes several more lines to describe the man.

> Art thou so bare and full of wretchedness
> And fearest to die? Famine is in thy cheeks,
> Need and oppression starveth in thy eyes,
> Contempt and beggary hangs upon thy back.
> (V.i.68–71)

68

The scene is protracted in the words that Romeo speaks. The narrative does not require it, yet Shakespeare gives us two descriptions of the Apothecary. This peculiar extension of scene has been noticed by critics over the years, and they offer various rationales to explain it in psychological terms. G. Wilson Knight, discussing a production he had seen in 1932, prescribed this antidote:

[Romeo's] description of the Apothecary is very important, and should be done slowly. New worlds are swiftly swimming into his ken. Observe how deepest tragic experience at once, and for the first time, opens his eyes to suffering and impoverished humanity: Lear's purgatory is forecast. He now recalls having seen the Apothecary; partly because he needs him, partly because his consciousness is tuned in to such things, unnoticed before. That is, Shakespeare uses the Apothecary to strike the required tragic note. Watch how Romeo's values are reversed during the conversation with the man; the world's gold becomes poison, life a sickness. Even so, beyond pleasure himself, he takes a selfless pleasure in the Apothecary's advantage: 'Go, buy food and get thyself in flesh'. This is the first purely selfless thought he has uttered: Juliet's death has made a Christian of him.[3]

Following his criticism of Zeffirelli's 1960 stage production, quoted above, John Russell Brown offers these interpretive comments:

The scene should surely be directed in a way that can show how grief *and* resolution have entered deeply into Romeo's soul, making him precise, understanding, compassionate, sharp, subtle and even cynical: it is a complex moment, that cannot be presented by a simple pursuit of energetic expression.[4]

In a more recent essay, Clifford Leech also stresses the psychological changes Romeo undergoes as he seeks out the Apothecary:

Left alone, with the desire for poison in his mind, he turns his attention to the apothecary's shop and to the situation of poor men. This is psychologically true, for in a moment of anguish we naturally tend to take refuge in a thought of something other than a demand that is immediately on us. After that, Romeo's recognition that the gold he gives is a worse poison than the one he buys is largely a Renaissance common-place, but the eloquence with which he expresses it gives him an authority he previously lacked.[5]

Widely variant interests in this particular scene have found different points of emphasis. In a lengthy essay appearing in *Shakespeare-Jahrbuch* in 1901, Julius Cserwinka focuses on the Apothecary scene to show that it is pivotal for the play's concluding death scene: because the Apothecary sells Romeo the poison, Romeo dies. Due to its deliberation, the Apothecary scene brings to immediate reappraisal the meaning of death, which, according to Cserwinka, has become an empty word for the theater audience by this point in the play. At the other extreme of prolixity and point of view, Ralph W. Condee notes in *Shakespeare Quarterly* in 1952 that Shakespeare gave the Apothecary a holiday ("a small but puzzling point") in order to allow the props for the next scene in the Friar's cell to be placed within the inner stage while Romeo purchases his poison.[6]

Whatever the measure of its significance, there seems to have been a persistent recognition that something of importance is occurring in the Apothecary scene. Precisely what that is may have been obscured by not considering one significant fact: the Apothecary scene is part of a *continuum* of scenic development, not simply a *shift* to something new because it moves the play to Act V and Mantua from Act IV's Verona.[7]

II

If we can consider what leads up to and what leads away from the Apothecary scene, we can define the dramatic context in which to read its significance. It would be considerably easier to limit the context to scenes immediately preceding and following, except in this case such limits would result in a *trio* of excludable scenes. Prior to Act V, scene 1, Peter and the Musicians appear with what most critics term "nonsense," and following the scene is Friar John's explanation of how he happened to miss delivering the important secret that Juliet is not dead. Each of these scenes has a relationship to the rest of the play's narrative structure, but each is less than essential to that structure.

Therefore, let us reconstruct the scenic sequence leading up to the Apothecary scene, beginning after the slaying of Tybalt: (III.iii) Romeo hides and weeps in the Friar's cell and is persuaded to go to Juliet; (III.iv) Capulet and Paris arrange the marriage; (III.v) Juliet and Romeo say goodbye, after which her parents inform her of the impending marriage to Paris and she, left completely alone, resolves to die if Friar Laurence can find no remedy; (IV.i) Paris arranges the time of the marriage with Friar Laurence; Juliet arrives to speak with the Friar, encounters Paris (for the only time onstage), and then agrees to take the sleeping potion; (IV.ii) as Capulet instructs the servants concerning the wedding party, Juliet appears to repent her stubborn rejection of the plans, and Paris is sent for; (IV.iii) left alone, Juliet takes the potion; (IV.iv) the bustle of the Capulet household anticipates the joyful event of Juliet's wedding while Juliet sleeps within the curtain; (IV.v) the Nurse attempts to waken Juliet but discovers her apparently dead, all lament, and Peter jests with the Musicians; (V.i) Romeo recalls his happy dream, is met with news from Verona that Juliet is dead, and goes to the Apothecary to secure poison.

The dominant visual image of Romeo's scene in the Friar's cell, which begins this sequence, is that of Romeo tearing his hair (l. 68), "on the ground, with his own tears made drunk" (l. 83), and, having risen, attempting to stab himself with a dagger (ll. 108–9). He has completely reversed the hope and optimism that followed his marriage to Juliet. To anyone familiar with the iconographical and emblematic literature that was part of the heritage of Shakespeare's audience, it would be hard to miss the visual recreation by Romeo of the emblem of despair. Excessive weeping, tearing of the hair, and self-destructive dagger wounds are attributes of the despairing suicide.[8] The dagger itself is a favorite weapon of suicides, as the episode at the Cave of Despair in Spenser's *Faerie Queene* testifies: both Sir Terwin and the Red Cross Knight accept a dagger from Despair.[9] Comparison with Spenser's employment of similar materials is useful, primarily because of the difference in allegorical scope. Rather than having a theological implication of supernatural focus as does Spenser's account,[10] Romeo's scene in the Friar's cell substitutes Juliet as the center of spiritual being, a point made by both Romeo and the Friar: "Heaven is here/ Where Juliet lives," Romeo says after hearing of his banishment, and the Friar's persuasion away from suicide depends on "Thy Juliet is alive,/ For whose dear sake thou wast but lately dead./ There art thou happy" (ll. 29–30, 135–37). There is no direct argument that suicide is sinful, such as Una makes in her chastisement of the Red Cross Knight:

> Come, come away, fraile, feeble, fleshly wight,
>> Ne Let vaine words bewitch thy manly hart,
>> Ne diuelish thoughts dismay thy constant spright.
>> In heuenly mercies hast thou not a part?
>> Why shouldst thou then despeire, that chosen art? (I.ix.53)

Instead, "Juliet is alive" is the grace and the faith that stays Romeo's hand.

Earlier in his speech the Friar refers to his religious office, "By my holy order," but this is only a mild oath that precedes "I thought thy disposition better tempered" (ll. 114–15). He does question Romeo's suicidal wildness as "doing damned hate upon thy self" (l. 118); however, he manages to curb Romeo's self-destructive intent by an appeal to reason, manliness, and practical action, rather than by reminding him of God's grace as Una does for the Red Cross Knight. The Friar, who might appropriately stress the error of substituting Juliet's life as the source of Romeo's salvation, himself fails to distinguish the world created by the lovers from the world created by God.

Aside from the purely emblematic interest of the scene, Shakespeare has intruded on it several comic moments, as if to suggest that Romeo thus far has not truly reached the essence of despair but is still playing an externalized role. Romeo's excessive punning throughout the scene objectifies his grief, even for an audience that by this time is used to puns and wordplay. To list only the most obvious: "What less than doomsday is the Prince's doom?" (l. 9); "Flies may do this but I from this must fly" (l. 41);

"what says/ My concealed lady to our cancelled love?" (ll. 97–98).
The Nurse's presence, too, mitigates the seriousness of the scene;
she has not yet violated Juliet's dreams of love by advising her to
take a second husband, although she may have impugned Juliet's
dignity in grief with

> O, he is even in my mistress' case,
> Just in her case! O woeful sympathy!
> Piteous predicament! Even so lies she,
> Blubb'ring and weeping, weeping and blubb'ring.
> (III.iii.84–87)

At the same time, of course, she reduces Romeo's evident grief to
posturing even as she describes what she sees. After the Friar
exhorts Romeo to be a man and go to Juliet rather than self-
indulgently to destroy himself, the Nurse deflates both the seriousness of the Friar's speech and the impact of Romeo's grief:

> O Lord, I could have stayed here all the night
> To hear good counsel. O, what learning is!
> (III.iii.159–60)

There is as well the disputable stage direction from Q1 that
indicates it is the Nurse who snatches Romeo's dagger away
from him. If Q1 is a memorial reconstruction by actors, as
Harry R. Hoppe argues, then such a staging note may be justified—it is likely that the actors would remember who grabbed
the dagger to prevent Romeo's suicide even if the Friar's lines
would suggest that he himself does the snatching." If Shakespeare did intend for the Nurse to grab the dagger after she
advocates that Romeo "stand up and be a man" (l. 88), her
performance of the stronger action as the Friar stands passively
by and verbally stresses "Hold thy desperate hand" (l. 108)
pushes the entire scene toward parody.

Whatever the tone, the scene stands midway between Romeo's
affectation of despair with his initial love for the unseen Rosaline
and the final despair that drives him to his actual suicide once he
perceives that Juliet is dead. Clearly there is a difference in the
kinds of despair Romeo exhibits in the three scenes. In his des-

pair over Rosaline, we see an empty posturing, a Romeo who cannot convince himself of his own emotions:

> Alas that love, whose view is muffled still,
> Should without eyes see pathways to his will!
> Where shall we dine? . . .
> This love feel I, that feel no love in this.
> Dost thou not laugh? (I.i.169–71, 180–81)

His questions to Benvolio betray his lack of self-confidence, a hesitance that changes with the death of Tybalt and word of his "banishment." His reaction to his decreed separation from Juliet (III.iii), though it still sounds postured, has a more substantial quality. With his final commitment to despair, however, role and feeling equate: "O true apothecary! Thy drugs are quick. Thus with a kiss I die" (V.iii.119–20). The three situations in which Romeo's despair is central are analogical: through incremental repetition they create dimension for despair and for death. The accumulation of energy that accompanies realization of the self—even if it is *within* a role—has persuasive power over the audience, so that by the final suicide we are made to feel satisfaction in the completed identification of Romeo with his role.

In the scene following Romeo's decision not to kill himself, *while* Capulet assures Paris of his impending marriage with Juliet, Juliet and Romeo are consummating their marriage. Capulet's " 'Tis very late; she'll not come down to-night" (III.iv.4) emphasizes for the audience that the time is exactly coincidental with Romeo's and Juliet's union. The juxtaposition of Capulet's farewell to Paris (who is impatient for *his* wedding day to arrive), "it is so very very late/That we may call it early by and by" (III.iv. 34–35), with Juliet's opening line of the next scene, "Wilt thou be gone? It is not yet near day" (III.v.1), delineates the opposing points of view, and the contrasting echo welds her double betrothal together despite her intent.

When Juliet, in exact contrast to her father's sense of time's speeding by, appeals to Romeo to ignore the evidence of a new day, Romeo (having been persuaded by the Friar to become realistic) metaphorically describes what he sees: the unpleasant truth that day is dawning. This is capped by his literal acceptance of the Prince's "doom," which he uses to create a figurative and sexual pun: he says, "I must be gone and live, or stay and die" (III.v.11). Juliet protests, "Yond light is not daylight, I know it I," somewhat after the fashion of Petruchio when he insists that the sun is the moon and forces Kate to agree, only to reverse himself and swear it is "the blessed sun."[12] And Romeo, like Kate, agrees against his better knowledge:

> I'll say yon grey is not the morning's eye,
> 'Tis but the pale reflex of Cynthia's brow;
> Nor that is not the lark whose notes do beat
> The vaulty heaven so high above our heads.
> I have more care to stay than will to go.
> Come, death, and welcome! Juliet wills it so. (III.v.19–25)

But Juliet cannot agree, not for the same reasons that Petruchio has, but because she knows that to ignore reality is to summon her lover's death. Still, the parallel is instructive—in the comic mode, reality can be ignored in order to reshape it according to the lover's eye; in the tragic mode, the lover's creation ignores reality only at the cost of his own life.

On their leavetaking, Juliet comments on Romeo's pale complexion, a look traditionally associated with melancholy, and he concurs in his analysis of their common cause to look so:

JULIET Either my eyesight fails, or thou lookest pale.
ROMEO And trust me, love, in my eye so do you.
Dry sorrow drinks our blood. (III.v.57–59)

This is only one of many instances where the psychological situation manifests itself physically and in "humoral" terms. According to M. Andreas Laurentius in *A Discourse of the Preservation of the Sight: Of Melancholike Diseases, etc.,* "All passions of the minde doe much hurt the sight, but above the rest, melancholicke dumpes and much weeping."[13] Both the lovers have wept openly and profusely in recent scenes, Juliet when she learns that Romeo has slain Tybalt, and Romeo when he discovers his banishment. According to the Nurse, both alike were "blubb'ring and weeping, weeping and blubb'ring." And now, even more susceptible to love-inspired melancholia, they must part. Their pale complexions, the sorrow that drinks the blood from their faces, are but one of an entire complex of physical signs of those afflicted by melancholia.[14]

When Lady Capulet intrudes on her daughter to tell her of her new betrothal, she mistakes Juliet's lamentations as grief over Tybalt and speaks of the "villain . . . which slaughtered him" (III.v.80). Since Tybalt has made such a contextually inappropriate point of calling Romeo a "villain" at the Capulet ball and again before the fatal street brawl (I.v.64 and 75, III.i.60), such reference creates ironic echo. Lady Capulet's reiteration of Tybalt's "villain" reminds us that Tybalt's then-inaccurate perception of Romeo was nonetheless dramatically predictive; likewise, Lady Capulet's plan to "send to one in Mantua" for poison to kill Romeo anticipates what is to be, although the agent turns out to be Romeo himself. She promises Juliet that

> We will have vengeance for it, fear thou not.
> Then weep no more. I'll send to one in Mantua,
> Where that same banished runagate doth live,
> Shall give him such an unaccustomed dram
> That he shall soon keep Tybalt company.
> (III.v.88–92)

Juliet's response, too, is ironically predictive, even though we know that the meaning she intends is not what her mother supposes: "Madam, if you could find out but a man/ To bear a poison, I would temper it;/ That Romeo should, upon receipt thereof,/ Soon sleep in quiet" (97–100). Her metaphorical double entendre becomes literal truth when her own sleeping potion, which would temper Romeo's poison, fails because it appears to be what it is not. Thus, on viewing her under the narcotic's effect, he drinks his poison and "sleep[s] in quiet." The play's ironic tension is developed through such puns in dramatic action, and from this point they multiply.

Juliet's response to both parents in this scene is a dramatic pun that the audience and Juliet share. When her mother informs her that she has been betrothed to Paris, Juliet resists:

> I will not marry yet; and when I do, I swear
> It shall be Romeo, whom you know I hate,
> Rather than Paris. (III.v.122–24)

In response to her husband's fulsomely metaphoric description of Juliet's tears and "tempest-tossed body," which he had expected to be relieved by news of the impending wedding, Lady Capulet again speaks with unintentionally predictive irony: "I would the fool were married to her grave!" The scene is built on a comic formula, parents defied by their child's opposing will; Capulet, the *senex* father, initially uncomprehending of Lady Capulet's meaning—"Soft! take me with you, take me with you, wife./ How? Will she none?"—swiftly shifting into rage and superficial misreading of his daughter's meaning—"Thank me no thankings, nor proud me no prouds." The strangely contrapuntal play of Juliet's own weighted oxymorons, "Proud can I never be of what I hate,/ But thankful even for hate that is meant love," against the comically superficial readings her father gives them, is the serious underside of comic routine. Compare for contrasting effect the scene in which the illiterate Servant-Clown fails to comprehend Romeo's postured metaphor: "I pray, sir, can you read? ROMEO Ay, mine own fortune in my misery" (I.ii.57–58). Here the surface misreading is an adequate commentary on Romeo's depth of feeling. Juliet is verbally abused by both her parents after the manner of clown's play, but because Juliet is suffering real pain, the discrepancy between comic routine and actual meaning strikes an unusually discordant note. Capulet makes a comic Lear in his rejection of Juliet, to which the Nurse responds that he is "to blame . . . to rate her so," and then he castigates the Nurse in comic terms. Capulet's description of Juliet, "A wretched puling fool,/ A whining mammet," disagrees so violently with our apprehension of Juliet's depth of character that his rage is comic even while it is an actual threat to Juliet's welfare. After he leaves her with threats of disowning and banishing her, Lady Capulet imitates him in more concise phrase:

"Talk not to me . . . for I have done with thee." Then Juliet, bereft, turns to the Nurse for comfort and counsel and gets instead a worldly wisdom that sees a husband at hand (even if it be a second husband) better than one absent who is effectively dead. Because the scene is structured on recognizably comic oppositions, the profundity of Juliet's sense of tragic isolation has greater impact.

This same counterpoint of comic form imposed on tragic material continues into the next scene when Juliet encounters Paris at Friar Laurence's cell. Their stychomythic exchange, again filled with puns that the audience shares with Juliet, we could imagine Rosalind speaking to Orlando. It is witty and sophisticated, yet it is not superficial. Juliet's release of control, once the door is shut on Paris, reveals the huge discrepancy between the role she has been forced into playing and her true feelings. In this instance, Juliet under pressure has assumed the role-playing that Romeo chose at the beginning of the play, a point that intensifies the actuality of their love.

In Friar Laurence's cell, Juliet re-enacts, but with a difference, Romeo's earlier attempt at suicide: rejecting marriage to Paris, she is willing to listen to an alternate plan.

> Tell me not, friar, that thou hearest of this,
> Unless thou tell me how I may prevent it.
> If in thy wisdom thou canst give no help,
> Do thou but call my resolution wise
> And with this knife I'll help it presently. (IV.i.50–54)

Friar Laurence comes up with an alternate plan based on her "strength of will to slay thyself," subtly reversing his reasoning with Romeo in the earlier scene. There, desperate threats of self-violence were condemned; here they are the basis of condoned action. Further, the visual impact of Juliet's drinking the potion anticipates Romeo's death by poison: the only difference is between appearance and reality, concepts that have become confused for both the characters in the play and the audience. The audience has been drawn into the play's action despite its superior knowledge.

In order to persuade all but the knowing ones—the lovers, the Friar, and the audience—that Juliet is in fact dead, the Friar must adopt the role of commiserating spiritual father: "Now heaven hath all,/ And all the better is it for the maid." In order to gain the freedom to appear dead, Juliet has had to assume the role of obedient daughter. Remembering how we have been asked to judge role-playing from the play's beginning, what anticipations are warranted by this? Earlier we are instructed to laugh at disguised emotions; now we are asked to encourage them.

After her need for disguise has passed, Juliet is filled with fatal premonitions; her "Farewell! God knows when we shall meet again" emphasizes her anticipation of joining Romeo in exile, but proves ironically to seal her total absence—she does not meet again with those she is now bidding farewell. She describes her physical recognition of fear in terms that are associated with "melancholia"; it "freezes up the heat of life." She reminds the audience of the dagger, the suicide's weapon—in case the "mixture do not work at all." Her vision of the tomb, if she should wake before Romeo comes "to redeem" her, resembles nothing so much as the Cave of Despair, where melancholia reigns.[15] What we see, Juliet with the alternate weapons of the vial and the dagger, and what we hear her describe, reinforce the development of the despair/melancholia theme that we have been conscious of since the play's opening scene.

III

Interlocking Juliet's "farewell" speech and the discovery of her "death" is a curious bit of comic business between the Nurse and Capulet and his wife. The Nurse encourages Capulet to retire (it is after three), but he insists that he has stayed up "all night for lesser cause," to which his wife knowingly agrees: "Ay, you have been a mouse-hunt in your time;/ But I will watch you from such watching now." That parents should joke about the father's former extra-marital sexual adventures on the eve of their daughter's wedding has an ordinary kind of appropriateness. Capulet's response to his wife's warning that his "mouse-hunting" days are over sees her wearing a "jealous hood"—at this point in their marriage, no doubt, jealousy seems a compliment. Despite this good-natured banter, however, the audience is aware that they are all three trying to force Juliet to violate her wedding vows to Romeo.

Preparations for the festive occasion are only briefly displayed, but the visible bustle with the servants carrying "things for the cook" is important—it reminds us of the scene before the ball where Juliet was first to meet Paris and fell in love with Romeo instead (I.v.1–15). Capulet takes the time to make a pun out of one of the servant's assurances that he has "a head, sir, that will find out logs." His pride in his own abilities to serve (rather than to call on Peter's supervision) is turned into a verbal quip at his expense when Capulet says, "Mass, and well said; a merry whoreson, ha!/ Thou shalt be loggerhead." All is meant in convivial spirit, and immediately music is heard from within that announces Paris's arrival. This small bit of a scene creates a domestic perspective of would-be happiness and harmony that increases our awareness of the discrepancy between what we know these characters will soon discover and what they think they will find.

The editorial division of this scene would seem to separate it from IV.iii (Juliet's drinking of the potion) and IV.v (the Nurse's discovery of her apparently dead body). But it seems quite clear that all three of these "scenes" are one scene, and that we are meant to be visually aware of Juliet's drugged body behind the curtains on the stage as the Capulet household joyfully prepares for her wedding to Paris. Simultaneous staging is one of the advantages of Shakespeare's stage, and here he puts it to powerful ironic use.[16]

The Nurse's discovery of Juliet's lifeless body is another display of her comic attitude. Totally unsuspecting at first, she calls Juliet a "slug-abed" and bawdily suggests that Paris will make her bed time more active from now on. The sexual bluntness of the Nurse's suggestions is in keeping with her character, and it is appropriate to sexual aspects of Juliet's being Death's bride, talked about earlier and finally summarized by Romeo when he finds her in the tomb. But for the audience, very much aware of

Juliet's precarious situation and anticipating the horror of the Capulet household on their discovery of what we know, the Nurse's anticipation of Paris's vigorous sexual attack on the body of Juliet suggests a terrible violation, much worse than her lewd suggestion to Romeo earlier that "there is a nobleman in town, one Paris, that would fain lay knife aboard" (II.iv.189–90). All of the happiness anticipated for Juliet by the Capulet household would mean a violation of Juliet, who has in fact violated her own body by taking the potion in order not to submit to their wills.

From this rather jarring emotional situation, the scene moves into its much-discussed "lamentation." S. L. Bethell, in an effort to right the "astonishing ineptitude of Victorian criticism," describes the "burlesque" tone of this section as necessary to keep the audience from joining in with the Capulet household over the mourning of Juliet's supposed death.[17] Other instances have been observed from Shakespeare's plays in which the audience knows that "the decedent is *not* dead" and in which "a sincere outburst of grief . . . would be out of place and a rude assault on the audience's feelings."[18]

It would be difficult to ignore the similarities between the Nurse's "O woe! O woeful, woeful, woeful day!" speech and Pyramus's lament over the supposedly dead Thisby in *A Midsummer Night's Dream*. Whether Shakespeare wrote the latter as a specific parody of *Romeo and Juliet* before or after he wrote the tragedy is yet a question, but the similarities between the play that Bottom and the mechanicals present, "The most lamentable comedy and most cruel death of Pyramus and Thisby," and *Romeo and Juliet* are clear.[19]

The excessive grieving over Juliet's death is predictive in a comic mode of the grief that leads Romeo to actual death: one effect of this parody that precedes the serious action is to release through laughter the hesitations an audience might have about the excesses of Romeo's grief, also mistakenly inspired.[20] Compared with this scene of comic mourning, Romeo's mourning creates an even greater effect than it would otherwise. The parodic rehearsal implies a warning: Romeo may be no more immune to mistaken causes for grief than Juliet's parents, the Nurse, and Paris.

The Friar's interruption of their lamentations with his question "Come, is the bride ready to go to church?" releases an elaboration of grief by each of the four mourners. They sound almost as if they were in a contest to see who could form the best oxymoron or other recognizably rhetorical figure, not very different from the way Romeo sounds in Act I when he affects his emotion for Rosaline.[21] Friar Laurence, after allowing each mourner to utter grief, calls a halt to it by shaming them with their neglect of Juliet's spiritual welfare, sounding like Feste when he questions Olivia about her brother's death in *Twelfth Night* and proves her the fool for mourning his soul, which is in heaven.[22] Friar Laurence says:

> Peace, ho, for shame! Confusion's cure lives not
> In these confusions. Heaven and yourself
> Had part in this fair maid—now heaven hath all,
> And all the better for the maid. (IV.v.65–68)

One distinction, however, makes the effect quite different. In *Twelfth Night,* Olivia's brother is dead; here we know, as does the Friar, that Juliet lives. Thus, his spiritual guidance for those caught in excessive grief is based on hypocrisy, and we may find ourselves discounting the truth he speaks as mere casuistry.[23] The Friar's double purpose, in other words, undercuts both the mourning and the consolation of the scene's surface.

As part of the funeral ceremonies, so suddenly changed from those planned for the wedding, the Friar advises the mourners to "stick your rosemary/ On this fair corse." This detail is more than a ceremonial decoration for the scene. It relates this rehearsal of grief and the combination of wedding and funeral to the general theme of melancholia and its cures with which the play is concerned throughout.

John Parkinson, appointed the Apothecary of London by James I, describes the virtues of rosemary as almost universal for curing all kinds of diseases, noting that it is used for civil purposes as well as physical cures.

Rosmary is almost of as great use as Bayes, or any other herbe both for inward and outward remedies, and as well for civill as physicall purposes. Inwardly for the head and heart; outwardly for the sinewes and ioynts: for civill uses, as all doe know, at weddings, funerals, &c. to bestow among friends: and the physical are so many, that you might bee as well tyred in the reading, as I in the writing, if I should set down all that might be said of it.[24]

In his later "Compleate Herball," *Theatrum Botanicum, The Theater of Plantes* (1640), he expands on its physical uses as a help for "all cold diseases, both of the head, stomack, liver, and belly . . . [by] drying up the cold moistures of the braines, and quickening the senses."[25] Pierre de la Primaudaye also praises this particular quality in *The French Academie:*

It would be very hard to finde out in one plant onely more vertues and properties, then they who haue trauelled to publish the science of simples, have attributed to rosemarie. . . . The flowers thereof confected in sugar, are good for all things aforesaide, particularly against cold passions of the hart.[26]

Melancholy is a disease associated with excessive cold, both physically and psychologically.

We are familiar, of course, with Ophelia's association of "rosemary, that's for remembrance" in *Hamlet*.[27] Philip Williams points out that the flowers Queen Gertrude scatters over Ophelia's grave would likely be rosemary; as she says, "I thought thy bride-bed to have decked, sweet maid,/ And not have strewed thy grave."[28] In his speech over his daughter's body, Capulet also stresses their ironically double use: "Our bridal flowers serve for a buried corse." Earlier when the Nurse asks, "Doth not rosemary and Romeo begin both with a letter?" she is trying to recall what Juliet has made of that: "she hath the prettiest sententious of it, of you and rosemary, that it would do you good to hear it" (II.iv.195–200). It is tempting to extrapolate that Juliet, though obviously not the Nurse, was aware that rosemary had such healing qualities as she then attributed to Romeo.[29]

By calling attention to rosemary in the Friar's directive, "stick your rosemary/ On this fair corse," and in the actions of the mourners as they leave the stage (Q1 stage direction specifies their "casting Rosemary on her and shutting the Curtens"), Shakespeare may want us to be aware of all these properties. Rosemary's virtue as a cure for melancholy, a disease that may be both psychologically and physically induced, is especially appropriate for the situation at hand, for, as Capulet puts it, "All things that we ordainèd festival/ Turn from their office to black funeral—/ Our instruments to melancholy bells" (IV.v. 84–86).

IV

Music also was thought to be a cure for melancholy, as Laurentius notes in his second discourse: "The old writers doe commend Musicke in all Melancholike diseases."[30] And Timothy Bright, in *A Treatise of Melancholie* (1586), specifies what kind of music is appropriate:

not only cheerfull musicke in a generalitie, but such of that kinde as most reioyceth is to be sounded in the melancholicke eare: of which kinde for the most part is such as carieth an odde measure, and easie to be discerned, except the melancholicke have skill in musicke, and require a deeper harmonie. That contrarilie, which is solemne, and still: as dumpes, and fancies, and sette musicke, are hurtfull in this case.[31]

The Musicians in *Romeo and Juliet* obviously know that a "dump," as Peter requests, would be the worst cure for the situation. Of course, Peter asks for a "merry dump," which as F. W. Sternfeld points out is "intentionally self-contradictory."[32]

The Musicians' verbal play that completes this scene has long been viewed as an anomaly and frequently as an embarrassment.[33] Perhaps the easiest explanation for its being is that Will Kemp wanted something more to do and Shakespeare complied by giving him this comic bit of business (the stage direction in Q2 reads "*Enter Will Kemp*"). Even if this is true, there is an aspect that has not been fairly noticed—the segment of the scene is thoroughly appropriate to several facets of the theme of melancholia developed in this scenic sequence.

The switch from the mirth of marriage celebration to the dirge of funeral is an oxymoron of action; we have been led to expect death in marriage all along. At last, with the discovery of Juliet's body, the rituals of wedding and death combine. At the same time that the Capulet household's expectations are thwarted, the audience's expectations are fulfilled, and, as a result, the audience is both satisfied and anxious—satisfied that so far the Friar's plan is working, and anxious about its final resolution.

After the mourners depart, the Musicians enter[34] and realize that they have no office to perform. Prepared for wedding entertainment, they now must "put up our pipes and be gone." The Nurse agrees:

> Honest good fellows, ah, put up, put up!
> For well you know this is a pitiful case. (IV.v.97–98)

At least one level of punning is clear—Juliet's case is pitiful, and the instruments must be put up in their cases. An underlying pun on sexual casing may also be present, since it is recurrent throughout the play and one that Juliet realizes in her final sheathing of the dagger in her own flesh.[35] Considering the Nurse's remarks on her discovery of Juliet's body and her earlier warning to Romeo that "there is a nobleman in town, one Paris, that would fain lay knife aboard" (II.iv.189–91), the bawdy suggestiveness is fitting for her characterization.

Given this possibility, the Musicians' response to the Nurse's pun continues for the audience a multileveled awareness of meaning: "Ay, by my troth, the case may be amended." The audience knows that Romeo may discover Juliet and rescue her, replacing the semblance of death as her bridegroom, and thus amending her pitiful case. Since "pipes" are frequently used to refer to "penis,"[36] the casing of the pipes initials this segment as multiplicit. If we recognize these puns, and certainly post-Victorian audiences have been trained not to, what is their effect? For one thing, the scene is released from the restrictions of mourning that have been artificially imposed on the facts. For another, we can enjoy the anticipation of a happy reunion between the lovers.

One of the few critics who has commented on the "possible bawdy" of the Nurse's two lines, discounts it, if there, because "it is quickly lost from sight on the arrival of Peter immediately afterwards. Peter's wit contest with the Musicians has an engaging quality. . . . the result is that for these three or four minutes we all but *forget* Romeo and Juliet."[37] Peter's engagement of the Musicians in a verbal duel certainly is diverting, and it follows a standard comic formula. I am convinced, however, that the whole of this segment keeps our focus on the main events by way of its parodic perspective.

Peter enters with a lament that echoes that of the Nurse and the others in the preceding segment, and he asks the Musicians to play a song to comfort him; they refuse. He then promises to requite them, not by giving them money, but by mocking them, and challenges them, through a series of puns on musical terms, to solve a riddle. Each Musician responds except the third, who has nothing to say. Peter answers the riddle himself, sings a few bars of a song, and leaves. One Musician comments that this is a "pestilent knave," and the other says, forget it, let's go in and wait for dinner.

What happens here is not nearly as important as how it happens. Part of the puzzle of this bit of action might be resolved if we consider it in the light of fencing rules. Dueling is, of course, a controlling metaphor for the play. The language that Peter uses after the Musicians refuse to play "a merry dump" for him is exactly that employed in the language of challenge and reply in fencing: "I will then give it you," "Then have at you," "Answer me like men."

Vincentio Saviolo published a fencing manual in English in 1595 that caused a considerable stir among the English, especially with fencing master George Silver, who scorned Saviolo's Italian techniques as not only unpatriotic but also unsafe.[38] Although Sir William Segar, an Englishman, had published a detailed description of the different kinds of lies to be recognized in challenging by gentlemen in his *The Booke of Honor and Armes* (1590), Saviolo's fencing manual created more excitement, probably because he was a foreigner who was changing a way of socially acceptable behavior. Whether Shakespeare was more familiar with Segar or Saviolo, whose list of "lies" accords exactly with Segar, is not as important as the fact that Touchstone's seven kinds of lies in *As You Like It* (V.iv.92ff.) recognizes the current fashion for the observance of precise protocol in such affairs. S. P. Zitner, noting Touchstone in an essay on the duel in *Hamlet*, remarks that Shakespeare "was not the only dramatist to laugh at a pedantry of violence."[39] Mercutio's remarks about Tybalt, preceding his verbal duel with Romeo in II.iv—"a duellist, a duellist! a gentleman of the very first house, of the first and second cause. Ah, the immortal passado! the punto reverso! the hay!"—also suggest that Shakespeare was amused by the extraordinary interest in the rules, in a very technical sense, of the sport of fence.

When Peter says, "I'll re you, I'll fa you," the Musicians respond as if he has threatened to beat them, and his weapon, named three times as the dagger, is one that Saviolo describes in detail in his first book on "the use of the Rapier and Dagger." Egerton Castle comments that, "Twenty years before Saviolo wrote his treatise, a small hand buckler or target was the usual complement of the sword in the costume of a gentleman walking abroad, but when the foyning play came into fashion, it was discarded in favor of the dagger, which was at once more elegant and better fitted to ward off a thrust to either side, and cover the enemy's blade."[40] In this instance, it is not the gentleman's dagger but the "serving-creature's dagger" that Peter employs. The Second Musician's request to Peter to "put up your dagger, and put out your wit," Peter answers by substituting his "iron wit" for his "iron dagger," and then he offers them the challenge.

Peter has earlier displayed his knowledge of the rules of fencing and the grounds for "honorable quarrels"[41] when the Nurse berates him for not challenging Mercutio's disrespectful classification of her as "a bawd." She complains, "And thou must stand by too, and suffer every knave to use me at his pleasure!" Peter protests:

I saw no man use you at his pleasure. If I had, my weapon should quickly have been out, I warrant you. I dare draw as soon as another man, if I see occasion in a good quarrel, and the law on my side. (II.iv.148–50)[42]

The question of lawful quarreling is primary in fencing manuals, as a chapter title from Saviolo's second book indicates: "How Gentlemen ought to accept of any Quarrel, in such manner that they may combat lawfully."[43] Even Sampson and Gregory in the opening scene seem to be aware of this in giving the challenge. Sampson, encouraging Gregory to incite the other to quarrel, says, "Let us take the law of our sides, let them begin." When Abram asks, "Do you bite your thumb at us, sir?" Sampson checks with Gregory before he answers, "Is the law of our side if I say ay?" Gregory says it is not and then asks Abram, "Do you quarrel, sir?" Gregory is the one who manipulates Abram to give the lie, which then results in a brief fight until Benvolio parts them (I.i.38–65). The language makes it clear, however, that they all are aware of the rules of fencing.

Both scenes, the opening "serving-creatures' " combat and Peter's engagement of the Musicians, are comic imitations of Mercutio's dueling with his wit and with his rapier, engaging at different moments Romeo, Benvolio, and finally Tybalt. Peter's echo of the play's opening line, "Gregory, on my word, we'll not carry coals," in his "I will carry no crochets," and the echoes of Benvolio's repeated "Put up your swords; . . . put up thy sword" (I.i.62–65) and Romeo's "Gentle Mercutio, put thy rapier up" (III.i.82) in the Second Musician's "Pray you put up your dagger, and put out your wit" bring the scenes into a similar perspective under what appears to be comic irrelevancy. The opening duel between the servants has often been recognized as a parody of the whole feuding principle of the play—the servants have no cause but habit to fight. In that instance, the feud has lost its content and has become merely a repetition of formula. The contest be-tween Peter and the Musicians occurs after the embattled houses have witnessed the fatal consequences of their irrelevant enmity in the deaths of Mercutio and Tybalt, but it provides a renewed focus on that essential pattern of causeless hostility.

The pattern of repetition itself signals thematic development, complementing the effect of the analogous scenes.[44] The street brawl involving Gregory and Sampson precedes Romeo's first appearance when he is suffering from superficial love-melancholia. The brawl between Mercutio and Tybalt precedes Romeo's despair in the Friar's cell. The scene with Peter and the Musicians, imitating the dueling pattern aurally with words and visibly with the dagger, precedes Romeo's final encounter with despair, induced by news of Juliet's death. To look at all three sets of scenes under the same light underscores the difference in their emotional substance and heightens the effect of Romeo's embrace of death.

The business between Peter and the Musicians concludes with his riddle. After he either says or sings twelve bars of a popular song, "In Commendation of Music,"[45] he interrupts himself to ask them, "Why silver sound, why music with her silver sound?" This question brings to mind several answers for one acquainted with Renaissance philosophy, musicology, and cosmology,[46] and the First Musician's answer recalls Romeo's comment about Juliet's voice in the first balcony scene:

> How silver-sweet sound lovers' tongues by night.
> Like softest music to attending ears! (II.ii.166–67)[47]

The First Musician says, "Marry, sir, because silver hath a sweet sound." Peter calls each Musician by a name, incidentally, that is a part of a stringed instrument, an interesting point since they have put up their "pipes" earlier in the scene. Thus, Peter is classifying them according to instruments they do not play (although in Q1 they are called "fiddlers"). His classification of them according to instrument parts resembles the comic flyting he challenges them with initially, substituting "minstrel" for "the lie." He says he will give them "No money on my faith, but the gleek. I will give you the minstrel." Their retort indicates that his substitution of their professional name as "the lie" in quarreling is an insult, and they in turn substitute his profession in their reply: "Then will I give you the serving-creature." Peter's "minstrel" echoes Mercutio's puns after Tybalt's accusation earlier that "thou consortest with Romeo":

Consort! what, dost thou make us minstrels? And thou make minstrels of us, look to hear nothing but discords. Here's my fiddlestick, here's that shall make you dance. 'Zounds, consort! (III.i.46–49)

In both cases, "minstrel" seems to be a challenging term, either as a diminution of Mercutio's gentlemanly high spirits or as a diminution of the Musicians' profession. The echo of these challenges emphatically connects the two scenes, both in words and action.[48]

Peter wryly accepts the First Musician's response, "Marry, sir, because silver hath a sweet sound," and turns to the Second, who puns on the reason that musicians play—and one that has not worked out for them in this particular situation, unless of course Paris has paid them beforehand: "I say silver sound, because musicians sound for silver." The Third Musician has no answer: "Faith, I know not what to say." And Peter with what I would imagine to be an obsequious bow says, "O, I cry you mercy, you are the *singer*; I will *say* for you" (my italics). In other words, the Musicians will not play for Peter's comfort and cannot be expected to have wit enough to "say" instead of to "sing," so Peter will have to do both jobs for them. He then answers the riddle—"it is music with her silver sound, because musicians have no gold for sounding"[49]—and returns to the twelfth bar of "In Commendation of Music," picking up where he had left off to ask the riddle, and sings "Then Music with her silver sound/ With speedy help doth lend redresse." Considering that he had asked for a "merry dump" to comfort him at the beginning, the fact that he supplies one when the professional Musicians refuse is a further aspect of his self-sufficient expertise.[50]

This part of the scene has provided in its musical emphasis one of the approved cures for melancholia, if not for the mourners over Juliet's corpse, at least for the audience. That Peter has to create it rather than receive it from the Musicians has ironic relevance as well: he is able to provide what Romeo cannot do for himself, his own cure for melancholia. The emphasis on recovery in the words of Peter's song as well as the music itself carries us into Romeo's hope-filled dream that immediately follows. Taken together, both segments of the scene, the lament over Juliet's body and Peter's dialogue with the Musicians, are preparative parody that heighten Romeo's final encounter with melancholy and its desperate consequences.

V

Whether or not there is a pause between this scene and the next, as G. K. Hunter argues there should be, a sequential heightening is in progress and it might be experienced most readily in the theater without a pause, as Harley Granville-Barker advises.[51] If the pause, as Hunter suggests, were of such a length as to "cause tension to increase rather than elapse" (p. 31), there would be no problem; but for the modern audience a break before the Apothecary scene seems to obscure the sense of continuity and of rising action in the arrangement of the scenes to this point. Act IV does complete a "phrasing of plot," as Hunter says, but the beginning of Act V continues Peter's musical adjustment of mourning, and then it repeats, with Romeo's reaction to Balthasar's news, the melancholy over Juliet's death in deeper terms.

The dream that Romeo narrates at the beginning of Act V exactly inverts Juliet's anticipation of what the tomb would be like before she drinks the sleeping potion: his dream presages "joyful news"—it is a vision of resurrection from death through Juliet's kisses; she has foreseen the horrors of awakening without Romeo "come to redeem me" (IV.iii.32). It also accurately predicts Juliet's actions when she discovers him dead;[52] but her kisses do not revive him nor do his lips retain enough poison to speed her death when she kisses him. The dream narration emphasizes the possibilities of resurrection, of joy, of the uselessness of mourning; it extends the effect created in the scene between Peter and the Musicians, and increases in the audience a hope, against its own foreknowledge, that love will extricate these passionate lovers from their "inevitable" deaths.

The ironies operative in the audience's response to this dream are complex. We suspect, having been through it with the Capulets, the Nurse, and Paris, that Romeo will accept the appearance of her death as reality and will act on it. Yet, the dream, which is illusory, may also suggest a way out of the trap of accepting appearance as reality. Whereas we fought against the realization of Juliet's vision of the tomb, we hope that somehow Romeo's dream may come true.

Romeo's manner in this scene marks a difference from the Romeo of earlier scenes: he has become more contemplative. He pauses to consider that it is a "strange dream that gives a dead man leave to think"; he seems to have grown in patience since his exile in Mantua. His attitude may remind us of the new calm with which he greeted Tybalt's insults after his marriage with Juliet: "Tybalt, the reason that I have to love thee/ Doth much excuse this appertaining rage/ To such a greeting" (III.i.61–63). But, just as his newly gained patience was too new for him to rely on in that situation, this contemplative potential dissolves into action of a desperate kind. The difference is that now Romeo is able to maintain his external calm; he has learned to persuade with his role-playing.

The suddenness of the switch from joyful expectations to dread-filled realities is something the audience has experienced before, but now it is total. We have seen Romeo's resolution alter with various forms of persuasion earlier: his "never" turns to "yes," as Benvolio promised, when he sees a beauty fairer than Rosaline at the Capulet ball; his moderation in resisting quarrel with Tybalt changes into fatal revenge with Mercutio's death; his desperation in the Friar's cell becomes hope in "Juliet is alive." We have been prepared repeatedly for Romeo's swift change from one extreme to the other, but after the news of Juliet's entombment turns his dream-inspired hope to despair, we know there will be no further change: he commits himself to death.

The news from Verona is couched in a pun that is both literally true and figuratively false. In answer to Romeo's "How fares my Juliet?", Balthasar says, "she is well. . . . her body sleeps in Capel's monument." Compare this with the doubleness of Juliet's reply when her mother is pushing her into marriage with Paris: "I will not marry yet; and when I do, I swear/ It shall be Romeo whom you know I hate." Or compare Mercutio's departing jest in the face of Romeo's disbelief: "Ask for me to-morrow, and you shall find me a grave man." The pun's effect in all these situations is immense. In his discussion of the play's use of puns, Michael Goldman comments:

The fury of the pun is the fury of our submerged innocence. . . . Punning restores to us—under certain very narrow conditions, and for a brief interval—our freedom to change names and to make connections we have been taught to suppress, to invent language, to reconstitute the world as we please.[53]

In this case, Goldman's observation applies to the audience alone, but it applies vehemently. Because Balthasar is unaware that his euphemisms ("she is well" and "her body sleeps" for "Juliet is dead") are literally true—Juliet is well, she *is* but sleeping in the tomb—Romeo understands only what Balthasar intends. The audience, however, apprehends the power of Shakespeare's pun that, if perceived, is capable of reconstituting "the world as we please." Our superior knowledge therefore intensifies that quixotic combination of hope and despair that has been building throughout the play. Romeo, hearing Balthasar's words figuratively as they are intended, loses the hope that has sustained him, and acts accordingly.[54]

When he acts, he acts carefully, instructing Balthasar to bring him paper and ink (so that he may write his suicide's explanation) and to hire posthorses to make the journey to Juliet's tomb—details easily overlooked by those in the grips of rash passion. Romeo has had his rehearsal in rashness. In contrast to his earlier performances under stress, he now deliberates and calculates consequences. When Balthasar cautions him to "have patience./ Your looks are pale and wild and do import/ Some misadventure," Romeo offhandedly denies his appearance, "Tush, thou art deceived." But we know that Balthasar is correct—Romeo is contemplating a desperate act and he has denied patience as a mode of procedure.[55] The conflict between described appearances—Romeo's "wild looks"—and his manner—deliberate, careful, "Let's see for means"—divides our sense of what is happening. We are caught paradoxically by the information our eyes receive, governed by Balthasar's eyes (and how Romeo plays the scene), and what our ears hear.

Comparison with Arthur Brooke's narration of this scene in his poem *The Tragicall Historye of Romeus and Juliet* (1562), a source Shakespeare follows closely at times, provides useful information about Shakespeare's choices in his dramatic presentation. Brooke's Romeus, seeking to hide his sorrow after hearing of Juliet's death,

> Straight, wery of the house,/ he walketh forth abrode:
> His seruant, at the maisters hest,/ in chamber styll abode;
> And then fro streate to streate/ he wandreth vp and downe
> To see if he in any place/ may fynde, in all the towne,
> A salue meete for his sore,/ an oyle fitte for his wounde;
> And seeking long (alac too soone)/ the thing he sought, he
>   founde.
> An Apothecary sate/ vnbusied at his doore,
> Whom by his heauy countenaunce/ he gessed to be poore.[56]

Shakespeare's Romeo, on the other hand, has already seen the Apothecary's shop and has previously thought that such a man might sell a poison if one had a need for it. Different requirements for the presentation of action on a stage and in a narrative poem account for some of the changes, of course; even so, Shakespeare's version emphasizes premeditated, deliberate action, whereas Brooke stresses the haphazard rashness of Romeus's passionate grief. Shakespeare's Romeo sees that "Being holiday, the beggar's shop is shut," and calls the Apothecary forth; Brooke's Apothecary happens to be sitting in front of his shop, unbusied. Romeo's elaborate description of the Apothecary's shop, quoted earlier, takes seven lines; Brooke uses two unspecific lines:

> And in his shop he saw/ his boxes were but fewe,
> And in his window (of his ware)/ there was so small a shew.

Brooke's Apothecary has a "heauy countenaunce," and from this Romeus concludes that he is "poore"; Romeo has seen the Apothecary

> In tatt'red weeds, with overwhelming brows,
> Culling of simples. Meagre were his looks,
> Sharp misery had worn him to the bones.

Noting the "penury" of both his shop and his person (in detail), Romeo concludes that such "a caitiff wretch" might succumb

to pressure. Shakespeare's Romeo, like Brooke's Romeus, realizes the compelling motive of the Apothecary's poverty to
make him accept gold for poison, but Shakespeare changes the
amount offered from "fiftie crownes of gold" in Brooke to
"fortie duckets." Whereas the poem's Romeus takes "the nedy
man apart/ And with the sight of glittring gold/ inflamed hath
his hart," Romeo persuades the Apothecary by philosophical
argument.

> Art thou so bare and full of wretchedness
> And fearest to die? Famine is in thy cheeks,
> Need and oppression starveth in thy eyes,
> Contempt and beggary hangs upon thy back:
> The world is not thy friend, nor the world's law;
> The world affords no law to make thee rich;
> Then be not poor, but break it and take this.

And this Apothecary, no more casuistical than Romeo, accepts
with a reservation: "My poverty but not my will consents." He is
not inflamed by avarice, as Brooke describes his Apothecary, but
is persuaded by Romeo's appeals to injustice and poverty and by
his apparent sympathy. Having convinced the man to sell him
what he wants, Romeo then becomes moralistic and speaks an
epigrammatic dictum on gold's being worse poison to men's
souls than poison itself. In Brooke, the narrator intrudes whatever moral cautions there are; for example, he tells us that Romeus finds the Apothecary "(alac too soone)" and warns that the
Apothecary's sale "too late, he doth repent." In the poem's conclusion, the narrator's prophecy is fulfilled when "Thapothecary
high/ is hanged by the throte" (l. 2993). Shakespeare chooses not
to punish his Apothecary. The traditional emblematic attributes
of Despair (and the sub-category Melancholia) give rationale and
meaning to this cluster of changes in emphasis, indicating that
Shakespeare was attempting to present this brief scene as a visually recognizable emblem.

Romeo's lengthy description of the Apothecary and his shop
before the man enters creates a pause in the action, which now
has begun to move swiftly toward its disastrous climax. As it

slows down the motion of the scene, the description emphasizes what we are to see before we see it and therefore heightens the pictorial quality of the encounter. Once we have seen the Apothecary in person, Romeo again describes his appearance. Romeo's two verbal insistences on the Apothecary's appearance (something Brooke pays almost no attention to) ask the audience to become pointedly conscious of the visual aspects of the man, to look at him closely. The Apothecary's attributes are those traditionally associated with figures of Despair, and they especially recall Edmund Spenser's description in *The Faerie Queene*. After having heard the fatal results of Sir Terwin's encounter with Despair from Sir Trevisan, Una and the Red Cross Knight approach him:

> That darkesome caue they enter, where they find
>> That cursed man, low sitting on the ground.
>> Musing full sadly in his sullein mind;
>> His griesie lockes, long growen, and vnbound,
>> Disordred hong about his shoulders round,
>> And hid his face; through which his hollow eyne
>> Lookt deadly dull, and stared as astound;
>> His raw-bone cheekes through penurie and pine,
> Were shronke into his iawes, as he did neuer dine.

> His garment nought but many ragged clouts,
>> With thornes together pind and patched was,
>> The which his naked sides he wrapt abouts.[57]

The similarities between the two descriptions do not mean that Shakespeare was intentionally using Spenser, but their figures seem to be drawn from the same tradition.[58] One major difference in Shakespeare's evocation of this figure of Despair is that Romeo seeks him out rather than the other way around, and Romeo is aware that he is doing so:

> Lets see for means. O mischief, thou art swift
> To enter in the thoughts of desperate men!
> I do remember an apothecary.

Despair and Melancholy are closely associated, frequently in a cause-effect relationship, as Robert Burton observes in his *Anatomy of Melancholy:*

> But melancholy and despair, though often, do not always concur; . . . and yet melancholy alone again may be sometimes a sufficient cause of this terror of conscience.[59]

Laurentius also associates the two, as did most of the writers who discussed the nature of melancholy:

> The melancholike man . . . is ordinarilie out of heart, . . . he goeth alwaies sighing, troubled with . . . an unseperable sadnes, which oftentimes turneth into dispayre. . . . To conclude, hee is become a savadge creature, haunting the shadowed places, suspicious, solitarie, enemie to the Sunne.[60]

The thin face and body and sunken eyes are attributes of both figures as described in emblem literature and medical treatises of the period. Timothy Bright in his *Treatise of Melancholie* (1586) describes the melancholic person thus:

> the melancholick sheweth it self, either in the qualities of the body, or in the deeds. Of the qualities which are first taken from the elements, the melancholick without adustion, is cold and drie: of such as are second, rising from the first, of colour blacke and swart, of substance inclyning to hardness, lean, and spare of flesh: which caseth hollownes of eye, and unchearfulness of countenance.[61]

In their major study, *Saturn and Melancholy,* Raymond Klibansky, Erwin Panofsky, and Fritz Saxl examine the historical background of Dürer's "Melencolia I" and discuss the traditional motifs that his engraving employs. They conclude that "among the medieval descriptions of the melancholic there was none in which he did not appear as avaricious and miserly," a characteristic symbolically suggested by the attribute of the purse.[62] This traditional association appears in Cesare Ripa's grouping of the four humors in his influential *Iconologia,* which appeared in the first two editions without woodcuts. In the 1603 edition, expanded and illustrated, the figure of Melancholia appears with a purse in one hand and a book in the other, his mouth bound to signify his silence, a figure that Henry Peacham imitated in his depiction of the four complexions of man in *Minerva Britanna* (1612).[63]

Although Geffrey Whitney's *A Choice of Emblemes* (1586) does not include a specific grouping of the four humors, two of his emblems have to do with the avaricious nature associated with the melancholic. The first is the emblem, "In Auaros." Following the motto, a picture shows an ass, bearing all sorts of good things to eat on his back, eating a thistle. The picture is then followed by its explanation, which draws this moral point about the miser "Septitus":

> This Caitiffe wretche, with pined corpes lo heare,
> Compared right vnto the foolishe asse,
> Whose backe is fraighte with cates, and daintie cheare,
> But to his share commes neither corne, nor grasse,
>   Yet beares he that, which settes his teeth on edge:
>   And pines him selfe, with thistle and with sedge.[64]

Romeo's moral evaluation of the Apothecary's avarice echoes the motto that precedes another Whitney emblem: *Saepius in auro bibitur venenum*—oftener in gold is poison drunk. The verbal echo reflects moral cliché and need not be taken as evidence that Shakespeare was consciously employing specific emblems or emblem writers to assist his picture of the Apothecary, but it does offer evidence of a common awareness of emblematic tradition.[65]

The particular awareness of the dictum Romeo speaks, that gold is worse poison to men's souls than the actual poison he buys, is exemplified in an earlier literary analogue, Chaucer's *The Pardoner's Tale*. The Old Man has much in common with the figures of Despair and Melancholia: like Spenser's Despair, Chaucer's Old Man cannot die, though he wishes to; and his appearance, "ful pale and welked is my face," is usually associated with Melancholy.[66] Further, as Klibansky, Panofsky, and Saxl observe, the matching of the Four Ages of Man with the Four Humors, which has its roots in ancient empirical medicine and philosophy, was current in this period:

Plate 1: Illustration from Cesare Ripa, *Iconologia* (Rome, 1603).
Courtesy of the Folger Shakespeare Library.

H EERE *Melancholly* mufing in his fits,
   Pale vifag'd, of complexion cold and drie,
All folitarie, at his ftudie fits,
Within a wood, devoid of companie:
   Saue Madge the Owle, and melancholly Puffe,
   Light-loathing Creatures, hatefull, ominous.

His mouth, in figne of filence, vp is bound,
For *Melancholly* loues not many wordes:
One foote on Cube is fixt vpon the ground,
The which him plodding *Conftancie* affordes:
   A fealed Purfe he beares, to fhew no vice,
   So proper is to him, as *Auarice*.

Plate 2: Illustration from Henry Peacham, *Minerva Britanna*
(London, 1612). Courtesy of the Folger Shakespeare Library.

SEPTITIVS ritche, a mifer mofte of all,
Whofe liuinges large, and treafure did exceede:
Yet to his goodes, he was fo much in thrall,
That ftill he vf'd on beetes, and rapes to feede:
    So of his ftoare, the fweete he neuer knewe,
    And longe did robbe, his bellie of his due.

This Caitiffe wretche, with pined corpes lo heare,
Compared right vnto the foolifhe affe,
Whofe backe is fraighte with cates, and daintie cheare,
But to his fhare commes neither corne, nor graffe,
    Yet beares he that, which fettes his teeth on edge:
    And pines him felfe, with thiftle and with fedge.

Plate 3: Illustration from Geffrey Whitney,
A Choice of Emblemes and Other Devises (Leyden, 1586).
Courtesy of the Folger Shakespeare Library.

H EARE LAIS fine, doth braue it on the ſtage,
With muſkecattes ſweete, and all ſhee coulde deſire :
Her beauties beames, did make the youthe to rage,
And inwardlie Corinthus ſet on fire:
    Bothe Princes, Peeres, with learned men, and graue,
    With humble ſute, did LAIS fauour craue.

Not euerie one, mighte to Corinthus goe,
The meaninge was, not all mighte LAIS loue:
The manchet fine, on highe eſtates beſtowe,
The courſer cheate, the baſer ſorte muſt prooue:
    Faire HELEN leaue for MENELAVS grace,
    And CORIDON, let MABLIE ſtill imbrace.

And thoughe, the poore maie not preſume alofte,
It is no cauſe, they therefore ſhoulde diſpaire:
For with his choiſe, doth IRV's ioye as ofte,
As dothe the Prince, that hathe a VENVS faire:
    No highe eſtate, can giue a quiet life,
    But GOD it is, that bleſſeth man, and wife.

Plate 4. Illustration from Geffrey Whitney,
A Choice of Emblemes and Other Devises (Leyden, 1586).
Courtesy of the Folger Shakespeare Library.

Through the whole of the Middle Ages and the Renaissance this cycle remained virtually unchanged, apart from some controversy over its starting point: it could begin with "phlegmatic" childhood, passing through "sanguine" youth and "choleric" prime to "melancholic" old age (in certain circumstances returning to a "second childhood"); or else it could begin with "sanguine" youth, pass through a "choleric" period between twenty and forty and a "melancholie" period between forty and sixty, and end in a "phlegmatic" old age.[67]

In other words, old age was frequently thought to be a man's "melancholic" age in terms of his progress through various periods of domination by each of the four humors.

The climax of *The Pardoner's Tale* stresses avarice, after the three young men discover the gold florins, and death by the dagger and poison, familiar weapons of suicide, as well as an apothecary who sells strong poison. The similarities to the scene in Shakespeare's play are clear, and again they point out a common background of emblematic awareness. For the young men in *The Pardoner's Tale*, gold becomes both literally and figuratively what Romeo says it is as he exchanges his purse filled with forty ducats for the Apothecary's poison:

> There is thy gold—worse poison to men's souls,
> Doing more murder in this loathsome world,
> Than these poor compounds that thou mayst not sell.
> I sell thee poison; Thou hast sold me none.

The fact that the notion of avarice is muted in Shakespeare's version until after the actual sale is made, as distinct from Brooke's immediate emphasis, suggests that Shakespeare was attempting to present a visual recreation in dramatic action of the familiar humoral figure, Melancholia. The Apothecary scene, in other words, acts out an emblem. Romeo's motto-like statement of theme—"O mischief, thou art swift/ To enter in the thoughts of desperate men"—announces the meaning that Shakespeare wants us to read from the scene. The dialogue with the Apothecary, accompanied by the handing over of the purse of forty ducats, constitutes the stage picture, which is analogous to the illustrative picture in an emblem; and then Romeo's drawing of the moral is equivalent to the explanatory verse. All three parts are mutually illustrative, bringing Romeo's emblem to life.

There is an important discrepancy, however, between the motto and the moral. Romeo comes to the Apothecary, himself the figure of Despair, persuades him to accept the gold, and then tells the Apothecary that his soul is in danger, denying what is obvious to anyone: Romeo's soul is in greater danger, as despair leads him to suicide, the final denial of God's grace in the secular world. Shakespeare seems to be creating an emblem that ironically contradicts its moral explanation.[68]

The discrepancy is subtle because the force of Romeo's proverbial pronouncement insists on an almost automatic affirmation. Yet, if we see the discrepancy between the emblematic message of the scene and Romeo's evaluation of it, we perceive that Romeo is projecting a moral cliché onto a situation that contradicts his view of it. Avarice is typically associated with Melancholy, and Romeo sees the Apothecary as a figure of Melancholy. On the other hand, Romeo does not seem to recognize himself as the figure of Despair who persuades the melancholic to self-destruction through the offer of gold. The audience, however, is able to see both emblematic figures simultaneously. Our double vision allows us to see more than Romeo does: the ironic inversion of Romeo's perceiving the Apothecary as emblematic of his own moral choice, creating in him a dramatic projection of his own nature, and then cautioning him about the state of his soul.

The Apothecary, with his "overwhelming brows," his almost fleshless bones, his obvious misery, is a recognizable figure of the "natural melancholic," one whose nature is overbalanced by that humor. Romeo, despite his profession of love-melancholia at the play's beginning, is by nature sanguine; through the death of Mercutio, he becomes choleric; in the Friar's cell he resembles the phlegmatic indulgence of childhood in excessive self-pity, although his rashness is choleric; momentarily, he regains his naturally sanguine attitude in Mantua; but after news of Juliet's death and his encounter with the Apothecary, he symbolically assumes the nature of melancholy: he has passed to the Fourth Age of Man. The emblematic impact of this scene, as it provides an analogical conclusion to previous despair scenes, forces us to accept the finality of his decision and the inevitability of his self-willed destruction.

VI

Consideration of scenic sequence thus reveals some of the dramatic purposes not always apparent to modern audiences. Because producers of the play have failed to recognize that there is consistency in the building thematic demonstration of melancholia/despair in Romeo, which is heightened by attempts to dispel it through comic and musical means, they have often cut the little scenes. Rather than detracting from the plot line by way of diversion, these scenes enhance it by reinforcing and clarifying the actions of the primary characters. The effect of the Apothecary scene is greater because we see Romeo's decision for suicide analogically, that is, because of Romeo's preceding rehearsals for this scene, his absolute commitment to despair takes on the quality of heroic action.

His earlier encounters with despair begin with his first appearance, where his contrived melancholy voices itself in oxymorons. His speech on seeing the evidence of the street brawl is surely one of the best Elizabethan parodies of Petrarchan rhetoric (I.i.174–82); it distills by excess the absolute simplicity of a mind driven into a corner by the apprehension of love. Encouraged by Benvolio's good-humored allowance of these histrionics, Romeo continues to elaborate on Rosaline's overwhelming control of his thoughts, until he laments:

> She is too fair, too wise, wisely too fair,
> To merit bliss by making me despair.
> She hath forsworn to love, and in that vow
> Do I live dead that live to tell it now.
> (I.i.220–23)

This is one of two occasions where Shakespeare uses the word "despair" to form a rhyme. The second occurs during Romeo's first encounter with Juliet, as they are sharing their spontaneous sonnet:

JULIET Ay, pilgrim, lips that they must use in prayer.
ROMEO O, then, dear saint, let lips do what hands do!
  They pray; grant thou, lest faith turn to despair.
  (I.v.102–4)

The "fair/despair" rhyme, as so much else associated with Romeo's agony over Rosaline, promotes reverberations of an orthodox religion of love, grown hollow through overuse. The "prayer/despair" rhyme of Juliet's and Romeo's first meeting also echoes clichés of love, especially because they are employing religious rituals of the pilgrim and the enshrined saint to express their mutual infatuation. Yet the introduction of the concepts of "sin" and of "prayer" signifies a more substantial intuition of the problems that such a passionate and hasty love incurs. This added dimension is a step toward the play's ultimate questioning of the nature of human love, but it is still incomplete. The echo of the despair rhyme, however, does connect Romeo's parodic rehearsal of love for Rosaline and his true emergence of feeling for Juliet. He has not yet passed from his posturing as the rhetorical lover into the real lover: his words and his gestures, as Juliet herself notes—"You kiss by th' book" (I.v.110)—are still in the stage of rehearsal.

In neither case is Romeo really desperate. He is playing games, encountering girls at the level of winning or losing. At the same moment, he unwittingly introduces the problem of the soul's ultimate engagement with reality, a problem that he finally answers with suicide. Because there is such a progression, from silly-enamored to semi-serious enamored to soul-committed enamored, the posturing of Romeo at the end of the play no longer reverberates hollowly. The working out of the silliness in the parodic preparation tends to decrease the suspicions that an audience no doubt always feels about the Romeos of this world: Does he know the difference between what he wants to feel and what he actually feels—the difference between being in love with the idea of love and actually loving someone other than himself?

His desperate scene with the Friar, III.iii, articulates this question in one way: there the Friar reminds him that, above all else,

"Juliet is alive"; and Romeo subsequently accepts this as a reason for his continuing. The scene with the Apothecary, similar to the one in the Friar's cell, articulates the question differently. What does one do when "Juliet is dead"?

Analogically planned scenes may often seem the product of coincidence, but Shakespeare makes sure that we recognize his parallel between the Apothecary and the Friar by having Romeo describe the former's "culling of simples." The Friar's initial appearance shows him at the same task, and he delivers a soliloquy on the ambiguous properties of Nature's plants, that both give and destroy life.

> I must up-fill this osier cage of ours
> With baleful weeds and precious-juicèd flowers. . . .
> O, mickle is the powerful grace that lies
> In plants, herbs, stones, and their true qualities. . . .
> Virtue itself turns vice, being misapplied,
> And vice sometime's by action dignified.
> (II.iii.7–22)

The Friar is knowledgeable in the Apothecary's art, and when he gives Juliet her sleeping potion he proves his adeptness as a culler of simples.[69] He may, in fact, be more adept at simples and their classification than he is in controlling human affairs through his counsel. The Apothecary, by paralleling the Friar in the final despair scene, visually illustrates Romeo's choice of a figure who represents Despair/Melancholia to aid him, rather than a figure who at least potentially represents Hope and Patience—the Friar.

The brief scene that follows provides another link between the Friar and the Apothecary. Friar John's calling Friar Laurence forth from his cell echoes Romeo's calling the Apothecary forth from his shop. And Laurence's question "What says Romeo?" counterpoints Romeo's question of Balthasar in the preceding scene, "Dost thou not bring me letters from the friar?" In terms of "stage picture" the Friar replaces the Apothecary as the source of action, but now with significantly less power. Not only has Romeo determined his own course of action independent of "letters from the friar," but Friar John reveals that the plague has interfered with Laurence's manipulations—"virtue itself turns vice, being misapplied."

This scene is marked with haste in contrast to the slower, deliberative tempo of Romeo's scene with the Apothecary.[70] Yet the audience senses that the Friar's substitute plans to forestall disaster—his second letter to Romeo, his sending Friar John for a crowbar, his plan to get to Juliet's side before she awakens— cannot match Romeo's speed now that Romeo has committed himself to action. The Friar's preparations are as superfluous as the Capulet's preparations for Juliet's wedding to Paris were in the earlier scene.

The appearance of Paris and his page at the tomb provides a visual preparative parallel for Romeo's arrival with Balthasar.[71] In his obsequies Paris modulates the excesses of the earlier lamentation scene and creates an image of what Romeo would have been had this occurred in Act II. The audience has traveled with Romeo, however, through his stages of emotional development, and now Paris's flowers and sweet water are too little for the "true love's rite" we have been encouraged to anticipate. Romeo's "mattock and the wrenching iron" appropriately express his passionate intention to complete his mourning rites by joining his true love in the grave. Romeo's words to frighten Balthasar from spying on him are intensely savage:

> But if thou, jealous, dost return to pry
> In what I farther shall intend to do,
> By heaven, I will tear thee joint by joint
> And strew this hungry churchyard with thy limbs.
> The time and my intents are savage-wild.
> (V.iii.33–37)

Balthasar needs little more persuasion to leave him, but Romeo pauses to give him money, not as he did with the Apothecary, to abuse him for taking it, but to wish him good life and prosperity. After all, Romeo is performing his own last rites here.

Thinking himself alone, but actually being watched by both Paris, who is hidden, and Balthasar, who but "retires," Romeo addresses his enemy with words that evoke memories of medieval mystery plays at the confrontation of hell's mouth.

> Thou destestable maw, thou womb of death,
> Gorged with the dearest morsel of the earth,
> Thus I enforce thy rotten jaws to open,
> And in despite I'll cram thee with more food.
> (V.iii.45–48)

Romeo, in fact, is harrowing hell, not, as in the Christian mystery cycles, to redeem lost saints, but to add to the number lost.

Interference now is intolerable, not only to Romeo but to the audience. We are committed with Romeo, right or wrong, because his embrace of desperate action is so vital, much as we feel with Macbeth as he confronts nothingness in his final act.[72] Paris's challenge seems as unwarranted, from the audience's point of view, as Tybalt's was earlier, and Paris uses the same epithet: "Condemned villain, I do apprehend thee." Romeo, in contrast, as he had tried to do with Tybalt, controls his frustration and advises Paris to desist: "Good gentle youth, tempt not a desp'rate man. . . . By heaven, I love thee better than myself." But Paris will not leave, and Romeo is driven to destroy him. Perhaps a final duel is the natural climax to a play that has been so thoroughly immersed in the feuding principle. Romeo impatiently accepts the challenge, which he clearly finds irrelevant to his central purpose, and he responds with familiar language: "Then have at thee, boy!"

Romeo's use of the word "boy" to address Paris echoes Tybalt's disparaging use when he fought with Romeo earlier. There, when Romeo attempted to take his peaceful leave, Tybalt challenged him: "Boy, this shall not excuse the injuries / That thou hast done me." After Mercutio's death between them, when Romeo sought vengeance, Tybalt gave the challenge with that word again: "Thou wretched boy, that didst consort him here, / Shalt with him hence." Romeo does not know who it is that offers him the challenge, as his later recognition of the dying Paris shows, and so he resorts to the language of insult. His mistaking of Paris (whom we have recognized to be at least his peer, if not his elder, earlier in the play) as a "boy" has a function other than recalling past scenes of fatal duels: it reminds us that Romeo has progressed through the emotional and psychological stages of man. He sees Paris now as the audience saw Romeo at the play's beginning—then he was sanguine, only a boy. Romeo is now emblematically an "old man," Melancholia, committed to death as he informs Paris: "tempt not a desp'rate man. . . . For I come hither armed against myself." After seeing Juliet as Death's paramour, he confirms his sense of being in life's last age:

> O, here
> Will I set up my everlasting rest
> And shake the yoke of inauspicious stars
> From this world-wearied flesh. (V.iii.109–12)

Traditionally the melancholic figure was ambiguous in his potential for accomplishments of imaginative creativity or for diabolical self-destructiveness, as Thomas Walkington's metaphoric passage describes:

The melancholick man is said of the wise to be *aut Deus aut Damon,* either angel of heaven or a fiend of hell: for in whomsoever this humour hath dominion, the soule is either wrapt vp into an *Elysium* and paradise of blesse by a heauenly contemplation, or into a direful hellish purgatory by a cynical meditation: like vnto a huge vessell on the rowling sea that is either hoist vp to the ridge of a maine billow, or eft hurried down to the bottom of the sea valley.[73]

In Romeo's final actions both the "angel of heaven" and the "fiend of hell" seem to be present. Romeo is both creative and destructive in his love-melancholia at the tomb; he figures forth both the savage desperation and divine imagination simultaneously. Centuries of controversial criticism about the play would seem to indicate that both potentials are present. Usually, one is asked to go either one way or another. Yet Shakespeare may have been trying to have it both ways, and both ways were available to him in the traditional associations of melancholia.

Romeo's final words express both the creativity of his melancholic passion, as he puns on taking life from death, and the self-destruction of his despair.

> Thou desperate pilot, now at once run on
> The dashing rocks thy seasick weary bark!
> Here's to my love! [*Drinks.*] O true apothecary!
> Thy drugs are quick. Thus with a kiss I die.
> (V.iii. 117–20)[74]

Romeo's fusing of the extremes of hope and despair, which failed to combine in his role-playing rehearsals, makes him seem a powerfully cohesive, almost heroic figure. Juliet puns in a similar way at her moment of death: "O happy dagger,/ This is thy sheath; there rust and let me die." Each uses the word "die" in doubleness: their sexual union through which they have "died" and also "lived again" they now enact for the last time with attributes, poison and dagger, emblematically associated with Despair. As Juliet falls upon Romeo, the phallic dagger permanently sheathed within her flesh, the lovers make literal what has been metaphorical to this point. Love and death have merged.

Their tableau would make a fitting celebration of their love that cannot tolerate their world, but the play does not end with that tableau of human sacrifice. We are forced to return to the world of the ordinary when the Watch discovers the bodies, and the Prince, the Friar, and the surviving parents gather to "clear these ambiguities." In the process, despite his promise to "be brief," the Friar takes forty lines to detail the action for the *players*—the audience has witnessed all this and hardly needs the long-winded summary.

In his summary, however, the Friar reiterates a possibility for action that the lovers did not choose:

> I entreated her come forth,
> And bear this work of heaven with *patience:*
> But then a noise did scare me from the tomb,
> And she, too *desperate,* would not go with me,
> But, as it seems, did violence on herself.
> (V.i.260–64; my italics)

III

Patience demonstrates hope and faith in a higher design, and we have seen Romeo refuse this option in the Apothecary scene. Juliet, on discovery of his body newly dead beside her, follows him in refusal. But the audience is not released, as the lovers are, from the knowledge that another choice was open to them. The Friar's summary accomplishes other things as well as renewing the muted focus on supernatural possibilities for mitigation in human affairs. One effect is to give us time to pull back from our personal engagement with the lovers, to put our view in balance, to let us see the community reorganize itself after the loss. Yet to imagine the carrying out of Montague's and Capulet's plan to idolize the lovers in statues of "pure gold" depersonalizes them too rapidly and makes what was potentially transcendental into mercantilely evaluated objects:

MONTAGUE There shall no figure at such rate be set
   As that of true and faithful Juliet.
CAPULET As rich shall Romeo's by his lady's lie.[75]

The "ambiguities" of narrative may have been settled for the Prince and the Veronesi, but in that process of clarification the same old patterns of attitude on the part of the older generation re-emerge. They are now in contest over who shall outdo whom in display of regard for the other's lost child, but they are still in contest. The audience is therefore no more released to accept the restorative civil ceremony than we are to accept the lovers' deification of love.

In the Prince's closing words, the figure of Melancholia may be seen lurking over the play:

   A glooming peace this morning with it brings.
   The sun for sorrow will not show his head. . . .
   For never was a story of more woe
   Than this of Juliet and her Romeo.

Chapter 5

PARODY IN *RICHARD II*

Given a puzzling scene, like that of Peter and the Musicians or the Apothecary in *Romeo and Juliet,* one method for discovering its significance is to consider it as a part of a sequence of scenes that develops aspects of the same theme in different ways. Such a puzzle occurs in *Richard II* just before Richard's murder, that is, the scene in which the Duchess of York contends with her husband to win Henry's judgment over their son Aumerle (V.iii). York would have him killed for plotting treason; the Duchess would have him pardoned to save his life. The comedy of the scene has been called "grotesque" by some and, of course, unworthy of Shakespeare.[1] A few critics, at least, have countered the orthodox view to demonstrate that the comedy does fit into the play, despite its tonal difference.[2] I would add that it is consistent with Shakespeare's practice elsewhere in the canon.

Comparison of Shakespeare's probable sources in Hall and Holinshed makes clearer what the playwright intended his scene to effect. Hall's treatment of the incident describes the "duke of Exceter's" arrival in Oxford to join the other conspirators in their plan to murder King Henry:

when he came there, he founde ready al his mates and confederates well apointed for their purpose, except the Duke of Aumerle Erle of Rutland, for whom they sent messengers in great haste. This duke of Aumerle went before from Westminister to se his father the duke of Yorke, and sittyng at diner had his counterpaine of the endenture of the confederacie wherof I spake before in his bosome.

The father espied it and demaunded what it was, his sonne lowely and beningly answered that it myght not bee sene, and that it touched not him. By saint George quod the father I will see it, and so by force toke it out of his bosome, when he perceaued the content and the sixe signed and seales sette and fixed to the same, whereof the seale of his sonne was one, he sodainlie rose from the table, com[m]aundyng his horses to be sadeled, and in greate furie saied to his sonne, thou trayter thefe, thou hast bene a traitour to kyng Richard, and wilt thou nowe be falce to thy cosen kyng Henry? thou knowest wel inough that I am thy pledge borowe and mayneperner, body for body, and land for goodes in open parliament, and goest thou about to seke my death and destruction? by the holy rode I had leauer see the strangeled on a gibbet. And so the duke of Yorke mou[n]ted on horsebacke to ride toward Windsor to the kyng and to declare the hole effecte of his son[n]e and his adherented & partakers. The duke of Aumerle seyng in what case he stode toke his horse and rode another way to Windsor, riding in post thither (whiche his father being an olde man could not do.) And when he was alighted at the castel gate, he caused the gates to be shut, saying that he must nedes deliuer the keies to the kyng. When he came before the kynges presence he kneled downe on his knees, besechyng him of mercy and forgeuenes: The kyng demanded the cause: then he declared to him plainely the hole confederacie and entier coniuracion in manner and forme as you haue harde: Well saied the kyng, if this be trewe we pardon you, if it bee fained at your extreme perill bee it. While the kyng and the duke talked together, the duke of Yorke knocked at the castel gate, whom the kyng caused to be let in, and there he delyuered the endenture whiche before was taken from his sonne, into the kynges handes. Which writyng when he had redde, and sene, perceiuyng the signes and seales of the confederates, he chaunged his former purpose [to attend the lists at Oxford].[3]

Holinshed's account is much the same, with incidental altering of details and a slight tightening of narrative style.

The character of the Duchess is entirely Shakespeare's invention, and it is around her domineering femininity that he builds his two scenes, V.ii and iii. York's characterization may owe something to Hall's description, since there he waxes prolix in his reviling of his traitorous son, Aumerle. Holinshed's description seems muted by contrast:

The father espieng it, would needs see what it was; and though the sonne humblie denied to shew it, the father, tooke it out of his bosome; and perceiuing the contents thereof, in a great rage caused his horsses to be sadled out of hand, and spitefullie reproouing his soone of treason, for whome he was become suertie and mainpernour for his good abearing in open parlement, he incontinentlie mounted on horssebacke to ride towards Windsore to the king, to declare vnto him the malicious intent of his [1577 his sonne and his] complices.[4]

Hall's depiction of the domestic crisis is more detailed than Holinshed's, and Shakespeare elaborates on those details, not only with the "invention" of the Duchess's role. In Hall, the names on the indenture are "six signed and seales sette and fixed to the same, whereof the seale of his [York's] sonne was one." Shakespeare had York extend the number of conspirators to "A dozen of them here have taken the sacrament . . . To kill the King at Oxford." Hall notes that Aumerle, recognizing his own peril after his father's hasty departure, determines to reach King Henry first, "riding in post thither (whiche his father being an olde man could not do.)" Shakespeare assigns that discrimination to the Duchess, who instructs Aumerle to

> Mount thee upon his horse,
> Spur post, and get before him to the King,
> And beg thy pardon ere he do accuse thee.
> I'll not be long behind. Though I be old,
> I doubt not but to ride as fast as York.
> (V.ii.111–15)

Historically, this Duchess of York was stepmother to Aumerle, but Shakespeare changes that so that she may challenge York with her emotionally charged inquisition:

> Have we more sons? or are we like to have?
> Is not my teeming date drunk up with time?
> And wilt thou pluck my fair son from mine age,
> And rob me of a happy mother's name? . . .
>   Hadst thou groaned for him
> As I have done, thou wouldst be more pitiful.
> (V.ii.90–103)

The ageless appeal to motherhood, which Lady Macbeth uses to such different purposes in her persuasion of her husband, in this case has little effect on York. His fury over his son's treason overwhelms any claims of blood loyalty. Because of this, York has come under some unusual scrutiny by psychological critics, who attempt to find a consistent rationale for York's actions here and earlier in the play.[5] Too frequently, ingenious attempts to explain York's behavior, such as M.P. Taylor's, completely ignore the fact that the action is detailed in both Hall and Holinshed. I would prefer to examine this scene and the following one in terms of their comic patterning, keeping in mind the fact that Shakespeare found the outline of York's actions in the chronicles of Hall and Holinshed.

Act V, scene ii, opens with York's description of Bolingbroke's triumphal entry into London. For this description, Shakespeare seems to have drawn on Samuel Daniel's account in *The Civil Wars,* although Shakespeare switches the order of the scenes. In Daniel, most of the lengthy description of the procession comes from Isabel's view at the window, where she sees in the distance Bolingbroke on the "white Courser" and mistakes him for her husband: "I know him by his seate, he sits s'vpright";[6] after this mistaken witness, Isabel and Richard have their final meeting. Shakespeare places their last encounter before he has York describe the "two cousins coming into London" (V.ii.3), and by so doing presents an almost private leave-taking between Richard and his Queen that anticipates the discordant effects of Richard's lost kingship on other private and public affairs. The discord that develops between York and his Duchess in the next scene is a reflection, on a more domestic scale, of the separation between Richard and his Queen. York's iconic account of Henry's "triumph" reveals as well York's sense of divided loyalties between his two nephews. He seems to be in some awe of Henry's magnificence at the same time he sorrows for Richard's humiliation, but he resolves in his opening speeches both for him and his wife that they must affirm Henry's "state and honor" as the "new-made king."

York's description of Henry's triumphal procession sounds

very like the typical procession of a victor leading a "conquered king" into London.[7] Whereas Daniel describes Richard as "the Captive King [who] must ride,/ Most meanely mounted on a simple Steed" (Bk. II, 61), York describes only Bolingbroke on his horse:

> Then, as I said, the duke, great Bolingbroke,
> Mounted upon a hot and fiery steed
> Which his aspiring rider seemed to know,
> With slow but stately pace kept on his course,
> Whilst all tongues cried, 'God save thee, Bolingbroke! . . .
> Whilst he, from the one side to the other turning,
> Bareheaded, lower than his proud steed's neck,
> Bespake them thus, 'I thank you, countrymen.'
> And thus still doing, thus he passed along.
> (V.ii.7–20)

York's description of Richard's entry, in contrast to Bolingbroke's, includes no reference to his horse:

> No joyful tongue gave him his welcome home,
> But dust was thrown upon his sacred head.
> (V.ii.29–30)

Of course, we should infer that Richard also was mounted, since the Duchess asks, "Where rode he the whilst?", but Shakespeare's omission of any description of his horse is curious, considering Daniel's emphasis on Richard's being "most meanely mounted on a simple Steed" and the equally emphatic stress on Richard's "little horse" in both Creton's *Metrical History* and Le Beau's *Traison*, other sources Shakespeare may have used.[8]

Whatever the reason for this slighting of Richard's horse, the scene begins in a very serious manner, describing Bolingbroke "mounted upon a hot and fiery steed," and ends in another than serious tone with York mounting his horse in furious haste; Aumerle, on his mother's directive about to mount one of his father's horses; and the Duchess herself promising to mount a horse and outride her husband to prove not only that she is "right" but also that she has more "might."

Aumerle's entrance in V.ii changes the tone of York's review of the royal entry from a formal narrative to a domestic evaluation of the effects that the change of monarchs has made. Aumerle has fallen from favor at court and appears to be indifferent to his successors there. York asks if his son plans to attend the "justs and triumphs" to be held in Oxford in honor of newly kinged Henry. As Aumerle affirms his intention to be there, York spies the seal hanging from his bosom and then the comic routine begins. It is important to notice that the playwright has modulated the tone from a heightened recognition of Richard's royal tragedy to a domestic squabble through dramatically natural terms—domestic equivalents of "How do these national affairs affect you?" and "What are your plans for adjusting to the changes?" When York discovers, to the surprise of both father and son, that Aumerle is planning treason, the ordinary world created by the domestic commonplace vanishes into the melodramatic world of impending crisis.

The Duchess's part in this scene and the following one forces the material into a comic tone: her excessive protectiveness of her son polarizes York's zealous determination to destroy him, and their dialogue abounds in farcical formulations. After York plucks the sealed treasonous confederacy from Aumerle's bosom, he voices his consternation with violent expletives. The Duchess pleads to know "What is the matter?"—repeating her question four times—only to be hushed by York's "Peace, foolish woman," which compounds with his earlier opinion, "Wife, thou art a fool," and his later lines, "Thou fond mad woman . . . Away, fond woman," and finally, "Make way, unruly woman." His characterizations of her, as he refuses to clarify the matter, change her from concerned wife and mother into a virago. Throughout all of York's castigation of his son and the Duchess's queries to be informed of the matter, York is calling for his boots; when his servant brings them, the Duchess tells her son to strike the servant, and when Aumerle does not comply, she apparently hits him herself: "Hence, villain! never more come in my sight." However, York commands him to stay: "Give me my boots, I say." The servant is comically caught, like Francis the Drawer in *1 Henry IV* (II.iv), between two equally forceful commands; the potential for visual clowning is great. When York finally discloses the news that Aumerle is a traitor and the King's life is endangered by the conspiracy, the Duchess shows concern only for her son and nothing for the King: "We'll keep him [Aumerle] here, then what is that [the conspiracy] to him?" Her mother's practicality comically over-simplifies the consequences of Aumerle's plot and intensifies York's impatience with her. The Duchess completes the comic flyting after York pushes past her by advising Aumerle to take his father's horse and ride faster to the King while she follows, trusting that she can ride more swiftly than her husband despite her age.

Her taunting challenge of York's riding ability is not the last of her tongue's weapons in the familial contest, which almost becomes a pitched battle in the next scene. First Aumerle manages to closet himself with King Henry, exacting a promise of pardon before the facts of his plot are revealed; then York knocks on the door, threatening to break it open, and gains entrance to warn Henry of Aumerle's treason; and *then* the Duchess demands entry. One of the most recognized techniques of farce is repetitive action that, through its exact repetition, calls attention to its comic and deflationary nature. In this scene there is not only the repeated knocking at the door of Henry's private chambers but also the repeated kneeling in supplication of his favor. With the Duchess's demand, "open the door!/ A beggar begs that never begged before," even Henry realizes that "Our scene is alt'red from a serious thing,/ And now changed to 'The Beggar and the King.' "[9]

When Henry describes his own relationship to the comic supplications of the Duchess of York as a playlet, whether or not the title he gives is based on a contemporary farce no longer extant, he is shifting the audience's perception (as well as his own) to the awareness of his role as "player-king."[10] The difference between Henry's employment of the theatrical metaphor for his "real-life" situation and Richard's in Pomfret prison (V.v) is that Henry is controlling the scene despite the York family's being thrust on him; Richard, on the other hand, is still seeking a role and recognizes that Henry is in the position to assign him one: "and by and by/ Think that I am unkinged by Bolingbroke."

The parody involved here is complex: it is both retrospective and proleptic. At first glance, Henry seems to be the comic version of kingship, play-acting to complement the Duchess's announced role of beggar—and, as he fulfills his "actor's" role, he becomes the benevolent king, graciously absolving Aumerle's treason to the Duchess's applause: "A god on earth thou art." Visually, perhaps more than verbally, this action recalls the scene at Flint castle when Bolingbroke kneels before King Richard and in effect asks to be approved in his own treason. There, Richard grants the beggar's supplication, and the beggar in fact becomes the king, the king the beggar, a point ironically echoed in the deposition scene where Richard, having "beg[ged] one boon," perceives Bolingbroke's unconditional granting of it as flattery:

> I am greater than a king;
> For when I was a king my flatterers
> Were then but subjects; being now a subject,
> I have a king here to my flatterer.
> Being so great, I have no need to beg.
> (IV.i.305–9)

The scene wherein Henry enacts the King to his several beggars moves into the comic mode through reiteration: not only does Aumerle kneel after his entrance; when the Duchess enters, she kneels, then Aumerle kneels again, and finally York kneels. Henry asks the Duchess to rise (or stand) up three times before she does. He does not ask anyone else to "rise up," but that may be because no one else can interrupt the Duchess's extended protest that only *her* kneeling is sincere. Probably Henry realizes that accommodating her is the easiest way to resolve this serio-comic crisis.

This scene in which Henry pardons Aumerle for his plotted treason balances through parody Richard's scenes of deposition, first at Flint Castle (and then before the Parliament) and finally in Pomfret prison. Theatrical awareness of playing roles charges all these scenes. At Flint Castle, Richard's descent to the "base court"—"Down, down I come, like glist'ring Phaeton,/ Wanting the manage of unruly jades"—emphasizes not only his awareness of acting a part but also the symbolic associations inherent in the physical stage itself. His descent is both literal and metaphysical: when he moves physically from the upper playing level to the lower, he also wills to "undo himself" as a divinely anointed king, an act he later details with insistent anaphora before Parliament:

> With mine own tears I wash away my balm,
> With mine own hands I give away my crown,
> With mine own tongue deny my sacred state,
> With mine own breath release all duteous oaths.
> (IV.i.207–10)[11]

When Henry responds to the Duchess's plea for entry in V.iii, he too calls attention to stagecraft; he is aware of the action's theatricality.

Bolingbroke's kneeling before Richard at Flint Castle immediately following Richard's descent is but a show of obeisance that Richard recognizes for its hypocrisy, and is farcically reiterated in the later scene where the Duchess kneels "but for mine own" (as Henry says to Richard in III.iii.196). The Duchess's "own" is "my transgressing boy," whereas Bolingbroke's "own" is ostensibly his Lancastrian inheritance but actually the crown itself. Of that, Richard is ironically aware: "Your own is yours, and I am yours, and all." The Duchess of York's kneeling to Henry thus reiterates Bolingbroke's kneeling to Richard and provides a comic reduction for both actions. If the echo makes us see Richard's serious capitulation of kingly prerogative in a comic light, it also makes us see King Henry as a ruler whose powers are temporarily contained by comic routine. Richard knows he must give in to Bolingbroke because the force of "twenty thousand men" (III.ii.76) has moved over to Bolingbroke's side; yet King Henry gives in to the Duchess, who has no force except her indefatigable tongue. The situations seem extremely removed at the surface, but they both uncover treasonous plots to usurp the power of the King. Both apparently end in forgiveness, yet neither depicts the dispensation of unmitigated grace through the authority of God's reigning deputy: Richard requires time to be tutored "to this submission" (IV.i.167), and Henry condemns Aumerle's confederates. Similarly, when the Duchess calls Henry "a god on earth," can we help but be reminded of Richard's ineffectuality in that capacity?

Waldo McNeir says that "the joke ends" by Shakespeare's giving the Duchess "the last word"—"Come my old son. I pray God make thee new." McNeir comments, "She is allowed to think that only her intercession saved Aumerle from the same fate as the other conspirators."[12] Lawrence J. Ross, on the other hand, points out the relationship of her parting words to a long tradition of spiritually cognizant Pauline doctrine, as part of a list of instances that shows Shakespeare has "a very complete awareness of the concepts and imagery associated with the theological Old Man."[13] McNeir is in touch with the tone of the scene, but he overlooks the point of the Duchess's remark. She evokes a resonant body of theological knowledge at the same time she creates a parody of it (much after the manner of the Wife of Bath). Whether Aumerle undergoes regeneration of spirit, as she hopes, is something beyond this play to discover. In terms of immediate dramatic situation, we have nothing to indicate that Aumerle will be true to Henry in future (even though he dies on the King's side at the Battle of Agincourt in *Henry V* [IV.iv.7ff.]). Aumerle here is eager to save his own neck, but can hardly be truly penitent for his father's untimely discovery of his own malice against King Henry. Bolingbroke, too, when confronted by Richard's ironic penetration of his alazon at Flint Castle, pretends to have spiritual humility. Neither case can be assumed to illustrate spiritual regeneration; their close parallelism encourages us to see qualifications of the actors' intended idealizations of their roles.

King Henry's pardoning scene, "altered from a serious thing," provides yet another parodic focus with the seemingly frivolous word-play that passes between the Duchess and York over the word "pardon." In refusing to stand up until Henry says "pardon" first, the Duchess, as Polonius later does with the word "tender" (*Hamlet,* I.iii.108–9), cracks "the wind of the poor phrase,/ Running it thus":

An if I were thy nurse, thy tongue to teach,
'Pardon' should be the first *word* of thy speech.
I never longed to hear a *word* till now,
Say 'pardon,' king; let pity teach thee how.
The *word* is short, but not so short as sweet;
No *word* like 'pardon' for kings' mouths so meet.
(V.iii.113–18; my italics)

York, displeased with her verbal onslaught, asks Henry to "Speak it in French, king. Say 'pardonne moi,' " which only arouses the Duchess to further prolixity in her pleading:

Dost thou teach pardon pardon to destroy?
Ah, my sour husband, my hardhearted lord,
That sets the word itself against the word!
Speak 'pardon' as 'tis current in our land;
The chopping French we do not understand.
Thine eye begins to speak, set thy tongue there;
Or in thy piteous heart plant thou thine ear,
That hearing how our plaints and prayers do pierce,
Pity may move thee 'pardon' to rehearse.
(V.iii.120–28; my italics)

The Duchess recognizes that York's odd request for Henry to speak his pardon in French is an attempt to get Henry to deny pardon, since Henry in effect would be saying "Pardon me, I cannot." Perhaps it is because of the prolix tenacity of her eloquence more than because of her eloquence itself that Henry finally agrees: "I pardon him as God shall pardon me" (V.iii.132). This pardon is the third one Henry has given in this scene (one to Aumerle, a second to York against his wishes), and that repetition makes the Duchess's insistence comically superfluous. Despite its comic setting, Henry's resolution of the familial contest in favor of the Duchess's plea to pardon Aumerle reverberates strangely through the next lines, in which he dispatches "destruction" for Aumerle's confederates in the assassination plot. The swift change from comic forgiveness to inexorable execution both here and in the brief scene that follows, with Exton testing his reading of the King's desire to have Richard killed (V.iv), shocks us into an uneasy awareness that newly-kinged Henry can dispense grace with comic ease at the same time he is dispensing death for others who are no more culpable than Aumerle.

In Richard's soliloquy that soon follows (V.v) there are several echoes of the preceding comedy. First is the sense that he is establishing a theatrical role: Richard tries to grasp at identity almost in the playful mood of the comic disguiser. Shakespeare has him draw on the idea that he is now, for a brief moment, like the playwright, peopling this little world—the prison—with his thoughts. But he is inverting the commonplace use of "the world is a stage" metaphor by saying that his stage—the prison—is like the world. In Stoic philosophy, the stage metaphor was a favorite figure of speech, but always with the idea that a man chooses his role or discovers his appointed role and then, if he is a virtuous man, realizes it in action.[14] What Richard does here as he seeks an identity at the end of his life is directly opposed to the virtuous man's essence as defined by Seneca in an epistle to Lucilius:

There is no man that doth not daily change both his counsaile and his vow: now will he haue a wife, then a Lemman: now will he gouerne, presently he laboureth for this, that no man may be a more officious seruant. . . . Hereby especially is an imprudent minde discouered, euery one betrayeth him, and that which in my opinion is most base, He is vnlike himselfe. Repute thou it to be a great vertue for a man to be one. But no man but a wise man doth one thing, all the rest of vs haue many shapes. To day we will seeme to be modest and graue, to morrow prodigall and vaine: we oftimes change our maske, and oftentimes take a contrarie to that we haue put off. Exact thou therefore this of thy selfe, that to thy last breath thou maintaine thy selfe such, as thou hast reso-lued to shew thy selfe.[15]

Richard's confession that he is unable to determine a single "per-sona" under which to live his life could almost be a paraphrase of the imprudent, foolish man described by Seneca:

> Thus play I in one person many people,
> And none contented. Sometimes am I king:
> Then treasons make me wish myself a beggar,
> And so I am. Then crushing penury

Persuades me I was better when a king;
Then am I kinged again; and by and by
Think that I am unkinged by Bolingbroke,
And straight am nothing. (V.v.31–38)

One of Richard's changing sets of alternates for determining his identity is "the beggar and the king," which ironically echoes Bolingbroke's recent definition of his own theatrical role.

Another echo occurs when Richard says that even the "better sort" of thoughts "do set the word itself/ Against the word." The verbal similarities between Richard's lines and the Duchess's (V.iii.122) are not often noticed and, when discussed, are rarely seen as parodic parallels.[16] My point is that Shakespeare has infused the comic scene (V.iii) not only with situational stresses that parodically imitate what has preceded but also with verbal stresses that become referents for what is to follow. Exton and the Servant puzzle over the "words" Henry spoke about ridding himself of "this living fear." Both heard the words, but what is their meaning? Exton interprets them to mean "Kill Richard," and so he does. Yet Henry denies this was what his words meant; at least he tries to squirm out of the implication, despite the fact that he cannot wholly absolve himself of Exton's inference. When York asks Henry in V.iii to do a similar skirmish with meaning, by giving a French phrase for the English word to mean its opposite, the Duchess is there to prevent such ambiguous dalliance.

Richard's "word against word" sets apparently contradictory scriptural passages against each other in an attempt to define his own thoughts. Recalling the gospel verses from Matthew, Mark, and Luke in which Christ initially welcomes the little children to come unto him, for "of such" is the kingdom of heaven (or of God), and in the next moment tells his disciples that it is more difficult for a rich man to enter the kingdom of heaven than for a camel to pass through the eye of a needle, Richard ponders the paradox of the ease and the difficulty of entering heaven. His own situation, he realizes, is bringing him toward such a passage.[17]

His soliloquy, for all of its apparent shifts in point, turns out to be a surprisingly controlled, almost formal, meditation.[18] Richard creates a "composition of place"—his prison he compares to the world, his thoughts to people—and proceeds to a threefold consideration of the "affections" of these thought/people. He moves from "thoughts of things divine" that lead to paradox; to "thoughts tending to ambition" that, because they cannot effect deeds of wonder, die in their own pride; to "thoughts tending to content" that produce the flattering notion that no individual man is alone in humiliation—he is not the first, nor shall he be the last to suffer shame and misfortune. The resolution to which he then moves—"Thus play I in one person many people,/ And none contented"—does not seem to be the emotional conclusion recommended by the Jesuits in their instructions, but it is a formal conclusion, which in turn leads him to contemplate the nothingness of his own death—one of the foremost subjects for systematic meditation.[19]

The examination of the self is an important prelude to the meditation on death, yet just as Richard reaches the appropriate point in his meditative structure, his thoughts are interrupted by music. The music is provided by unknown sources, and it is hardly necessary to speculate that the groom who soon enters has either hired the musicians or played the music himself. It is a "sweet music," although to Richard's ears it is "sour," because its harmony reminds him of how he has broken his own. The mystery of the music's source is part of the value here. It could even suggest, as does Pericles' strange music, that at the point of selflessness reached through his meditative attempt, Richard can hear the music of the spheres. Whatever its source, it brings him back from a timeless realm of thought to thoughts about time. The world is still in motion, and Bolingbroke is dictating Richard's. His associations between musical time and temporal time, nonetheless, lead him to a fourth category of his thoughts that continues his earlier threefold division—"My thoughts are minutes"—and suggests that his meditative mode is still operative. This metaphor and the elaborate analogy of himself to a clock lead him once again to contemplation of Bolingbroke as controller of his time:

> But my time
> Runs posting on in Bolingbroke's proud joy,
> While I stand fooling here, his Jack of the clock.

He calls an end to the music, recognizing that all things work in contradiction for him: whereas music has helped "mad men to their wits," it "mads me." Even so, he blesses its source because it is a "sign of love" in a world where he perceives that all hate Richard.

At this point, en route to York from London, where he saw King Henry's coronation, the Groom enters to greet his former master. His "Hail, royal prince!" evokes from Richard complex word-play on "royal" and "noble," coins worth more than Richard estimates his current worth to be, and this is another instance of the leveling of estates on which he has meditated in his soliloquy.

The Groom, like the Duchess of York in V.iii, is one of Shakespeare's additions to the historical accounts. At first glance he may seem an odd intrusion on Richard's last search for identity. On closer consideration, however, we realize that the language and imagery of horsemanship have occurred frequently throughout the play. Beginning with Mowbray's response to Bolingbroke's challenge in scene one—

> The fair reverence of your highness *curbs* me
> From giving *reins* and *spurs* to my free speech,
> Which else would *post* until it had returned
> These terms of treason doubled down his throat.
> (I.i.54–57; my italics)

—through the Duchess of Gloucester's curse on Mowbray for the anticipated tournament—

> . . . if misfortune miss the first *career*,
> Be Mowbray's sins so heavy in his bosom
> That they may break his *foaming courser's* back
> And *throw* the *rider* headlong in the lists.
> (I.ii.49–52; my italics)

—and York's advice to the dying and indignant Gaunt—

The King is come. Deal mildly with his youth;
Young hot colts, being raged, do rage the more.
(II.i.69–70; my italics)

—we have been hearing words that relate not only to Richard's descent at Flint Castle, "like glist'ring Phaeton,/ Wanting the manage of unruly jades" (III.iii.178–79) but also to his surprise at being quite literally unhorsed and then *ridden* by Bolingbroke (V.v.84–94).

These instances of Shakespeare's references to horsemanship are by no means singular in *Richard II,* and other references illuminate pertinent associated values. Consider, for one example, the Dauphin's ecstatic praise of his horse in the concluding play of the tetralogy that *Richard II* begins:

Nay, the man hath no wit that cannot, from the rising of the lark to the lodging of the lamb, vary deserved praise on my palfrey. It is a theme as fluent as the sea. Turn the sands into eloquent tongues, and my horse is argument for them all. 'Tis a subject for a sovereign to reason on, and for a sovereign's sovereign to ride on.[20]

Again, in *Measure for Measure,* when Claudio is explaining to Lucio why he is being led to prison, he says:

Whether it be the fault and glimpse of newness,
Or whether that the body public be
A horse whereon the governor doth ride,
Who, newly in the seat, that it may know
He can command, lets it straight feel the spur;
Whether the tyranny be in his place,
Or in his eminence that fills it up,
I stagger in.[21]

Both of these passages could be read as glosses on Richard's remarks to the Groom. He has been unkinged and finally un-horsed by Bolingbroke, who was able to ride Richard's favorite horse, his "roan Barbary," in the coronation procession. The Groom as well as Richard seems surprised that such a favorite horse of them both—"That horse that thou so often hast bestrid,/ That horse that I so carefully have dressed!" (V.v.79–80)—could allow Bolingbroke its mastery. Not only that, the horse seemed proud to be so ridden.

Ability in horsemanship was a commonplace requirement in guides for gentlemanly conduct because it signaled innate nobility as well as learned skills. Sir Philip Sidney begins his *Defence of Poesie* with an amused account of the horse's stature as told to him by Jon Pietro Pugliano while Sidney and a friend were "at the Emperours Court togither." In Pugliano's opinion,

no earthly thing bred such wonder to a Prince, as to be a good horseman. Skill of government was but a *Pedanteria,* in comparison, then would he adde certaine praises by telling what a peerlesse beast the horse was, the only serviceable Courtier without flattery, the beast of most bewtie, faithfulnesse, courage, and such more, that if I had not bene a peece of a Logician before I came to him, I thinke he would have perswaded me to have wished my selfe a horse.[22]

In a letter to his brother Robert, date 18 October 1580, Sir Philip advises him to read Grison Claudio's book on horsemanship, "La gloria del cavallo . . . that yow may joyne the[e] through contemplation of it with the exercise."[23] Roger Ascham in *The Schoolmaster* (1570) also applauds skill in horsemanship as essential to a gentleman's upbringing:

for of all outward qualities, to ride fair is most comely for himself, most necessary for his country, and the greater he is in blood, the greater is his praise, the more he doth exceed all other therein.[24]

Castiglione in *The Book of the Courtier* has the Count say, "Therefore will I have our Courtyer a perfecte horseman for everye saddle. . . . And because it is the peculyer prayse of us Italians to ryde well, to manege with reason, especiallye roughe horses, to runne at the tynge and at tylte, he shall bee in this among the beste Italyans."[25]

Regard for horsemanship as a sign of nobility and heroic stature is ancient, as an examination of the equestrian monument testifies.[26] Nicholas Morgan in *The Perfection of Horse-manship* (1609) has a commendatory poem to a recently "deceased worthy & renowned Rider, Robert Alexander," in which he draws an analogy based on the last name:

Great Alexander *deerly lou'd his Horse,*
The Horse lou'd him, and suffered none to ride
Vppon his backe, by flattery or by force,
But his dread Lord, that halfe the world did guide.[27]

Morgan is clearly one of the more enthusiastic idealizers of the horse and of the loyalty between the noble beast and his rider, yet his belief that "euery Horse is created as man is of soule and bodie" and that "the gentillitie and noblenesse of the beast so manifest, whose heart is so highly set, that for to dye hee will not leave his master in danger" was commonly held. No doubt Richard's surprise that his "roan Barbary" failed in fidelity— "Would he not stumble? would he not fall down,/ Since pride must have a fall, and break the neck/ Of that proud man that did usurp his back?"—is due to similar assumptions. Richard quickly realizes that his railing on the horse's fickleness is inappropriate because the beast, "created to be awed by man,/ Wast born to bear." The dissimilarity of his created destiny and that of the horse reminds him finally of how totally he has been mastered by Bolingbroke:

> I was not made a horse;
> And yet I bear a burden like an ass,
> Spurred, galled, and tired by jauncing Bolingbroke.
> (V.v.92–94)

Gaunt's prophetic proverb—"He tires betimes that spurs too fast betimes" (II.i.36)—has been realized in his son's mastery of the King—not only of the King's body politic but of the King's natural body as well, both bodies being represented in the figure of the horse.[28]

The two descriptions of Bolingbroke on horseback, by York and by the Groom, are companion pieces that assert Bolingbroke's assumption of dynastic authority through his individual prowess. These portraits take on the power of an icon—the picture of Bolingbroke drawn from actual events becomes symbolic, much as Vernon's description of Prince Hal before the Battle of Shrewsbury takes on iconic and humanly impossible features:

I saw young Harry with his beaver on,
His cushes on his thighs, gallantly armed,
Rise from the ground like feathered Mercury,
And vaulted with such ease into his seat
As if an angel dropped down from the clouds
To turn and wind a fiery Pegasus
And witch the world with noble horsemanship.[29]

The force of the image is revealed in Hotspur's "No more, no more!" and his call for his "hot horse."

Richard's subjection to Bolingbroke thus has its final effect on him and on the audience in what is both a very personalized and a heavily symbolic recognition: the horse is quite simply Richard's favorite animal, more complexly the metaphor of Richard's state and ultimately of Richard himself. Bolingbroke rides both the literal and figurative horses with absolute authority, and the Groom's report of his so doing causes Richard's final acceptance of his deposition. The physical assault on him that follows produces a more authoritative, more dynamic Richard than any of his earlier acts as King have done—as if he discovers in "nothing" the paradoxical essence of his being.[30]

Throughout the scenes that begin with York's description of Henry "mounted upon a hot and fiery steed" and end with the Groom's stunned report of Bolingbroke's riding Richard's "roan Barbary" with complete mastery, we have been led to see more than a man on horseback. Henry has become idealized through these formal speeches into a conquering hero, a Marcus Aurelius or a Gattemelata: the picture is more than the man. When we have seen Henry in action as a king, however, he has been less than heroic. Not only is there the farcical encounter with the York family, an earlier scene shows him to be no more effective than Richard in resolving the question, "Who killed Thomas of Woodstock?"

Even before he has received Richard's public conveyance of the crown and the title of King, Bolingbroke has presumed the royal authority. To clarify the issue of "noble Gloucester's death" Bolingbroke calls forth the testimony of Bagot, who has nimbly evaded the execution of *his* confederates—Bushy, Green, and the

Earl of Wiltshire (II.ii.122ff. and III.ii.137–42)—by escaping to Ireland, and who has now returned to ingratiate himself with the soon-to-be-crowned Henry. Bagot asks that Aumerle be brought before him so that he may accuse him of plotting Gloucester's death. It is an exact replay of Bolingbroke's accusation of Mowbray in the play's opening scene, except that now Henry is in Richard's authoritative place.

The gage-throwing in the later scene (IV.i), however, gets out of control, so much so that Aumerle has to ask "Some honest Christian [to] trust me with a gage." The stage is actually littered with gages too numerous to identify, pushing the action through excessive repetition toward farce.[31] Ironically, the resolution of all these gages held in suspension by Henry depends on bringing his old enemy Thomas Mowbray, Duke of Norfolk, back from exile. That act, Henry discovers, he is impotent to perform, because Norfolk lies dead in Venice. In the first act, Richard cannot persuade Mowbray and Bolingbroke to desist from their mutual accusations of treason and so must call off the tournament in which they were to prove their innocence or guilt. Bolingbroke, as Richard's surrogate, is equally strapped. He cannot "prove" what is commonly "known" because Mowbray, his earlier opponent, did not violate his "banishment" as Henry himself has done. The confusion of Woodstock's murder remains unresolved, and is soon to be replaced by Henry's ambiguity in accepting his responsibility for Richard's murder by Exton.

In York's description of Bolingbroke's triumphal entry into London with Richard trailing behind, he uses a theatrical metaphor to explain how Richard could so easily be replaced by Bolingbroke in the people's favor:

> As in the theatre the eyes of men,
> After a well-graced actor leaves the stage,
> Are idly bent on him that enters next,
> Thinking his prattle to be tedious,
> Even so, or with much more contempt, men's eyes
> Did scowl on gentle Richard. (V.ii.23–28)

Yet even as York describes Richard's reception by the people as that of a poor player, the actual theater audience has begun to perceive Richard as the "well-graced actor" about to "leave the stage." Bolingbroke does not, therefore, become a tedious prattler, but his part in the rest of the play's action is not as theatrically powerful as Richard's.

Discussing "the actor in *Richard II*," Georges A. Bonnard assumes that "Shakespeare did not take much interest in him [Bolingbroke]. . . . He could only see him from the outside. . . . As a dramatic character he only comes to life for a brief moment in the Aumerle scenes of the Fifth Act." Bonnard concludes that *Richard II* is an unbalanced play because "its structure demanded two heroes in opposition" and Shakespeare's "imagination was quickened by one of the heroes and not by the other."[32] This seems to stretch unduly for a biographical fallacy based on an assumption, possibly erroneous, about the play's *intended* structure. If we allow that the play's structure does not intend to set up Bolingbroke and Richard as "mighty opposites" but as parallel entrepreneurs in kingship, we see more about why Shakespeare allows Richard's characterization to dominate the play's ending. Speaking of opposition between characters, we should more likely name Bolingbroke and Mowbray at the play's beginning, whose intended contest is disallowed by Richard, or Bagot and Aumerle, who submit a replay in Act IV, also suspended. But there is no dramatized contest between Richard and Bolingbroke. Bolingbroke advances, Richard capitulates. No battle is fought, as in the later plays of this tetralogy. This is not opposition of equally drawn characters, but usurpation by show of "might." By bringing Bolingbroke into a near parody of Richard's earlier scenes with the gage-throwing (I.i and IV.i) and with the Yorks' appeals for merciful judgment (I.iii and V.iii), Shakespeare suggests that Bolingbroke's effective action is not so different from Richard's, despite his more practical opportunism. Furthermore, as York has warned Richard on his confiscation of Bolingbroke's land and title, Richard sets a precedent in that action for Bolingbroke's usurpation of the throne:

> Take Hereford's rights away, and take from Time
> His charters and his customary rights;
> Let not to-morrow then ensue to-day;

Be not thyself—for how art thou a king
But by fair sequence and succession?
Now, afore God (God forbid I say true!)
If you do wrongfully seize Hereford's rights, . . .
You pluck a thousand dangers on your head,
You lose a thousand well-disposed hearts,
And prick my tender patience to those thoughts
Which honor and allegiance cannot think.
(II.i.195–208)

Shakespeare has clearly set up an imitation, not a progression from one kingly point-of-view to another, and the scenes that are precisely parallel in comic terms indicate that not only are Richard's actions diminished by reductive imitation but Bolingbroke's actions are also limited in themselves. The control and mastery that the images of King Henry on horseback suggest are contained by the comic routines he is forced into playing. The effect of this comic parallelism that shades into parody reminds us that the play ends where it began. The difference is that instead of the King's having murdered a royal uncle, Bolingbroke now has killed the King.

Chapter 6

TWELFTH NIGHT AND THE PARODIC SUBPLOT

The preceding chapters have examined individual scenes and sets of scenes that parody larger issues opening up within the entire play. These scenes usually distinguish themselves from their larger context by a change of tone, a change of pace, and a seeming narrative irrelevance. In *Twelfth Night,* Shakespeare employs the parody principle throughout the entire subplot, with the result that there is a sense of narrative necessity between these scenes and those they imitate in comic ways. Because the subplot is fully developed and ongoing, the interweaving of the primary plot with these scenes often creates a sense of cause and effect, although a given effect does not always have a direct cause. The tonal shifts are less jarring as well (despite lopsided productions that feature the farcical elements of the subplot as the major focus of the play and make the primary plot seem irrelevant and out of joint). Shakespeare has balanced the tones between the two so that one seems incapable of its point without the other.[1] The pace of the subplot scenes never slows the main plot (at least in good performances) but increases the momentum toward the climactic merger of the two when they become one "natural perspective that is and is not" (V.i).

To help the subplot's mimicry of the main plot seem even more integrated than it might otherwise be, Shakespeare incorporates a secondary gulling of Sir Andrew to set off the gulling of Malvolio. Both Sir Andrew and Malvolio futilely aspire to Olivia's hand in marriage, as does the Duke, but neither is accorded a more appropriate substitute for his desire such as the

Duke finds in Viola. Perhaps Sir Andrew's carousing with Sir Toby and the others in Olivia's household sufficiently distracts him from the recognition that his will has not been satisfied, but Malvolio has no such substitute. His hope of gaining Olivia results in public humiliation at the hands of Feste, who takes obvious satisfaction in being able to throw Malvolio's earlier haughty words back at him under their new context of Malvolio's demonstrated foolishness:

Why, 'some are born great, some achieve greatness, and some have greatness thrown upon them.' I was one, sir, in this interlude, one Sir Topas, sir; but that's all one. 'By the Lord, fool, I am not mad!' But do you remember, 'Madam, why laugh you at such a barren rascal? An you smile not, he's gagged'? And thus the whirligig of time brings in his revenges. (V.i.360–66) .

Feste's assertion that the "whirligig of time" has brought this revenge on Malvolio neglects the fact that Maria has been the instigator and Feste the enforcer of the plot to harass Malvolio. Time's design, insofar as Malvolio is concerned, depends primarily on Maria's and Feste's will,[2] which differs significantly from a central point that the main plot makes—that human will is not the controller of events. The characters in the main plot learn from the play's confusing action that human designs are frequently inadequate for securing "what you will" and that a design outside their control brings fulfillment in unexpected ways.[3] Feste's fallacy, of course, makes the results of the subplot *seem* to be the same as the results of the main plot, but time's revenges on Malvolio are primarily human revenges, and this particular measure for measure is thoroughly within human control.[4] Feste's justice allows no mitigation for missing the mark in human action; and the incipient cruelty that his precise justice manifests is felt, apparently, by other characters in the play.[5]

When Olivia and her company hear Malvolio's case, she responds with compassion: "Alas, poor fool, how have they baffled thee! . . . He hath been most notoriously abused" (V.i.359, 368). Duke Orsino, on hearing Malvolio's letter of explanation, comments, "This savors not much of distraction" (V.i.304). And even

Sir Toby has become uneasy about the harsh treatment of Malvolio in the imprisonment scene: "I would we were well rid of this knavery. If he may be conveniently delivered, I would he were; for I am now so far in offense with my niece that I cannot pursue with any safety this sport to the upshot" (IV.ii.66–70). Actually, to place the responses into this sequence reverses the play's order; and we should consider the fact that Shakespeare builds *toward* a compassionate comment, with Olivia's statement climaxing an unwillingness to condone the actions of Feste and Maria in gulling Malvolio—at least in its last phase. Feste's exact form of justice without mercy has always characterized revenge, and even the word "revenge" is stressed by several of the characters in the subplot. When Maria voices her apparently spontaneous plot to gull Malvolio, she says:

> The devil a Puritan that he is . . . the best persuaded of himself; so crammed, as he thinks, with excellencies that it is his grounds of faith that all that look on him love him; and on that vice in him will my revenge find notable cause to work. (II.iii.134–40)

Maria's successful implementation of her "revenge" elicits Sir Toby's enthusiastic, parodically gallant admiration. At the end of II.v, he exclaims, "I could marry this wench for this device" (168), and when Maria appears soon thereafter, he asks, "Wilt thou set thy foot o' my neck?" (174). The battlefield image of the victor and the victim is mock-heroic, of course; but in the final scene Fabian testifies to its literal fruition: "Maria writ/ The letter, at Sir Toby's great importance,/ In recompense whereof he hath married her" (V.i.352–54). Sir Toby's submission to Maria's will is a comic parallel for two actions: the pairing off of lovers, and the submission of the individual's will to a design other than his own. Yet the inclusion of a parodic version of marriage-harmony in the subplot does not fully ease the discomfort of the subplot's conclusion. Fabian tries to smooth it away when he suggests that the "sportful malice" of gulling Malvolio "may rather pluck on laughter than revenge" (V.i.355–58). Neither Feste nor Malvolio seems to be convinced, however. Feste's "whirligig of time brings in his revenges," and

Malvolio quits the stage with, "I'll be revenged on the whole pack of you!" (V.i.366–67). The forgiveness that should conclude the comic pattern is "notoriously" missing from the subplot and cannot be absorbed successfully by the Duke's line, "Pursue him and entreat him to a peace." Malvolio seems unlikely to return. The major difference between the subplot and the main plot is clearest at this dramatic moment: revenge is a human action that destroys; love, graced by the sanction of a higher providence, creates a "golden time."

Feste's "whirligig" seems to be a parody of fortune's wheel in its inevitable turning, particularly with its suggestions of giddy swiftness and change. It provides a perfect image for the wild but symmetrical comic conclusion of the play's action. Feste's speech that includes it gives the appearance of completion to a mad cycle of events over which no human had much control. Only in Malvolio's case was human control of events without impediment. In her forged letter, Maria caters to Malvolio's "will" and, by encouraging him to accept his own interpretation of circumstances as his desire dictates,[6] leads him not only into foolishness but also into a defense of his sanity. The discrepancy between Malvolio's assumption that fortune is leading him on his way and the fact that Maria is in charge of his fate manifests itself clearly in the juxtaposition of her directions to the revelers as she leaves the stage with Malvolio's lines as he enters:

MARIA Get ye all three into the box tree. . . . Observe him, for the love of mockery; for I know this letter will make a contemplative idiot of him. Close, in the name of jesting. [*The others hide.*] Lie thou there [*throws down a letter*]; for here comes the trout that must be caught with tickling. *Exit. Enter Malvolio.*

MALVOLIO 'Tis but fortune; all is fortune. Maria once told me she [Olivia] did affect me. (II.v.13–22)

The gulling of Malvolio that follows is hilariously funny, partly because Malvolio brings it all on himself. Even before he finds the letter, his assumptions of rank and his plans for putting Sir Toby in his place elicit volatile responses from the box tree. And after he finds the forged letter, Malvolio's self-aggrandizing interpretations of the often cryptic statements evoke howls of glee mixed with the already disdainful laughter.

One fascinating aspect of the comedy is the role played by Sir Andrew Auguecheek.[7] He is ostensibly a part of the plan to "gull" Malvolio "into a nayword" broached by Maria (II.iii.124), but he is not perceptive enough to participate fully. He is kept outside of the "gulling," even while he and the box tree audience respond to Malvolio's presumptiveness, because he cannot comprehend the integration of the parts with the whole of the action. Although he echoes Sir Toby's anger at Malvolio's fantasy of becoming "Count Malvolio" (II.v.32), Sir Andrew's responses indicate that he is not within the same realm of perception as the other two in the box tree. Just before Malvolio discovers the forged letter, he describes how he would reprimand Sir Toby for his many faults:

'Cousin Toby, my fortunes having cast me on your niece, give me this prerogative of speech. . . . You must amend your drunkenness. . . . Besides, you waste the treasure of your time with a foolish knight.' (II.v.65–73)

Sir Andrew, following as an audience would if it were completely taken in by Malvolio's fiction, anticipates his own role in the fantasy: "That's me, I warrant you." And when Malvolio goes on to name " 'One Sir Andrew'—" Andrew concludes with satisfaction: "I knew 'twas I, for many do call me fool."

Sir Andrew not only anticipates his being named as the fool in a hypothetical comic routine, he also calls attention to Malvolio's discovery of the peculiarity in Olivia's handwriting of special letters: "By my life, this is my lady's hand. These be her very C's, her U's, and her T's; and thus makes she her great P's. It is, in contempt of question, her hand." Andrew picks up the first three—"Her C's, her U's, and her T's? Why's that?"—as if these irrelevant letters had significance. In his mind these particular letters probably echo Sir Toby's earlier reassurance to him that, "If thou hast her [Olivia] not i' th' end, call me Cut" (II.iii.172–73). The letters' juxtaposition suggests an elusive meaning that Sir Andrew cannot quite grasp.[8]

Sir Andrew thereafter becomes a silent attendant on Malvolio's further reading of the forged letter, although his stage action may involve him in the voiced responses of Fabian and Sir Toby. Only after Malvolio leaves and Sir Toby praises Maria "for this device" does Sir Andrew speak again, and in succession he parrots five of Sir Toby's lines:

> So could I too. . . .
> Nor I neither. . . .
> Or o' mine either? . . .
> I' faith, or I either? . . .
> I'll make one too. (II.v.168–92)

On his own, Sir Andrew does not perceive Malvolio to be a comic butt, and significantly he has nothing to do with the further plot that involves Malvolio's imprisonment. In the first phase of the gulling, the forged letter, he is as much a naif as is Malvolio.

In the next scene Sir Andrew's fascination with Viola/Cesario's words—"Odors, pregnant, and vouchsafed"—suggests a disjunction between words and their meanings that resembles his intrigue with the single letters Malvolio chooses to ponder in the forged letter. Viola/Cesario, having engaged Feste in word games at the beginning of this scene (III.i), contemplates Feste's skill at playing the fool:

> This is a practice
> As full of labor as a wise man's art;
> For folly that he wisely shows, is fit;
> But wise men, folly-fall'n, quite taint their wit.
> *Enter Sir Toby and [Sir] Andrew.* (III.i.63–66)

Sir Toby's and Sir Andrew's entrance on the tag end of Viola's couplet embodies the point of her proverbial wisdom and emphasizes the difference between a "wise fool," a "folly-fall'n" fool, and a "natural." Both Sir Toby and Sir Andrew offer courtly greetings, but Andrew affectedly greets her in textbook French. When Viola responds in French, he switches to English, having progressed as far as he dare in a language for which he has not yet memorized the basic vocabulary (obvious in his question earlier:

"What is 'pourquoi'? Do, or not do?" [I.iii.83]).[9] Hearing Viola's flowery greeting to Olivia, Sir Andrew is impressed by her artificial diction and promises to memorize the words for his future exercises in gallantry: "I'll get 'em all three all ready" (III.i.87–88).

When Sir Andrew next appears, however, his admiration for Viola/Cesario has changed to anger, brought on by his perception that even the "Count's servingman" receives more favors from Olivia than he does. Toby and Fabian persuade him that such appearances are a deliberate ploy by Olivia "to exasperate you, to awake your doormouse valor, to put fire in your heart and brimstone in your liver" (III.ii.17–18). Convinced that he must display some show of valor, Sir Andrew goes off to compose a letter of challenge to Cesario, and thus misses the appearance of Malvolio in yellow stockings, cross-gartered.

The visual comedy of Malvolio's clownish appearance encourages a total release in the fun of the game—Malvolio is gulled and the audience need not feel the least bit guilty about their laughter because he is marvelously unaware of his own foolishness. Oblivious to any reality but his own, Malvolio thinks he is irresistibly appealing with his repugnant dress and his continuous smiles—so contrary to his usual solemnity—and Olivia concludes that he has gone mad. "Why, this is very midsummer madness," she says, and then, as she is leaving to receive Cesario, she commends Malvolio to Maria's care.[10]

Good Maria, let this fellow be looked to. Where's my cousin Toby? Let some of my people have a special care of him. I would not have him miscarry for the half of my dowry. (III.iv.55–58)

Malvolio miscontrues Olivia's generous concern as amorous passion and he thanks Jove for contriving circumstances so appropriately:

I have limed her; but it is Jove's doing, and Jove make me thankful. . . . Nothing that can be can come between me and the full prospect of my hopes. Well, Jove, not I, is the doer of this, and he is to be thanked. (III.iv.68–77)

Malvolio's scrupulous praise of a higher designer than himself is a parodic echo of Olivia's earlier submission to fate after she has begun to love Cesario: "What is decreed must be—and be this so!" (I.v.297). The impulses underlying Malvolio's speech (and to some extent, Olivia's speech as well) exert opposite pulls: Malvolio wants to attribute control of circumstances to Jove at the same time he wants to dictate circumstances himself. He attempts to simulate foreknowledge through predictive assertion: "Nothing that can be can come between me and the full prospect of my hopes." As long as events are in the hands of a non-human control, man cannot destroy or divert the predetermined order. But Malvolio cannot foresee the vindictive wit of Maria, nor can Olivia foresee the necessary substitution of Sebastian for Viola/Cesario. All must learn that they, like the characters they wish to control, are subject to an unpredictable will not their own.

Malvolio, still ecstatic over Olivia's display of concern for his erratic behavior, which he misreads as romantic love, encounters the tricksters responsible for his delusion, and finds their taunting suggestions that he has gone mad outside his comprehension. Unable to cope with their irrelevance, he angrily takes his leave, while Fabian remarks that "If this were played upon a stage now, I could condemn it as an improbable fiction" (III.iv.119–20).

S. L. Bethell observes that Fabian's line has a double purpose: "to justify an improbable situation, and to underline the essential unreality of the play-world. . . . We are reminded that the play is only a play, just when the reminder is needed to enable us to enjoy the comedy of Malvolio's imprisonment."[11] Fabian's self-conscious awareness of the theater probably does have that effect here. The anticipation of further fun with the gulling of Malvolio "in a dark room and bound" is complemented by the anticipation of Sir Andrew's duel with Cesario, which Fabian and Sir Toby develop next. Fabian's announcement of Sir Andrew's entrance, "More matter for a May morning," has the similar effect of signaling fun rather than painful abuse, as does his line following Malvolio's exit. Both the plots to gull Malvolio and Sir Andrew, however, move beyond their anticipated innocuous fun: not only is Malvolio notoriously abused, but also Sir Andrew receives a real blow from Sebastian that causes blood to flow.

The duel promoted between Sir Andrew and Cesario provides some of the funniest material in the play, and its onstage development precedes Malvolio's imprisonment. Sir Andrew's letter of challenge is a masterpiece in parodying the rules of fence, a point about which Sir Andrew is comically unaware. Sir Toby reads it to Fabian's amused approval:

TOBY . . . [*reads*] 'Youth, whatsoever thou art, thou art but a scurvy fellow.'

FABIAN Good, and valiant.

TOBY [*reads*] 'Wonder not nor admire not in thy mind why I do call thee so, for I will show thee no reason for't.'

FABIAN A good note that keeps you from the blow of the law.

TOBY [*reads*] 'Thou com'st to the Lady Olivia, and in my sight she uses thee kindly. But thou liest in thy throat; that is not the matter I challenge thee for.'

FABIAN Very brief, and to exceeding good sense-less.

TOBY [*reads*] 'I will waylay thee going home; where if it be thy chance to kill me'—

FABIAN Good.

TOBY [*reads*] 'Thou kill'st me like a rogue and a villain.'

FABIAN Still you keep o' th' windy side of the law. Good.

TOBY [*reads*] 'Fare thee well, and God have mercy upon one of our souls. He may have mercy upon mine, but my hope is better, and so look to thyself. Thy friend, as thou usest him, and thy sworn enemy,
'Andrew Aguecheek.' (III.iv.139–58)

Sir Andrew's letter of challenge violates almost every rule set down by Sir William Segar and Vincentio Saviolo in their treatises on the subject.[12] The letter of challenge was to follow the initial offense issued orally in order to formalize the challenge. In Sir Andrew's situation, this is reversed: he writes his letter before Cesario is aware of having offended him. Offering the lie, as Sir Andrew does, before the other has spoken categorizes his as what Saviolo describes as a "foolish Lye":

And heereupon it commeth, that euerye daye there riseth from the common sorte new and strange foolishnesses, as he who wil giue the lye ere the other speake, saying: if thou saye that I am not an honest man, thou lyest in thy throate. And this is a changing of nature, for the lye beeing but an answere, in this manner it commeth to answere that which was neuer spoken.[13]

Another point that Saviolo makes is that one should "speake honourably of his enemie" when writing the cartel,

for so a Gentleman or Caualier doth honor to himselfe, shewing thereby to haue quarrell with an honorable person: whereas otherwise, hee dishonoreth himselfe, and sheweth himself rather to haue minde to fight with the pen then with the sworde. (p. 370)

Sir Andrew's churlish opening of his letter defies such a perception.

In the writing of a cartel, or letter of defiance, Saviolo emphasizes that the writer must "come to the particulars" of the cause, "shewing well the persons, the thing, the times and places, which doe appertaine to the plaine declaration thereof, so that one maye well resolue to the answere" (p. 368). Andrew gives a particular, it is true: "Thou com'st to the Lady Olivia, and in my sight she uses thee kindly." But in the next sentence he denies that this is "the matter I challenge thee for." Instead of cause, he gives non sequitur. Furthermore, he promises ambush rather than assigning a specific place for the duel—"I will waylay thee going home"—and concludes with a nonsensical contradiction of good wishes and curses for his opponent, wishing that he himself will meet "with better" than God's mercy. It would be difficult to find a letter of challenge more opposite to the accepted rules.

Sir Andrew's presentation of his letter visually recalls the forged letter that encouraged Malvolio into his apparently mad behavior with the cross-gartered yellow stockings and smiles. In Sir Andrew's case, the letter is original, but so off the mark for appropriate rules of fence that Sir Toby has to forge the challenge orally: "This letter, being so excellently ignorant, will breed no terror in the youth. He will find it comes from a clodpoll. But, sir, I will deliver his challenge by word of mouth" (III.iv.174–77). What is done with words in both letters illustrates the dallying with words that "make[s] them wanton"

(III.i.14–15) about which Viola and Feste speak. The words Maria forges as Olivia's clearly dally with Malvolio and make him "wanton" in the sense that he forsakes his dignity to achieve his lady's favor. That letter's words are intentionally misleading in contrast to Sir Andrew's words in the cartel, which are uncomprehending echoes of a language and a set of social rules he has not yet got "without book" (I.iii.25). The two letters literally bring the two comic butts into a parallel visual focus, and, if they are not equivalent scenes, they are balancing ones. Sir Andrew provides a parody of Malvolio as an object for the tricksters' gulling, just as Malvolio provides a parody of Orsino's self-love.

All three characters are depicted in varying comic tones as they pursue Olivia, who wants none of them. Duke Orsino, although he pronounces himself love-sick, pursues his own heart more than Olivia's; Malvolio, apparently metamorphosed by her forged encouragement, desires social advancement more than he desires Olivia herself; and Sir Andrew, never in her company, seems to have no clear motive for wooing her. In diminishing degrees of seriousness, each figure presents a suitor who cares more for himself than for Olivia. None of these suitors is charmed by Olivia directly, but by what she represents for each of them: the ideal of love, social position, wealth. Olivia herself, misled by Viola's disguise, has qualified her power to charm by directing it toward an inappropriate object. Only when Sebastian happens into Illyria and responds directly to her physical beauty and social charm, without understanding any of the confusing circumstances, does the audience witness her dramatic validation as love object.

The encounter of the hesitant duelists Sir Andrew and Viola/Cesario provides sheer fun in terms of woman turned male without the accompanying knowledge of a gentleman's acquired courteous skills and of a "carpet knight" forced into a situation that tests his unproved gentlemanly mettle: Shakespeare again incorporates parody within a parody. Antonio's appearance and his assumption that Viola is Sebastian return the farcical worlds of the duelists who would prefer not to fight to a literal world where appearances are not double but single. The ambiguities of imagination's fancy—embodied equally though distinctly in Sir Andrew's and Viola's poses as knights gallant—Antonio brings into direct and threatening action. He, of course, is stayed by the Duke's officers, but his intrusion on the fabrication of Sir Toby's fictional creation has the same effect as Sebastian's later incursion into the world of romanticized love. Both hyperboles collapse into solid and literal correlatives.

Astonished by Antonio's mention of her brother's name, Viola quickly forgets the fabricated duel, but Sir Andrew, encouraged by Sir Toby and Fabian, regains his purpose of humiliating Cesario: " 'Slid, I'll after him again and beat him" (III.iv.361). Almost immediately he encounters Sebastian, whom he mistakes for Cesario, and, his original cowardice forgotten, strikes him. When Sebastian returns his blow in triplicate, Sir Andrew, less surprised than his cohorts, promises to "have an action of battery against him, if there be any law in Illyria. Though I struck him first, yet it's no matter for that" (IV.i.31–33). Because Sir Andrew has less facility to follow cause to consequence, he finds Sebastian's surprise response a matter of course. His purposed retaliation also is for him typically illogical.

After Olivia intervenes in this fracas, Sir Toby, Maria, and Feste proceed with Malvolio's inquisition. Feste adopts the disguise of Sir Topas to convince Malvolio that he is mad,[14] and the imprisonment scene evokes a different response from the letter that exploits Malvolio by encouraging him to wear yellow stockings and cross-garters. In the earlier phase of the gulling, Malvolio is unaware of his foolishness; however, imprisoned, Malvolio is a helpless victim, fully aware that he is being abused. With Olivia, his extraordinary costume and perpetual smiles make him a visible clown, and, as a result, he even seems good-humored. But with Maria and Feste in the imprisonment scene, he is not visible; we only hear him and his protestations of abuse. These different visual presentations produce a notable difference in comic effect because visual comedy often changes a serious tone in the dialogue.

In the imprisonment scene, Sir Topas keeps insisting that things are not as Malvolio perceives them; but Malvolio refuses to admit a discrepancy between what he perceives and reality. Accordingly, Malvolio insists that he is not mad.

Malvolio within.

MALVOLIO Who calls there?

CLOWN Sir Topas the curate, who comes to visit Malvolio the lunatic. . . .

MALVOLIO Sir Topas, never was man thus wronged. Good Sir Topas, do not think I am mad. They have laid me here in hideous darkness.

CLOWN Fie, thou dishonest Satan. I call thee by the most modest terms, for I am one of those gentle ones that will use the devil himself with courtesy. Say'st thou that house is dark?

MALVOLIO As hell, Sir Topas.

CLOWN Why, it hath bay windows transparent as barricadoes, and the clerestories toward the south north are as lustrous as ebony; and yet complainest thou of obstruction?

MALVOLIO I am not mad, Sir Topas. I say to you this house is dark.

CLOWN Madman, thou errest. I say there is no darkness but ignorance, in which thou art more puzzled than the Egyptians in their fog.

MALVOLIO I say this house is as dark as ignorance, though ignorance were as dark as hell; and I say there was never man thus abused. I am no more mad than you are. (IV.ii.20–48)

In the darkness of his prison, Malvolio literally is unable to see, and Feste makes the most of the symbolic implications of Malvolio's blindness. The audience perceives with Feste that the house is not dark (that hypothetical Globe audience would have been able to see the actual daylight in the playhouse), yet the audience also knows that Malvolio is being "abused" because he cannot see the light. The audience is therefore led to a double awareness of values in this scene: we are able to absorb the emblematic significance of Malvolio's separation from good-humored sanity and to know at the same time that Malvolio is not mad in the literal way that Feste, Maria, and Sir Toby insist. Although the literal action engenders the emblematic awareness, the literal action does not necessarily support the emblematic meaning.[15] This pull in opposite directions occurs simultaneously and places the audience in a slightly uncomfortable position. We prefer to move in one direction or in the other. Yet it seems that here Shakespeare asks us to forgo the either-or alternatives and to hold contradictory impressions together. Malvolio cannot be dismissed as a simple comic butt when his trial in the dark has such severe implications.[16]

The ambiguities of his situation are clear to everyone except Malvolio, but he rigidly maintains his single point of view. Because he refuses to allow more than his own narrowed focus, he is *emblematically* an appropriate butt for the harsh comic action that blots out his power to see as well as to act. He must ultimately depend on the fool to bring him "ink, paper, and light" (another letter) so that he may extricate himself from his prison, a situation that could have seemed to Malvolio earlier in the play "mad" indeed. Feste thus does force Malvolio to act against his will in submitting to the fool, but Malvolio fails to change his attitudes.[17] Malvolio remains a literalist—Feste's visual disguise is for the audience, so that we can see as well as hear the ambiguities of his performance, a point that Maria emphasizes when she says, "Thou mightest have done this without thy beard and gown. He sees thee not" (IV.ii.63–64).

In the very next scene, Sebastian presents a contrast that delineates even more clearly the narrowness of Malvolio's response to an uncontrollable situation. Sebastian, too, confronts the possibility that he is mad: his situation in Illyria is anything but under his control.

> This is the air; that is the glorious sun;
> This pearl she gave me, I do feel't and see't;
> And *though* 'tis wonder that enwraps me thus,
> Yet 'tis not madness. . . .
> For *though* my soul disputes well with my sense
> That this may be some error, *but* no madness,
> *Yet* doth this accident and flood of fortune
> So far exceed all instance, all discourse,
> That I am ready to distrust mine eyes
> And wrangle with my reason that persuades me
> To any other trust *but* that I am mad,
> *Or else* the lady's mad. (IV.iii.1–16; my italics)

Sebastian's pile of contrasting conjuctions ("though," "yet," "but") underlines his hesitance to form a final judgment, unlike

Malvolio, whose point of view never changes despite the on-slaught of unmanageable circumstances. The contradictions of his sensory perceptions lead Sebastian to a state of "wonder" in which he is able to suspend reason and delay judgment, and this signifies a flexibility of perception that Malvolio cannot attain. Malvolio is not stirred by the discrepancies of experience to con-sider that appearances may not be reality; but Sebastian can ap-preciate the undefinable workings of a power beyond the evi-dent. Sebastian's ability to sense the "wonder" in a world where cause and effect have been severed gives him a stature that Mal-volio cannot achieve.[18] (At the other extreme is Sir Andrew, who cannot perceive cause and effect when confronted with them.) The difference between Sebastian and Malvolio, however, is due to the source of their manipulation as well as to their response. Sebastian is manipulated by fate or by fortune; Malvolio, by Maria and Feste. Human manipulators parody suprahuman con-trol and because they do, Maria and Feste define both levels of action.

Feste, Maria, and Sir Toby are all in a set and predictable world of sporting gullery, and the rules for their games are known. Feste's "whirligig" associates time with a toy (perhaps even with an instrument of torture) and limits time to human terms of punishment. On the other hand, the Time that Viola addresses does untie her problematic knot of disguise. Feste's attribution of revenge to this "whirligig of time" points up the difference between the two controls. The whirligig becomes a parodic substitute for the larger providence that other char-acters talk about under other titles: time, Jove, fate, fortune, or chance. Significantly, Malvolio's humiliation is the only hu-manly designed action that fulfills itself as planned. Even Sir Andrew's contrived duel meets with unforeseen obstacles in the presence of Antonio and Sebastian. The subplot performs its parody in many other ways,[19] but in Feste's summary "whirli-gig" it displays the double vision that Shakespearean parody typically provides. The foibles of the romantics in Illyria are seen in their reduced terms through Sir Toby, Maria, and Sir Andrew, but the limitations of the parodic characters also heighten by contrast the expansive and expanding world of the play. Love, not revenge, is to be celebrated.

But even Feste's whirligig takes another spin and does not stop at revenge: in the play's final song the playwright extends an embrace to his audience. Feste's song creates an ambiguity of perspective that fuses the actual world with an ideal one: "the rain it raineth every day" is hardly the world described by the play. Romantic Illyria seems to have little to do with such realistic intrusions. Yet the recognition of continuous rain is in itself an excess—it does not rain every day in the actual world, at least not in the same place.[20] Thus the pessimistic excess of the song balances the optimistic excesses of the romance world of Illyria; neither excess accurately reflects the actual world. Despite its suggestions of a man's growing from infancy to maturity and to old age, the song remains something of an enigma.[21] The ambiguities of the first four stanzas build to a contrast of direct statements in the final stanza:

> A great while ago the world begun,
>   With hey, ho, the wind and the rain;
> But that's all one, our play is done,
>   And we'll strive to please you every day.

The first line of this stanza seems to imply that the world has its own, independent design;[22] and it also suggests that man's actions must take their place and find meaning within this larger and older pattern. The specific meaning of that larger design, however, remains concealed within the previous ambiguities of Feste's song. His philosophic pretensions to explain that design are comically vague and he knows it. He tosses them aside to speak directly to the audience: "But that's all one, our play is done." This is the same phrase Feste uses with Malvolio in his summary speech in Act V: "I was one, sir, in this interlude, one Sir Topas, sir; but that's all one." In both cases, Feste avoids an explanation.

Turning to the audience and shattering the dramatic illusion is typical in epilogues, but Feste's inclusion of the audience in his consciousness of the play as a metaphor for actual experience has

a special significance here. Throughout *Twelfth Night,* Feste has
engaged various characters in dialogues of self-determination. In
one game of wit, he points out that Olivia is a fool "to mourn for
your brother's soul, being in heaven" (I.v.65–66). By his irrefut-
able logic, he wins Olivia's favor and her tacit agreement that her
mourning has been overdone. The Duke also is subject to Feste's
evaluation in two scenes. Following his performance, at the
Duke's request, of a sad song of unrequited love, Feste leaves a
paradoxical benediction:

Now the melancholy god protect thee, and the tailor make thy doublet
of changeable taffeta, for thy mind is a very opal. I would have men of
such constancy put to sea, that their business might be everything, and
their intent everywhere; for that's it that always makes a good voyage of
nothing. (II.iv.72–77)

And later, when the Duke is approaching Olivia's house, Feste
encounters him with one of his typically unique and audaciously
applied truisms:

DUKE I know thee well. How dost thou, my good fellow?
CLOWN Truly, sir, the better for my foes, and the worse for my friends.
DUKE Just the contrary: the better for thy friends.
CLOWN No, sir, the worse.
DUKE How can that be?
CLOWN Marry, sir, they praise me and make an ass of me. Now my foes
   tell me plainly I am an ass; so that by my foes, sir, I profit in the
   knowledge of myself, and by my friends I am abused; so that, conclu-
   sions to be as kisses, if your four negatives make your two affirma-
   tives, why then, the worse for my friends, and the better for my foes.
   (V.i.9–20)

The Duke has in fact lacked some knowledge of himself, and
Feste's pointed remark makes it clear that he is using his role as
fool to point up the true foolishness of others. In the prison scene
with Malvolio, Feste provides a confusing game of switching
identities from the Clown to Sir Topas. In each situation, Feste
provides the other person with a different perspective for seeing
himself. Thus it is more than merely appropriate that at the end

of the play Feste engages the audience in its own definition of self. By asking them to look at their participation in the dramatic illusion, Feste is requesting them to recognize their own desire for humanly willed happiness.

The playwright, like the comic providence in the play, has understood "what we will" and has led us to a pleasurable fulfillment of our desires, but in ways which we could not have foreseen or controlled. The substitution of the final line, "And we'll strive to please you every day," for the refrain, "For the rain it raineth every day," is a crucial change. Like the incremental repetition in the folk ballad, this pessimistic refrain has built a dynamic tension that is released in the recognition that the play is an actual experience in the lives of the audience, even though it is enacted in an imagined world. The players, and the playwright who arranges them, are engaged in an ongoing effort to please the audience. The providential design remains incomplete within the play's action and only promises a "golden time"; similarly, the playwright promises further delightful experiences for his audience. The subplot's action, on the other hand, is limited within the framework of revenge; the revenge of the subplot characters elicits Malvolio's cry for revenge.

Although Sir Andrew and Sir Toby suffer "bloody coxcombs" as a result of Sebastian's realistic entrance into Illyria's fantasizing world, Malvolio is the only one who is truly excluded from the play's harmonizing conclusion. This is because Malvolio alone refuses to see that he is subservient to a larger design than his own will. True, Malvolio's larger design is limited to human manipulators and is therefore less acceptable than that of the play's other characters. But Malvolio's literal insistence that his "will" is all reminds us of the self-oriented limitations of the others at the play's beginning. They have grown beyond themselves; he has not. Feste's manipulation of Malvolio resembles the playwright's manipulation of his audience's will, but its similarity reminds us of the difference between merely human revenge and the larger benevolence that controls the play's design.

Chapter 7

Twelfth Night and *Hamlet* have much in common despite their different genres. Olivia and Hamlet are both accused of excessive mourning for a lost kinsman, but only Hamlet can say, "I know not seems." Feste and Hamlet both wear the "antic disposition," although in Feste's situation it is to point out the truth, and in Hamlet's to hide it. Whereas in *Twelfth Night* unmasking reveals identity, in *Hamlet* murder is the means for revealing true personality.

T. S. Eliot has J. Alfred Prufrock distinguish betwen "Prince Hamlet" and the "attendant lord"

> that will do
> To swell a progress, start a scene or two,
> Advise the prince; no doubt, an easy tool, . . .
> Almost, at times, the Fool.[1]

This "attendant lord" for the most part describes Polonius, yet both Hamlet and Polonius play the fool and, during the first half of the play, compete with each other for who can do it better.

Shakespeare employs Polonius to perform in a myriad of functions the same kind of clarifying parody that the whole of the subplot in *Twelfth Night* achieves. This is not the only secondary character Shakespeare uses this way, of course, but it seems to be the only time he uses a secondary character as a parodic figure who continues throughout a tragedy. Like Falstaff in the second *Henriad,* or Caliban in *The Tempest,* Polonius seems to draw into himself the larger terms of the play and through his literalizing and reductive effects creates a lens that enlarges the audience's vision of Hamlet.

Polonius is, first, a "father" in a play that is dominated by father figures. Second, Claudius appears to accept him as a chief counselor, and whether or not Polonius speaks foolish words, he speaks them into the ear of a king.[2] Third, Polonius tries to be a "wit" and a literary critic. In each aspect of his characterization, Polonius delivers a parody of the other, less "foolish" characters in the play.

The first scene in which Polonius appears is a public demonstration of Claudius's power as king of Denmark. Having boldly established himself as a proper surrogate for the elder Hamlet, both on the throne and in matrimony, Claudius turns to Laertes and says:

> What wouldst thou beg, Laertes,
> That shall not be my offer, not thy asking?
> The head is not more native to the heart,
> The hand more instrumental to the mouth,
> Than is the throne of Denmark to thy father.
> What wouldst thou have, Laertes? (I.ii.45–50)

On hearing Laertes's request to "bend again toward France," Claudius insists that Polonius have the final power over his son: "Have you your father's leave? What says Polonius?" And Polonius appears to be the generous father, flexible about his son's need for liberation, yet fully aware of his own control. He pleads that Laertes's wish be granted. Such a picture of filial concord precedes Claudius's own attempt to reconcile Hamlet to their new roles in relation to each other. Claudius is now technically father to Hamlet and justifiably concerned with Hamlet's attitudes and desires. Hamlet's response to his substitute father is, however, harshly rejective: "A little more than kin, and less than kind." Furthermore, when Claudius insists that Hamlet accept him as "father," his specious comfort inadvertently pronounces his own sentence: nature's "common theme," he says, "is death of fathers" (I.ii.101–8). We may not pay much attention to the fact that Polonius is to Laertes what

Claudius fails to be to Hamlet, but the basis of comparison is clearly laid.

Polonius continues to anticipate other, more serious actions. Moving from a public stance to a private domestic scene, Polonius clarifies his paternal control. He intrudes on his children, and his entrance seems to be a comic redundancy, a point that Laertes makes with loving mockery:

> But here my father comes.
> A double blessing is a double grace;
> Occasion smiles upon a second leave.
> (I.iii.52–54)

Polonius's advice to Laertes echoes his son's lecture to Ophelia both in content and tone. Each admonition suggests that—human nature being what it is—other people are likely to betray you. Laertes warns that Hamlet cannot be a faithful lover to Ophelia because he is first of all a prince; and Polonius warns Laertes against self-revelation: "Give thy thoughts no tongue. . . . Give every man thy ear, but few thy voice." Both speeches are Machiavellian in expressing the probability of betrayal and the importance of self-knowledge.[3]

Following Laertes's departure, Polonius reveals his true insensitivity to his children. He is a father guided by precept rather than emotion; and ultimately he is guided by self-regard. He pries into the conversation between his children, and Ophelia, obedient daughter that she is, reveals the nature of her conversation with Laertes: "So please you, something touching the Lord Hamlet." Polonius eagerly extends his son's attack on Ophelia's weak, feminine judgment with "I must tell you/ You do not understand yourself so clearly/ As it behooves my daughter and your honour": her honor takes a second place to her being his daughter. On discovering that Ophelia has received certain "tenders of his affection" from Hamlet, Polonius digresses, comically and unfeelingly, into a series of word-plays:

> Marry, I will teach you: think yourself a baby
> That you have ta'en these tenders for true pay
> Which are not sterling. Tender yourself more dearly,

Or (not to crack the wind of the poor phrase,
Running it thus) you'll tender me a fool.
(I.iii.105–9)

Advising her to set her "entreatments at a higher rate," Polonius commands her never to speak to Hamlet again. Ophelia meekly submits: "I shall obey, my lord."

The parodic nature of this scene becomes fully apparent only after we witness Hamlet's encounter with the ghost of his father (I.v), yet there are several significant parallels between these two scenes.[4] Polonius seeks out his children in a private situation in order to set down guides for their behavior, and he commands their obedience. The Ghost, seeking Hamlet for a more serious reason, insists on speaking with him privately. The triple injunction that he gives his son is more complex and more significant than Polonius's command to Ophelia, but eventually both commands lead to the death of the obedient children.

The comic nature of the first scene is due primarily to the characterization of Polonius—he is pompous in his pride of words and ridiculous in valuing wittiness above emotions. Even when he protests that he will not "crack the wind of the poor phrase,/ Running it thus," his multiple puns on the word "tender" show that Polonius is not emotionally attuned to his daughter's precarious social position (as he and Laertes present it), but rather that he is wittily intrigued by its corners.[5] This differs almost diametrically from the characterization of the Ghost in the later scene with Hamlet: the Ghost is concerned for his son's welfare despite his own need for revenge. "Taint not thy mind," he says, and compassionately adds, "nor let thy soul contrive/ Against thy mother aught." The scene with Polonius provides a diminutive parallel to the scene between the Ghost and Hamlet, and the precedence of the comic reduction enhances the awesomeness of the Ghost's appearance. In addition to heightening the stature of the Ghost as authority figure and as father, Polonius's action toward Ophelia qualifies an assumption that lies behind the Ghost's command—the assumption that a man can control the consequences of his actions. Most actions produce results that are not only outside the control of the human actor but also beyond his ability to predict.

Polonius quickly discovers, or so he thinks, that he has misread circumstances in regard to Hamlet and his daughter. Following Ophelia's description of the distraught Hamlet who "rais'd a sigh so piteous and profound/ As it did seem to shatter all his bulk/ And end his being" (II.i.94–96), Polonius concludes that her obedience in forbidding Hamlet access to her "hath made him mad": "I am sorry that with better heed and judgment/ I had not quoted him" (II.i.111–12). Clearly, Polonius could not predict or control the consequences of the action he commanded Ophelia to take. This limitation, which is immediately realized in the play's action, suggests that the situation that it parallels—the Ghost's threefold command to Hamlet—may have similar limitations in it.

Parody usually functions this way, but here the parodic scene takes an unusual position in the dramatic sequence. By preceding the serious scene, the parodic scene lays the grounds for qualification without actually imitating a scene that has gone before. This comic scene, although slowing the momentum of the play's action and allowing momentary relaxation from the anxieties and anticipations that force us forward, is not a digression or a diversion from the main action; it presents central concerns through another perspective and suggests, in advance, limitations that might not otherwise be apparent.

A third instance of Polonius's proleptic parodic role occurs in the opening scene of Act II. Reynaldo listens patiently, but with some surprise, to Polonius's plan for discovering what Laertes is up to in Paris. If there existed any question about Polonius as an idealist, in this scene the possibility is denied. A Machiavellian schemer who takes his plotting to absurd extremes, Polonius pursues "indirection" for its own sake. Ostensibly he wants to know what his son is doing, but from the wandering lecture he gives Reynaldo, Polonius makes it comically clear that he is more concerned with means than with ends. His efforts to discover Laertes's reputation in Paris assume that Laertes will not follow his earlier advice; thus, the later words become a comic reduction of his previous sermon to his son. Claudius, on the other hand, has good reason to discover what his stepson is thinking; and Claudius's employment of "indirections to find directions out" is necessary if he is to maintain his power. He therefore engages Rosencrantz and Guildenstern to "glean" from Hamlet, if they can, the cause of his "transformation" (II.ii.1–18).

The parody in this pair of scenes works in at least two ways. Polonius in his absentmindedness—"What was I about to say? By the mass, I was about to say something!" (II.i.49–50)—presents a comic figure of a Machiavel to contrast with Claudius's serious one. Furthermore, we know that if Reynaldo can find a clear picture of Laertes through the haze of indirection that Polonius is suggesting, it will be amazing. In a similar manner, it later becomes apparent that Rosencrantz and Guildenstern cannot penetrate the cover of indirections that Hamlet throws about himself with his "antic disposition." The suggestion of failure remains covert, but the limitations of Polonius in his scheming carry over to Claudius, no matter how much more perceptive the king may be.

These scenes also point up the parallel roles of Polonius and Hamlet; and this is perhaps the most complex of Polonius's parodic functions. Hamlet, like Polonius and Claudius, works by "indirections"—he is, in a way, forced toward deviousness by the discrepancies between Denmark's appearances and realities. For Claudius, "indirections" are a necessary subterfuge under which to hide his own culpability; for Polonius, "indirections" seem to be an appealing game for him to play; for Hamlet, in dealing with both the serious and the comic Machiavels, "indirections" are the only means through which he can confront his adversaries and retain a measure of personal safety. Yet Polonius seems oblivious to the possibility that anyone else might be playing his game, and he displays his comically narrow perspective by announcing:

> If circumstances lead me, I will find
> Where truth is hid, though it were hid indeed
> Within the center. (II.ii.156–58)

We have already witnessed Hamlet's announcement that he will "put an antic disposition on" (I.v.172),[6] and we know that Hamlet as well as Claudius is engaged in deceptive role-playing. Thus, we can only smile at Polonius's assumption that circumstances will lead him to the truth.

Hamlet, on the other hand, seems to be well aware of the ambiguity inherent in "circumstances," and for this reason he insists on "proof" of Claudius's guilt before he fully accepts the Ghost's command. Ironically, Hamlet never achieves such proof—though the audience does. He and Horatio interpret Claudius's response to "The Murder of Gonzago" as clear evidence of guilt, but they impose a predetermined reading on the circumstances (III.ii.73–85).[7] Of course, Claudius's confession, which follows (III.iii.36ff.), validates Hamlet's reading of circumstances, but Hamlet fails to hear that confession. Hamlet, therefore, with great caution, makes the same assumption that Polonius hastily makes: he assumes that ambiguous circumstances may be read narrowly and clearly, and that they will lead him to the truth. The error in Hamlet's assumption becomes dramatically realized as soon as he acts on it: he thinks that Claudius, kneeling in prayer, is successfully praying. The appearance hides the reality, a fact that Claudius confesses to the audience after Hamlet leaves the stage: "My words fly up, my thoughts remain below./ Words without thoughts never to heaven go" (III.iii.97–98). Misread circumstances thus delay Hamlet's revenge at the very moment that he fully commits himself to being a revenger.

Polonius's narrow pursuit of proof for his new theory that Hamlet is mad for love of his daughter illuminates how reduced Hamlet's single-minded role of revenger is. Compared to the complex being he was before the Ghost's command, Hamlet almost becomes, at the successful closing of his "mousetrap," a less than human mechanism. For the moment, he seems to be the mere instrument of a codified action called "revenge."

> Now could I drink hot blood
> And do such bitter business as the day
> Would quake to look on. (III.ii.375–77)

Realizing the dangers inherent in this kind of reduction, Hamlet warns himself against his dehumanization: "O heart, lose not thy nature. . . . Let me be cruel, not unnatural." Having finally focused his energies on revenge, Hamlet is in danger of losing the compassionate part of his nature: the Ghost's "commandment all alone" lives "within the book and volume" of his brain. Those two other parts of that commandment, "Taint not thy mind, nor let thy soul contrive/ Against thy mother aught," seem to have been forgotten. Yet his inability to fulfill all three parts of the command suggests their mutually exclusive nature, and points out unmistakably the ultimate limitations of a code of man-made vengeance.[8]

Both Hamlet and Polonius suffer dehumanization from their single-minded search for proof. Polonius's concern for Hamlet's well-being and his care for Ophelia's modesty fall by the way as he doggedly presents his evidence to the King and Queen. Prefaced by a comic prologue of such length that Gertrude pleads for "more matter with less art," Polonius's testimony loiters without compassion on the semantic games that any word suggests:

> Madam, I swear I use no art at all.
> That he is mad, 'tis true: 'tis true 'tis pity.
> And pity 'tis 'tis true—foolish figure.
> But farewell it, for I will use no art.
> Mad let us grant him then, and now remains
> That we find out the cause of this effect—
> Or rather say, the cause of this defect,
> For this effect defective comes by cause.
> (II.ii.96–103)

Even as he reads the letter, Polonius pauses to establish himself as a literary critic: he thinks that Hamlet's word "beautified" is a "vile phrase." Gertrude, too, is apparently surprised by Hamlet's naiveté in acting the gallant lover: "Came this from Hamlet to her?" Yet this is not the worst. Polonius reads on:

> 'Doubt thou the stars are fire;
> Doubt that the sun doth move;

> Doubt truth to be a liar;
>   But never doubt I love.

'O dear Ophelia, I am ill at these numbers. I have not art to reckon my groans, but that I love thee best, O most best, believe it. Adieu.

> 'Thine evermore, most dear lady,
>   whilst this machine is to him, Hamlet.'
> (II.ii.115–23)

This is not the Hamlet we know, not the serious-minded, philosophically tormented man incapable of putting aside moral questions for murder. This is another Hamlet, one who existed before the play begins and one whom we are never able to glimpse except through the critical and foolish eyes of Polonius. Still, this Hamlet of the letter is a charming young man, aware that the role of courtly lover fits him ill, and yet willing to make an effort at playing the wrong role. The letter is a record of an idealistic youth that is no longer possible in a world of murder and revenge. The contrast between this somewhat awkward but delightfully innocent Hamlet and the melancholy prince who is tormented by his father's death, his mother's apparent lust and infidelity, and his uncle's control of Denmark provides a measure of how far the garden of Denmark has decayed.

Polonius of course refuses to comprehend what the young lover Hamlet meant and tries to elevate himself on the earnestness of the clumsy letter. He then proceeds to "loose" Ophelia on Hamlet in order to prove his point that she is the cause of Hamlet's madness, denying his previous care of her modesty; and he becomes the comic butt of Hamlet's witty word-play. The amateur punster clashes headlong with the professed "antic," and Polonius has opportunity to notice only that Hamlet's madness seems to have a "method in 't" (II.ii.204). Their next encounter occasions a repetition of Polonius's affected pose as literary critic—he listens with Hamlet to the Player's recitation of some formally structured lines from an unpopular play about the fall of Troy. The passage that Hamlet requests details the bloody vengeance Pyrrhus takes against Priam for his own father's death.

Just as the Player reaches the invocation to the gods to take away Fortune's power, Polonius comments, "This is too long." Hamlet scornfully responds, "He's for a jig or a tale of bawdry, or he sleeps," and urges the Player to come to the speech describing Hecuba. Hamlet reacts to the phrase, "The mobled queen," *perhaps* with aesthetic unease (II.ii.497), but Polonius, having been reprimanded for his lack of poetic appreciation, misinterprets the pause: "That's good; 'mobled queen' is good." As usual, Polonius takes precisely the wrong stance, and he emphasizes it. His part in the scene is rather a small one, a carping critic, a misinterpreter of nuance, yet it manages to support by its contrast Hamlet's aesthetically responsible comments, here and later, on how to speak the speech. In other words, Polonius's parodic parallelism furnishes dramatic resonance for Hamlet's discourse on theatrical good taste.

Hamlet's attitude toward Polonius in this scene is an odd mixture of scorn and concern. When he tells the First Player to "Follow that lord," he adds, "and look you mock him not." Polonius obviously has left himself open for mockery, considering his imperceptions about the nature of acting, but Hamlet allows only himself to play the mocking game.[9] Even as the tension is building before his presentation of the play for the royal audience, Hamlet takes a moment to jest with Polonius.

HAMLET My lord, you played once i' th' university, you say?
POLONIUS That did I, my lord, and was accounted a good actor.
HAMLET What did you enact?
POLONIUS I did enact Julius Caesar. I was killed i' th' Capitol;
    Brutus killed me.
HAMLET It was a brute part of him to kill so capital a calf there.
    (III.ii.94–102)

As has been noticed, this jest of Hamlet's is predictively ironic.[10] Without his realizing it, Hamlet is to fulfill the brute part and kill Polonius while the would-be informer eavesdrops on him and his mother. But there are other ironic potentialities at work here as well.

For one thing, the self-conscious reference to the actor's playing a role, the performance of which would still be fresh in the memory of Shakespeare's audience, recalls for them the particular awareness that they too are participating in this fiction. Quite probably the same actor who had played Julius Caesar in that season's production of Shakespeare's play was now performing the part of Polonius; and just as probably the actor now playing Hamlet was Brutus.[11] Thus, the audience would recognize an integration of their ongoing role as audience into the performance of these repertory plays. The lines function somewhat similarly to Fabian's in *Twelfth Night,* "If this were played upon a stage now, I could condemn it as an improbable fiction": they underline the paradoxical conjunction of actuality and fiction.

In addition to the multiplication of levels through which the audience sees itself as participant in the play's referential scheme, the badinage between Hamlet and Polonius pulls in another frame of reference, one that is highlighted in Horatio's speech in the opening scene. In between the Ghost's two silent but ominous appearances to the guards and Horatio on the battlements, Horatio likens the situation to a former time:

> In the most high and palmy state of Rome,
> A little ere the mightiest Julius fell,
> The graves stood tenantless, and the sheeted dead
> Did squeak and gibber in the Roman streets;
> As stars with trains of fire and dews of blood,
> Disasters in the sun; . . .
> And even the like precurse of feared events,
> As harbingers preceding still the fates
> And prologue to the omen coming on,
> Have heaven and earth together demonstrated
> Unto our climatures and countrymen. (I.i.113–25)

What Horatio does not know is that current odd events point not to a "prologue" but to an epilogue. Denmark has already suffered the assassination of its ruler before the signs of it appear. Hamlet's questioning of Polonius about the part of Julius Caesar that he acted in the university connects through parodic echo the ominous atmosphere following the elder Hamlet's death and the subsequent accidental murder of Polonius.

After the "Murder of Gonzago" has presented both a reitera-tion of the murder of the elder Hamlet and a warning of Ham-let's intent to revenge that murder on Claudius, Polonius hurries off to Gertrude's closet, delighted with the chance to prove fur-ther his worth to the King as interpreter of Hamlet. His final effort is appropriately an "indirection" as well as the means of revelation through parody. Polonius is a substitute for Claudius in death, a point that both Hamlet and Claudius emphasize. Without knowing whom he has killed, Hamlet asks Gertrude, "Is it the king?" (III.iv.26); and Claudius, when he learns of the murder, realizes, "It had been so with us had we been there" (IV.i.13).

One of the shocking things about the death of Polonius is the ease with which Hamlet assimilates it:

> Thou wretched, rash, intruding fool, farewell!
> I took thee for thy better. Take thy fortune;
> Thou find'st to be too busy is some danger.
> (III.iv.32–34)

And perhaps the most famous line of reductive evaluation is Hamlet's method of removing Polonius from the stage: "I'll lug the guts into the neighbor room" (III.iv.212). Hamlet's jest about the death of Polonius as the common death of man—"Your worm is your only emperor for diet: . . . your fat king and your lean beggar is but variable service—two dishes, but to one table" (III.iv.21–25)—sounds remarkably like the Gravedigger's com-ments in a later scene, even to the use of the general pronoun "your" (V.i.165–68). The difference, of course, is that Hamlet speaks of a man whom we know who is only recently dead and the Gravedigger speaks in generalities of the body of mankind. The Gravedigger is a professional handler of corpses and Hamlet is not, yet Hamlet adopts the professional tone that drains death of its emotional context. The actual murder of Polonius, as it happens, is a thoughtless accident. Hamlet responds to the in-truder's cry for help without thinking of what he does or of his victim. Thought follows the action, and by that time Hamlet has moved beyond the possibility of premeditated meaning. He completes, in fact, a totally impersonal, abstract murder, and reveals in performing it that revenge requires just such an action from just such a man.

Deep thought, intricate moral questions, complex emotional responses all get in the way of effecting revenge when revenge requires murder; yet all along Hamlet has been bringing to bear precisely these pressures on his adopted role of revenger. His self-castigation after the Player's speech about Hecuba's tears registers his own sense of impotence within the driving force of knowledge:

> What would he do
> Had he the motive and the cue for passion
> That I have? He would drown the stage with tears
> And cleave the general ear with horrid speech, . . .
> Yet I,
> A dull and muddy-mettled rascal, peak
> Like John-a-dreams, unpregnant of my cause,
> And can say nothing. (II.ii.544–54)

The impotence in the images he chooses to describe this state of frustration turns into powerful aggression by the time he goes to his mother's chamber, and he has to remind himself to merely "speak daggers to her, but use none" (III.ii.378–79). He has arrived, in other words, at a state of physical, emotional, and psychological brutality: he has almost become the simplified instrument he needs to be to kill. And kill he does—not the King, because the King might be praying and he might send his soul to heaven, but Polonius, the King's substitute. Hamlet wishes that the body he uncovers will prove to be the King's and thus end for him the horrendous tension of his vow to revenge his father's murder. His discovery of that "rash, intruding fool" instead of the King is for Hamlet the ultimate frustration. He had not meant to kill Polonius, but now that he has, the fact itself is irrelevant. Polonius in death becomes a parody of what Claudius, the man, would be as Hamlet's victim, and perhaps this accounts for the emphasis on his body *per se*. In terms of the parody, the body of Polonius, the "natural person" of the King's two bodies, becomes a literal "thing" to be handled and manipulated.

The confusing game of hide-and-seek that Hamlet plays with Polonius's body is one that neither Claudius nor his messengers Rosencrantz and Guildenstern can decipher. It seems to them to be further evidence of Hamlet's madness, and it certainly is a further instance of Hamlet's deliberate display of his "antic disposition." As usual, however, there is a method in Hamlet's mad playing.

In defining the concept of the "King's Two Bodies," Ernst H. Kantorowicz cites Edmund Plowden's *Reports:* the "Body natural . . . is subject to Passions and Death as other Men are"; and the "Body politic," an incorporation of the subjects and the king, "is not subject to Passions as the other is, nor to Death," but is conveyed from one king to the next at the point of death. Moreover, the "Body politic is a Body that cannot be seen or handled."[12]

In his attempts to keep the body of Polonius hidden, Hamlet seems to be using Polonius's body as a literal demonstration of the figurative separation of the King and his body politic:

ROSENCRANTZ My lord, you must tell us where the body is and
  go with us to the king.
HAMLET The body is with the king, but the king is not with
  the body. The king is a thing—
GUILDENSTERN A thing, my lord?
HAMLET Of nothing. Bring me to him. Hide fox, and all after.
  (IV.ii.24–30)

"The body is with the king" recognizes that Claudius's natural body is the King's, no matter how that kingship was acquired; "but the king is not with the body" acknowledges Claudius's metaphysical violation of the relationship between the rightful king and his body politic.[13]

Nonetheless, to kill Claudius is to kill more than the man, or the king's natural body, and the act involves much more than the hasty murder of Polonius. Hamlet may wish after the deed is automatically accomplished that the *man* he has killed is Claudius, and he asks, "Is it the king?" Polonius is a man just as Claudius is a man, but Polonius is not the king. Hamlet's enterprise involves the "cess of majesty," as Rosencrantz inadvertently reminds us (III.iii.15), and for it he must have philosophical clarity.

The game with Polonius's body provides both the time and the action for Hamlet to contemplate the philosophical exigencies in which the fact of death involves every man. Perhaps the sound of Hamlet's comments on death that anticipate those more literalized views of the Gravedigger, especially the pre-echoes of the verbal idiom, are necessary considerations not only for the prince-avenger but for the audience as well. We may need to be reminded when Polonius dies that there is, in fact, very little difference between the beggar and the king. Polonius, the politician, in diminution parallels the fall of a monarch: "Your worm is your only emperor for diet."[14] Yet simultaneously we also need to recognize with Hamlet the living difference between the king and all other classifications of human beings. All may be reduced to this same dust, fit to "stop a hole to keep the wind away," in death, but in life there remains a significant difference.

Hamlet's inadvertent murder of Polonius therefore clarifies several philosophical questions that had remained ambiguous before, both for Hamlet and for the audience. It proves that Hamlet's delay is not the result of his inability to act: he can act and in the most violent way. It is true, of course, that he resists killing Claudius almost the moment before he kills the unknown eavesdropper behind his mother's arras, but this is hardly a weakness of the will to act. Everything is perfect for Hamlet to act in the case of Claudius's prayer scene, but Hamlet ratiocinates himself out of the deed, precisely at the moment that he has discarded all previous moral dilemmas concerning the killing of a king, because at last he is convinced that this false king has murdered his father, the true king. Thinking analogically, he cannot enact a revenge that does not equal the act to be revenged. His self-conscious review of how such an act of unequal reprisal "would be scanned" calls our attention to his insistence on *precise* revenge, as well as to his sense of acting not only for the moment but also for history's appraisal. His attitude here is consistent with his dying words to Horatio:

> O God, Horatio, what a wounded name,
> Things standing thus unknown, shall live behind me!
> If thou didst ever hold me in thy heart,
> Absent thee from felicity awhile,
> And in this harsh world draw thy breath in pain,
> To tell my story. (V.ii.333–38)

Hamlet obviously has a sense of historical "destiny" even before his rescue by the pirates leads him to verbalize it.

In addition, the murder of the person behind the arras, if it were Claudius, would fulfill in exact terms Hamlet's wish to kill Claudius while he is "about some act/ That has no relish to salvation in't" and would in some sense suggest that "there's a divinity that shapes our ends,/ Rough-hew them how we will." The playwright has contrived a delectable ironic parallel for what has preceded and for what is to follow. Hamlet has to *wait* for circumstances to accord with his will once he recognizes that Polonius is not the King, and this required patience leads him into a different philosophical perspective: "If it be not now, yet it will come. The readiness is all" (V.ii.210–11).

Polonius's accidental death, then, is a crucial axis on which the play moves. It is the first comic perspective on death that the play has offered, by diminishing a man's value to a parcel of guts to be lugged into the neighbor room, and almost simultaneously it provides a renewal of the spectral father figure who inspires his son to revenge. The fact that the ghost of Hamlet's father reappears in the same scene in which Polonius is killed may be a dramaturgically planned coincidence. Visibly present on the stage are a father newly dead—Polonius—and another dead father—the Ghost.

The way in which the play moves from this point subtly elaborates the parallel between Polonius as spectral father figure and the Ghost. Many readers of the play wonder how it is that Polonius, who has so many comic limitations, could evoke such absolute responses from his children. The serious effects of his death—his daughter's insanity and drowning and his son's self-destructive revenge—are hardly anticipated by their scenes together. It is therefore something of a surprise that Polonius, whom we did not take seriously before his death—"an attendant lord, that will do/ To swell a progress, start a scene or two"—becomes a major figure in the plot's movement after his death. "Look you mock him not" takes on a new meaning in Ophelia's mad scenes and in Laertes's haste to avenge his father's death.

What most of us sense is a melodramatically simplified reprise of the play we have already witnessed, but the difference is that now we understand the causes and consequences of events. Hamlet killed Polonius and is sent away; Ophelia goes mad and dies; Laertes returns from Paris to kill his father's murderer. When Hamlet returned from Wittenburg after his father's sudden death, none of the facts surrounding that event were clear. Hamlet reached for clarity through his feigned madness, but he could not reduce to action, as Laertes does, the will for vengeance. Because the strong reactions of both Ophelia and Laertes to their father's death seem excessive, given what Polonius has seemed to be in life, we are reminded of how much more appropriate Hamlet's apparent extremes are for the person who inspired them. Polonius's children take to the literal extremes what Hamlet has been trying to adopt as roles for the first half of the play. What Hamlet was incapable of committing to action, they manifest spontaneously. Ophelia in her madness and suicide and Laertes with his single-minded, self-annihilating vengeance are able to fulfill Hamlet's frustrated emotional intentions. At the point where their situations become parallel, we are able to see clearly the difference between Hamlet, the complex, tentative perceptor of ambiguous situations, and those characters who fail to comprehend at his level. Because they are there, we have another way to view the complexity of Hamlet.[15]

The Polonius nexus therefore extends beyond his physical death as he parodies the Ghost's relationship with Hamlet in his effect on his children. The discrepancy between what the audience sees of Polonius in his life and after his death causes us to reexamine the parallel situation between the Ghost and Hamlet.

When a Polonius evokes from his children such extreme responses to his death, how much more to be appreciated are the violent swings in Hamlet's attitudes over the loss of a father he likens to Hyperion, and how much more does his control of those violent changes seem heroic.

Chapter 8

CLOTEN AND CALIBAN: PARODIC VILLAINS

I

There are figures like Polonius who present an inclusively parodic perspective on many aspects of their plays before and after *Hamlet*'s appearance in the canon. Falstaff is the example who stands out in the earlier plays, and, as Shakespeare progresses toward his final group of plays, he seems to experiment with the figure: Lucio in *Measure for Measure*, Thersites in *Troilus and Cressida*, and Parolles in *All's Well That Ends Well* share a common heritage as comic stage types. In a similar way, each remains outside the play's primary action, although both Lucio and Parolles suffer a form of public humiliation.

By the time Shakespeare was writing *Cymbeline*, *The Winter's Tale*, and *The Tempest*, however, he seems to have become intrigued with a more flagrantly parodic type who is also integrated into the causal aspects of the main plot's development. Both Cloten and Caliban differ from Polonius because of their self-announced roles as villains. Autolycus in *The Winter's Tale* also announces himself to be a rogue, "a snapper-up of unconsidered trifles" who fears "beating and hanging" (IV.iii.25–29),[1] but he finds that his con-game turns out to benefit his intended victims: "Here come those I have done good to against my will" (IV.vi.118).[1] Nonetheless, Autolycus is much less depraved in his roguishness than Cloten and Caliban, whose intentions to rape and murder also are thwarted.

In tragicomedy, as Guarini and Fletcher defined it,[2] death should be a real danger but should remain unrealized in action. Shakespeare embodies that threat in comic types who parody not only serious villainy but also the "heroic" figures in each play. Cloten has an intricate parodic relationship with Posthumus and Imogen as well as with Iachimo and the evil Queen, and Caliban shares a parallelism with Ferdinand and Miranda and with Prospero and Ariel as well as with Antonio and Sebastian.

Both characters seriously threaten to rape and murder people we care about. In Caliban's case, Prospero controls the monster's potential deeds earlier and more obviously than the providential power in *Cymbeline* constrains Cloten's attempts on Imogen:

> With that suit upon my back will I ravish her; first kill him, and in her eyes. He on the ground, my speech of insultment ended on his dead body, and when my lust hath dined—which, as I say, to vex her I will execute in the clothes that she so praised—to the court I'll knock her back, foot her home again. (III.v.135–42)

Nevertheless, at first Cloten is amusing, and we must feel some gratitude that there is a worse fool than Posthumus to elicit our disfavor.

Shakespeare employs a subtle strategy of displacement in his introduction of Posthumus (already exiled at the play's beginning) and Cloten, his on-the-scene "understudy." The two Gentlemen who begin the play immediately draw a comparison between Cloten and Posthumus:

> He that hath missed the Princess is a thing
> Too bad for bad report; and he that hath her—
> I mean, that married her, alack, good man,
> And therefore banished—is a creature such
> As, to seek through the regions of the earth
> For one his like, there would be something failing
> In him that should compare. (I.i.16–22)

The initial contrast between the "thing/ Too bad for bad report" and the "creature" that surpasses hyperbolic praise continues through the minimal presentation of Posthumus. Although he has but a moment to exchange love tokens with his bride before

taking his leave, he fulfills the formulaic expectations of a romantic lover-hero, whereas Cloten, the would-be lover-hero, is persistently present but thoroughly inept. What we hear about in
glowing terms is Posthumus; what we see in his place is Cloten.
Shakespeare presents this contrast in several ways; for example,
Imogen's response to her father represents the thorough disdain
with which all the reasonable characters in the play look upon
Cloten in comparison with Posthumus: "I chose an eagle,/ And
did avoid a puttock" (I.i.139–40). Immediately thereafter, Cloten
makes his first appearance, and we must agree with Imogen that
he is a foolish figure, unworthy of entertaining any notions of
her as a mate.

Thus far, we are filled with Posthumus's good reports and
with Cloten's obvious foolishness. The scene moves to Rome
with reiterations of Posthumus's good report by Philario and
the others, excepting Iachimo; and then, incredibly, we watch
Posthumus fail to match his good report. He *agrees* to allow
Iachimo to test Imogen's fidelity. To this point, Shakespeare has
carefully paired Posthumus and Cloten as exact opposites on a
scale of potentially heroic nobility; now he begins to bring
them together through the disintegration of the delicate equation between Posthumus's external reputation and internal integrity, so that we can eventually see *with* Imogen the same
noble frame in Cloten's headless corpse. This is a remarkable bit
of psychological stagecraft.

The realization that Imogen's description of Cloten's headless
corpse is a factual, if idealized, description of the body of the man
she loves beyond life itself is stunning. Cloten, the fool, turns out
to be identical with Posthumus in external terms, as he has
boasted all along he was:

. . . the lines of my body are as well drawn as his; no less young, more
strong, not beneath him in fortunes, beyond him in the advantage of
the time, above him in birth, alike conversant in general services, and
more remarkable in single oppositions; yet this imperceiverant thing
loves him in my despite. What mortality is! Posthumus, thy head,
which now is growing upon thy shoulders, shall within this hour be
off. (IV.i.9–17)

Many readers of the play as well as many who have seen it in live performance fight Imogen's identification of Cloten with Posthumus. They assume that she is, at this moment, uncharacteristically a foolish girl, misguided by her love for an unworthy man, dazed by the hardships of her wandering in Wales and by her sleeping potion, not to mention Pisanio's report of Posthumus's rejection of her. So she cannot be held responsible for her assumption that this corpse is in fact Posthumus:

> A headless man? The garments of Posthumus?
> I know the shape of 's leg; this is his hand,
> His foot Mercurial, his Martial thigh,
> The brawns of Hercules; but his Jovial face—
> Murder in heaven? How? 'Tis gone. (IV.ii.308–12)

It often becomes an uncomfortable moment in the play for the audience.

If we examine the implications involved in our continuing acceptance of Imogen as a reasonable heroine, we are forced to acknowledge that, paradoxically, bodies have little to do with love. Cloten is transformed in death because of his headlessness into the physical twin of the man Imogen loves. And precisely because Posthumus has lost his head—his reasonableness—he is the figure that Cloten represents. We know that there is a substantial though elusive difference, but we are chagrined by the blunt, comic confutation of our knowledge in this scene. What occurs in the way of our readjustment is fascinating. Because we must retain our respect for Imogen, we modify our disgust for Cloten, and, as a by-product, Posthumus seems to recover some of the respect he has lost. A psychological tendency is to compensate for a compensation, and because we must give an inch to Cloten's former boast in order to exonerate Imogen's mistaken view of his headless corpse, we are eager to give a mile to Posthumus, whom we wanted to like from the start, but who has proved so unlikable. This is a masterly maneuver of a playwright intent on changing his audience's point of view from complacent morality to disturbed compromise.[3]

We know that Shakespeare failed on occasion to change narrower and more secured perspectives. Samuel Johnson, in his famous denunciation of the "unresisting imbecility" of the play's artifices,[4] was not the last to voice discomfort with the play. I suggest, however, that Shakespeare here challenges a new kind of potential in his audience's awareness. We are asked *not* to look at Posthumus as a romance hero, although he starts out according to formula; *not* to see the plot as a romance (nor as history); *not* to be confined by formulas of any kind, be they comic, satiric, pastoral, or tragic. Instead we are asked to accept evidence that life is a continuing, dilemma-ridden confrontation with perplexities. In the use of an absurd figure like Cloten to represent literally a potentially noble figure like Posthumus, Shakespeare takes the technique of parodic parallel further than he has in earlier plays. What started out as parody ends as identification. When we accept the identification, as Imogen has, it is possible for Posthumus to be reborn out of the visibly present corpse of his counter-person. After the removal of the parodic fool, Posthumus regains the stage and gains as well a new, if not entirely regenerated, perspective on life, love, and the pursuit of tolerance.

Cloten also parallels Imogen in parodic ways as they both wander about Wales, feeling "faint," dressed in clothing not their own. Cloten gets Posthumus's clothes from Pisanio in the scene immediately preceding Imogen's appearance in boy's clothing when she describes the tediousness of a man's life. She discovers the cave of Belarius, Guiderius, and Arviragus and is soon discovered by them. Their generous response in offering her not only their food and shelter but also their love contrasts with their reception of Cloten, whom Belarius recognizes as the son of the Queen (IV.ii.61ff.). Both Imogen and Cloten are ignorant about country people and both expect them to be "savage." After she befriends the country trio, Imogen recognizes that she has been deceived by reports:

> These are kind creatures. Gods, what lies I have heard!
> Our courtiers say all's savage but at court.
> Experience, O, thou disprov'st report! (IV.ii.32–34)

When Guiderius asks Belarius and his brother to leave him alone to challenge Cloten, Cloten sees the other two depart and says:

> Soft, what are you
> That fly me thus? Some villain mountaineers?
> I have heard of such. (IV.ii.70–72)

Both Imogen and Cloten have believed the court's view that all people living outside the court are savage, but Imogen's experience belies that report while Cloten's affirms it. The difference in their experience of the strange land and its people is due to the difference in their own natures. The brothers and Belarius instinctively love the good in Imogen and instinctively hate the evil in Cloten.

The manner in which Guiderius dispatches Cloten by cutting off his head and sending it down the "creek" to the sea is both violent and comic. The echo of Orpheus's demise in the death of Cloten and the disposal of his head[5] is appropriate because of Cloten's earlier association with music in his hiring a group of musicians to serenade Imogen on the morning after Iachimo's visit to her bedchamber. Set on by advice that music will "penetrate" Imogen's resistence to him, Cloten's remarks concerning the function of music reveal his perversion of the art. He does not understand that music has its own integrity and is not simply a tool to be used by anyone for any reason. In order to represent what it conventionally may—that is, concord in human relationships that signifies harmony with the larger cosmic order—music must be played from appropriate motives.[6] Cloten, however, sees the aubade as a limited, manipulable tool for "penetration" (with all of that word's bawdy innuendoes); as a result, the music's figurative, metaphysical values are not only unrealized, they are parodied. Cloten perverts music's potentialities, and his echo of Orpheus's beheading is an ironically appropriate diminution of the prototypical musician.

Immediately following Guiderius's description of having "sent Cloten's clotpoll down the stream/ In embassy to his mother" (IV.ii.184–85), he and Belarius hear the sound of music from the cave. The music from Belarius's "ingenious instrument" has not sounded since the death of the boys' presumed mother, Euriphile, and now it precedes Arviragus's entrance carrying the apparently dead body of Imogen. The use of music here is totally appropriate to the men's expression of grief over the loss of their new friend, Fidele, and it creates one of the play's more memorable moments.[7] That Belarius insists on including Cloten's headless body at the end of their obsequies for Imogen lends dignity to the recently dead would-be villain and twins Imogen with Cloten momentarily in death. Thus, in his death, Cloten has in some sense merged with each of the nobler figures that he has parodied in life.

Other parodies occur between Cloten and the recognizably villainous characters in the play. With Iachimo, the parody is situational and is set up by the juxtaposition of scenes in which they both attempt to "penetrate" Imogen's chastity. Iachimo's villainy is enhanced by his awed perception of Imogen's beauty both at their initial meeting and in his surreptitious observation of her sleeping:

> All of her that is out of door most rich!
> If she be furnished with a mind so rare,
> She is alone th'Arabian bird, and I
> Have lost the wager. (I.vi.15–18)

> . . . Cytherea,
> How bravely thou becom'st thy bed, fresh lily,
> And whiter than the sheets! That I might touch!
> But kiss, one kiss! Rubies unparagoned,
> How dearly do they do 't! 'Tis her breathing that
> Perfumes the chamber thus. (II.ii.14–19)

For the villain to voice observations appropriate to a lover turns the romantic formula around. It is true, of course, that Iachimo recovers from his rapt apprehensions of Imogen's physical and symbolic beauty in order to steal from her the bracelet that wins him the wager with Posthumus concerning her chastity. Yet the awe with which he perceives her in her innocent and chaste beauty almost causes him to falter in his mission. As Milton did with Satan and Eve years later, Shakespeare creates a magical scene of intense beauty through the eyes of one determined to defile all the beauty he perceives.

In the next scene the totally imperceptive fool, Cloten, wants to violate Imogen's chastity, but he has no apprehension of the beauty he intends to profane. "If I could get this foolish Imogen, I should have gold enough" (II.iii.7–9) is Cloten's perception of the "heavenly angel" Iachimo saw. No eschatological apprehensions are his. Cloten proceeds with instructions for his musical assault:

Come on, tune. If you can penetrate her with your fingering, so; we'll try with tongue too. If none will do, let her remain, but I'll never give o'er. . . . [Song: "Hark, hark, the lark"] So, get you gone. If this penetrate, I will consider your music the better; if it do not, it is a vice in her ears which horsehairs and calves' guts, nor the voice of unpaved eunuch to boot, can never amend. (II.iii.13–31)[8]

No greater bathos could be achieved between villains with similar purpose than the apprehensions of Imogen by Iachimo and by Cloten.

Cloten also seems to be an extension of his mother's villainy reduced to parodic terms. One of the Lords analyzes it thus:

That such a crafty devil as is his mother
Should yield the world this ass! A woman that
Bears all down with her brain, and this her son
Cannot take two from twenty, for his heart,
And leave eighteen. (II.i.49–53)

The discrepancy between the Queen's conniving wit and Cloten's blunt, unsubtle responses to people and situations is a source of comic fun. Both the Queen and Cloten are dangerous in their intentions—she would kill Pisanio (and perhaps Imogen) with the "cordial" (I.v.64) she thinks is poison and hopes that Imogen will at least die of despair and Cymbeline of grief; Cloten promises to kill Posthumus and rape Imogen. What makes both villainous figures comic rather than tragic (tragicomic is perhaps a better classification) are the moments that provide huge discrepancies in their perceptions, not only of themselves but of the world around them.

The Queen thinks that she has outguessed everyone at court, all of whom she considers inferior to herself, and yet the physician Cornelius, Imogen, and even Pisanio are aware of her duplicity. Cornelius supplies her with a harmless compound because he does "not like her. . . . I do know her spirit/ And will not trust one of her malice with/ A drug of such damned nature" (I.v.33–36). Imogen sees right through her "dissembling courtesy" (I.i.84) when the Queen pretends to be solicitous of her last moments with Posthumus; and Pisanio, after he accepts the box containing the sleeping potion as a sign of her favor, promises to think on her words, "But when to my good lord I prove untrue,/ I'll choke myself. There's all I'll do for you" (I.v.86–87). Even the Lords of the court are aware that she is a "crafty devil" (II.i.40). It seems that only Cymbeline is deceived by her appearance:

> Mine eyes
> Were not at fault, for she was beautiful;
> Mine ears, that heard her flattery; nor my heart,
> That thought her like her seeming. (V.v.62–65)

Like his mother, Cloten assumes an appearance that his actions belie: "Is it fit I went to look upon him [Iachimo, the stranger in the British court]? Is there no derogation in't?" (II.i.40–41). Cloten's affectations of nobility are swiftly undercut by the Second Lord's aside: "You are a fool granted; therefore your issues, being foolish, do not derogate" (II.i.44–45). All of Cloten's actions—his drawing of a sword on the exiled Posthumus (I.i); his breaking of his bowl on his opponent's pate (II.i); his gross misuse of the aubade (II.iii); his rude bravado in front of the Roman ambassador (III.i)—consistently present him literally as a fool, perhaps even retarded. That his mother pins all her idealistic hopes on this foolish son makes comic villains of them both, despite their truly vicious and threatening intentions. When Cloten has failed to "penetrate" Imogen with his morning song, the Queen advises him:

> Frame yourself
> To orderly solicits, and be friended
> With aptness of the season. Make denials

Increase your services. So seem as if
You were inspired to do those duties which
You tender to her; that you in all obey her,
Save when command to your dismission tends,
And therein you are senseless. (II.iii.46–53)

Cloten fails to understand the subtlety of her advice and protests
that he will not be "senseless." As in the case of Imogen's rejection of him, he picks up a word or a phrase ("His meanest gar-
ment"—"senseless") and reacts to it out of context. In both cases
he literalizes the figurative through his actions, wearing Posthumus's garments and becoming "senseless" by losing his head.

To watch the Queen and Cloten onstage together is to realize
how effectively Shakespeare has arranged their duet of super-
charged evil intentions and comic ineffectuality. After her two
first appearances, as the watchful but ostensibly solicitous moni-
tor of Posthumus's and Imogen's leavetaking (I.i) and the procurer of the "poisonous" compound from Cornelius (I.v), the
Queen is never without her counter, Cloten, the son she insists
on seeing as the extension of her own will to power. The scene in
which the Roman ambassador, Caius Lucius, is received at Cymbeline's court is perhaps the most interesting counterpoint between the two. Both are encouraging Cymbeline to withhold
tribute from Rome, but whereas the Queen waxes figuratively
eloquent in her appraisal of Britain's glory, Cloten is literal about
Britain's strength, since there are "no moe such Caesars" as Julius. The Queen speaks to Cymbeline:

Remember, sir, my liege,
The kings your ancestors, together with
The natural bravery of your isle, which stands
As Neptune's park, ribbèd and palèd in
With rocks unscalable and roaring waters,
With sands that will not bear your enemies' boats
But suck them up to th' topmast. A kind of conquest
Caesar made here, but made not here his brag
Of 'Came and saw and overcame.' With shame,
The first that ever touched him, he was carried
From off our coast, twice beaten; and his shipping,

> Poor ignorant baubles on our terrible seas,
> Like eggshells moved upon their surges, cracked
> As easily 'gainst our rocks. For joy whereof
> The famed Cassibelan, who was once at point—
> O giglet fortune!—to master Caesar's sword,
> Made Lud's town with rejoicing fires bright
> And Britons strut with courage. (III.i.16–33)

Cloten apparently interrupts his mother with his literal evaluation of the situation:

Come, there's no more tribute to be paid. Our kingdom is stronger than it was at that time, and, as I said, there is no moe such Caesars. Other of them may have crook'd noses, but to owe such straight arms, none. (III.i.34–37)

Not only does Cloten's prosaic evaluation deflate his mother's rhetoric, his jest about the shape of the Roman nose is thoroughly indecorous. Cymbeline seems to object to Cloten's intrusion into his wife's more appropriate speech of defiance—"Son, let your mother end"—but Cloten, having reached his peak of self-assurance, continues to admonish his king against paying the tribute. The Queen is silent for the rest of the scene, perhaps happy to see her son reiterate her own advice to Cymbeline. But for the audience, Cloten's usurpation of diplomatic prerogative continues the ill-bred oafishness of his preceding characterization. Caius Lucius's "So, sir," in response to Cloten's conclusion of the scene, is cryptic enough to indicate displeasure not only of content but also of form.[9]

Cloten and his mother disappear from the play as active characters with his death. We hear of her failing health from Cymbeline: "A fever with the absence of her son,/ A madness, of which her life's in danger" (IV.iii.2–3).[10] She meets the fate she had wished for both Imogen and Cymbeline—to die of despair. In the concluding scene, Cornelius announces her death together with her full confession of the evil deeds she had contrived but not effected. In context, the report of the Queen's death is as comic as Guiderius's casual report of having "sent Cloten's clotpoll down the stream/ In embassy to his mother" (IV.ii.184–85). Both deaths are contained by their matter-of-fact reportage and become harmonious pieces of the play's tragicomic conclusion.[11]

Cloten appears at opposite ends of the spectrum both of nobility and of cunning villainy as he is paired with each of the villains and heroes at particular points in the play, and in this he may remind us of Shakespeare's characterization of Falstaff in the second *Henriad*.[12] What has changed with Cloten, however, is that he does not always retain comic distance from those he parodies. In his figure, the fool is not only a threatening villain, in a way that Falstaff never is, but he is also identified with the hero. Falstaff's impersonation of the King and of Prince Hal is never taken for anything but play-acting, but Cloten is mistaken for Posthumus by Imogen.

II

Caliban, the magically monstrous villain of *The Tempest*, shares many similarities of situation and characterization with Cloten.[13] They both are offspring of evil mothers who at one point control their worlds. Caliban's mother has died by the time the play begins, yet Sycorax and Cymbeline's Queen are very much alike under the flesh tones. With Cloten we see the Queen's attempts to place the British crown on her son's inheriting head, whereas with Caliban we can only guess that Sycorax assumed he would control her island after her death. Caliban at least voices a disinherited son's claim: "This island's mine by Sycorax my mother,/ Which thou tak'st from me" (I.ii.331–32).

In the same way that Cloten shares parallels of situation despite being opposite to Imogen in his wit and in his actions (such as being disguised and alone in a strange land—Wales), Caliban shares with Miranda the ignorance of an islander who has never seen people from the civilized world, other than Prospero. Miranda's response to Ferdinand when she first sees him—"I might call him/ A thing divine; for nothing natural/ I ever saw so noble" (I.ii.418–20)—closely parallels Caliban's response to Stephano and Trinculo—"These be fine things, an if they be not sprites./

That's a brave god [Stephano] and bears celestial liquor. . . . Thou wondrous man" (II.ii.114–15; 160). Each point of view is tempered, one by Prospero's evaluation of Ferdinand—"To th' most of men this is a Caliban,/ And they to him are angels" (I.ii.481–82)—and the other by Trinculo's comments on Caliban's credulity—"A most ridiculous monster, to make a wonder of a poor drunkard!" (II.ii.161–62). In addition, because Caliban's "god" is obviously unworthy of admiration, the audience is cautioned to look for flaws in Ferdinand's "nobility." Miranda's adoration of such a noble creature might win our approval because romantic convention dictates that "love at first sight" is acceptable; and we might therefore think Prospero an unnecessarily difficult and disapproving father when he belittles the love-match to their faces and demands that Ferdinand pass some tests of his "virtue." Certainly Miranda thinks her father is excessive in requiring Ferdinand to carry logs like a slave. When Stephano, without trial, becomes Caliban's "new master," we see a parody of Miranda's simple adoration and witness its potentially dire results.

Caliban parodies several characters and situations throughout the play. He is like Miranda in his ignorance of the world outside their island, and so his responses, like hers, are innocent. Yet his nature, unlike hers, is base and he is attracted to baseness in Stephano, the drunken butler, and Trinculo, the drunken jester. Miranda, whose name designates her wonderful beauty and perfection (as Ferdinand reminds us [III.i.37–39]), is attracted to like nobility and beauty in Ferdinand. Yet, if we disregard the "call" of like-to-like natures, we see that Caliban and Miranda are basically similar, responding without experience and in ignorance, and both might easily be misled. Prospero's interference in making sure of Ferdinand's worthy intentions is therefore necessary to contain the potential lust that exists not only in Caliban but also in the Prince.[14]

To further increase our recognition of the similarities between Caliban and Ferdinand, but always within the measure of parody, Shakespeare draws several marked parallels. Caliban's initial appearance reminds Miranda what a beast this being is. When Prospero tells her, "We'll visit Caliban," she responds, " 'Tis a villain, sir, I do not love to look on" (I.ii.308–10). Prospero insists that he must be considered, nonetheless, ostensibly because he performs services that make their existence more comfortable, but also to prepare a contrast for Ferdinand's appearance. In the ensuing exchange with Caliban, Prospero recalls how, after caring for Caliban as his own child and lodging him in his "cell," Caliban repaid him by trying to rape his daughter. Caliban's laughing recollection tells us that for him the violation of Miranda's virginity is insignificant, but it is a point that Prospero later makes deliberately significant as he speaks to Ferdinand. Miranda recalls how she tried to teach Caliban language and he jests that "my profit on't/ Is, I know how to curse" (I.ii.363–64).

Recalcitrant and unregenerate, Caliban leaves the stage at the same moment Ferdinand enters for the first time, following the "invisible" Ariel's haunting song. The visual pairing of the two brings them into parallel focus not only for the audience but also for Miranda, all of whom cannot help but see the vast difference between a Caliban and a Ferdinand. Enhanced thus, Ferdinand appears as "a thing divine," which makes Prospero's denigrating comparison between him and Caliban (I.ii.481–82) seem entirely unreasonable. In addition, there is Prospero's assumption that Ferdinand is a "traitor," having "put thyself/ Upon this island as a spy, to win it/ From me, the lord on 't" (I.ii.455–57). Prospero lets the audience know, of course, that his negative reaction to Ferdinand is contrived to test the Prince's nature, and the audience also knows that such a charge is contrary to fact. Caliban has already charged Prospero with taking the island from him (I.ii.331–34) and later makes a similar claim to Stephano and Trinculo—"A sorcerer, that by his cunning hath/ Cheated me of the island" (III.ii.42–43). Prospero echoes Caliban's accusations when he wrongly accuses Ferdinand of treason, and the parallel encourages us to discount Caliban's claims as we do Prospero's, realizing that each speaker alters the facts to suit his purposes of the moment.

Visual parallels between Caliban and Ferdinand occur in II.ii and III.i, successive scenes that begin with Caliban's carrying "a burden of wood" and with Ferdinand's "bearing a log." Both characters discuss the terms of their servitude grudgingly, Caliban cursing Prospero and Ferdinand noting that only Miranda's presence "makes my labors pleasures" (III.i.7).[15] Their different attitudes toward Prospero's imposed authority are made clearer because their physical, visible actions are the same. Similarly, their common acceptance of slavery leads us to see a crucial difference. Ferdinand, whose nature is to rule, accepts slavery because of his love for Miranda:

> The very instant that I saw you, did
> My heart fly to your service; there resides,
> To make me slave to it; and for your sake
> Am I this patient log-man. (III.i.64–67)

Caliban proves that he is by nature a slave when he encounters Stephano and determines to cast off Prospero's authority in order to subject himself to his new "god": "I'll kiss thy foot. I'll swear myself thy subject" (II.ii.148).

The two are paired also in their praise of Miranda's beauty. In order to reach the conclusion that Miranda is "so perfect and so peerless" Ferdinand admits that he has known "full many a lady," and that "many a time/ Th' harmony of their tongues hath into bondage/ Brought my too diligent ear" (III.i.39–42). Caliban, in contrast, "never saw a woman/ But only Sycorax my dam and she;/ But she as far surpasseth Sycorax/ As great'st does least" (III.ii.97–100). Each is aware of Miranda's superior beauty, but one speaks out of prior knowledge of this world's beauties and the other out of ignorance. Ferdinand speaks hoping to win Miranda's love for himself, whereas Caliban is pandering to Stephano's lust, setting up a breeder-queen to people the island once Prospero is dead. The contrast between the motives of lover and pimp creates different effects in the descriptions of Miranda's beauty, but their external similarities encourage us to see beyond the present moment with Prospero's prescience and to realize the danger of lust that could mar the perfect union between the lovers and stain the generations to come.

This theme is one focus of the masque that Prospero presents to celebrate the betrothal of his daughter and Ferdinand. Iris, the rainbow, calls on Ceres, the goddess of plenty, to bless this nuptial, but Ceres wants to be sure that Venus and her son Cupid will have no part in the ceremony. As Ceres says, she is mistrustful of those two ever since they conspired in abducting her daughter Proserpine to join Dis in the underworld for a part of each year. Iris assures Ceres that Venus and Cupid will not be present, although they did have a plot, since broken,

> to have done
> Some wanton charm upon this man and maid,
> Whose vows are, that no bed-right shall be paid
> Till Hymen's torch be lighted. (IV.i.94–97)

With such assurance that lust will not mar the ceremony, the masque proceeds, only to be interrupted when Prospero remembers "that foul conspiracy/ Of the beast Caliban and his confederates/ Against my life" (IV.i.139–41). Once more the figure of lust intrudes on the harmonious celebration of love's ideal perfection.

Prospero needs to remain alert in order to contain Caliban's threats to deter the fulfillment of his purposes. In the past, he had to learn that with Caliban's attempt to violate Miranda, even as he had to learn about his brother's treachery in ousting him from his dukedom. The fact that Caliban is replaying, with less subtlety and more directly intended violence, the pre-play usurpation is another instance of his parodic function. Prospero describes Antonio's usurpation in I.ii when he fills in for Miranda the heretofore secret history of their journey in exile. Antonio and Sebastian replay that plot in their thwarted attempt to kill Alonso and Gonzalo (II.i), and Caliban plays it yet again in his recruiting of Stephano and Trinculo to kill Prospero and gain control of the island. The repetitions of the original crime occur in the play's present action in comically contained forms. Sebastian must have a final word with Antonio *after* they have drawn their swords, and Stephano and Trinculo must try on the deceptively glittering clothes before they proceed (much to Caliban's distress). In each instance, Prospero has Ariel ready to insure that the plots will not be realized, but in each case the characters themselves provide their own crucial delays because of comic pendantry and comic vanity. In effect, the usurpation/regicide plot is reduced from evil threat to farcical inertia, and this parodic reduction allows the villainous plotters to be included in the play's final harmonious vision, despite the fact that not all of them are repentant.[16]

Yet another instance of Caliban's comic focusing occurs in the surprised reactions of Ferdinand and of Stephano on finding that these "natives" of the island can speak their own language. Ferdinand is already charmed by Miranda's beauty, thinking her a "goddess," and when she answers his question whether she "be a maid or no" in his language—"No wonder, sir,/ But certainly a maid"—he is overwhelmed (I.ii.422–29). When Stephano stumbles over Caliban, under whose gaberdine Trinculo has hidden from the storm, and Caliban cries out, Stephano likewise is surprised: "Where the devil should he learn our language?" (II.ii.65–66). Not only does Caliban speak, but when Trinculo recognizes the other voice as Stephano's, he calls out, and Stephano is further astonished: "Four legs and two voices—a most delicate monster!"[17] Thus what appears in Ferdinand as sublime wonder is broadened under Stephano's response to comic absurdity. The two attitudes, so similar to begin with, collide because of the disparity in the objects that generate them. On recognition of the analogy, however, the audience may see how each modifies the other.

Caliban clearly resides at the opposite pole from the "spirit" Ariel. He is of earth and melancholic elements and exudes "a very ancient and fishlike smell" (II.ii.25–26), whereas Ariel is of air and fire—as Ariel so aptly describes his role in the opening tempest: "now on the beak,/ Now in the waist, the deck, in every cabin,/ I flamed amazement" (I.ii.196–98). Yet both share attitudes that draw them into the parodic mirror. Both Caliban and Ariel desire freedom and both rebel against Prospero's constraints. Whereas Caliban continues in dark bitterness to oppose Prospero's control, Ariel, once Prospero reminds him of Sycorax's cruelty, eagerly submits to Prospero's commands.

Furthermore, there is a tenderness between Ariel and Prospero that Caliban's brutal hatred deepens by contrast. Prospero would have encompassed the beast when he harbored Caliban in his own cell with his daughter and tried to teach him civilized ways. Caliban refused to be "nurtured," but Ariel has become Prospero's trusted servant, with an occasional reminder that he must obey the master rather than follow his own will. The tortures that Prospero proposes to Ariel in I.ii when Ariel retreats from "more toil" are mental reminders of the imprisoned state in which Prospero found him, bound by Sycorax's evil spell. The tortures that he administers to Caliban are physical, and they continue *in order* to remind him, in the only way he will apprehend, that Prospero is in control. The punishment is adjusted to the nature of the two servants. Prospero retains his control over both, but at some expense of energy in each case.

Prospero's ill temper often has been difficult for critics to accept, especially when he is seen to be a surrogate for Providence.[18] His irascibility makes good sense dramatically, however. He has always preferred a distanced role in terms of governing, but no situation has allowed him distance with immunity. He literally was forced to gain distance from his dukedom, but only to find his natural leadership called into action on the island. To keep his "natural" servants in control requires constant attention, and frequently distracts him from what he prefers to think about. The parallel rebellion of Ariel and Caliban in I.ii displays his potential for anger in terms of the energies he must expend simply to insure his control.

Later, of course, his momentary forgetfulness when he would rather enjoy the masque his spirits are presenting for Miranda and Ferdinand causes him extreme discomfort. His agitation at remembering the "foul conspiracy" of Caliban and the others on his life is so intense that both Ferdinand and Miranda are startled by it. "Never till this day," Miranda says, "saw I him touched with anger so distempered" (IV.i.144–45). Prospero immediately reassures them that he is once more in control and removes himself in order to still his "beating mind"; but for that brief moment we are allowed to see into the extraordinary alertness and self-control that his mastery involves.

Perhaps one of the greatest pains Caliban himself must suffer is to understand the lack of diligence and control that his newly found "god" and conspirators display. Caliban's recognition of true leadership at the end of the play causes him to reconsider his allegiance to Prospero in a way that is surprising not only to the audience but also, I think, to Prospero:

> I'll be wise hereafter,
> And seek for grace. What a thrice-double ass
> Was I to take this drunkard for a god
> And worship this dull fool![19] (V.i.295–98)

Caliban's contrast with Ariel is finally dramatized with Prospero's commands to each. To Caliban: "Go to! Away!" To Ariel: "Then to the elements/ Be free, and fare thou well!"

There are so many parallels between Ariel and Caliban by way of inversion that it seems redundant to name them all, but the Pied Piper analogy deserves comment. In II.ii, a drunken Caliban leads his new master and Trinculo off stage, singing a cacaphonous song of freedom:

> 'Ban, 'Ban, Ca-Caliban
> Has a new master: get a new man.
> Freedom, high-day! high-day! freedom! freedom,
> high-day, freedom! (II.ii.179–82)

In III.ii, Ariel, invisible to the others, plays a game that resembles a classic farcical routine by placing his invisible voice where one of the visible characters stands, thus encouraging their incensed reactions.[20] Having wrought his indignities on their somewhat blighted sensibilities, Ariel leads them off the stage; they are aware that "the picture of Nobody," the invisible "taborer," is the musical leader of their group. Ariel's leading suggests the control of revolt by reason, whereas Caliban's leading dramatically signifies the loss of reason through drunkenness. In both cases, those being led are drunk and reasonless—or as Peter Seng puts it, they are the "rats" being led off the scene.[21]

The pair of scenes might remind us of Ariel's leading of Ferdinand to his meeting with Miranda—the ethereal music being not only beautiful but also indicating divine control—and at the other extreme, the penultimate scene with the drunkards being driven out by "divers Spirits in shapes of dogs and hounds hunting them about" (S.D. IV.i.253).

The loss and achievement of "control" may be the major thematic exploration of the play, and Caliban's attitudes and actions re-present all efforts toward "control" under the perspective of parody. He would rule the island; he would not serve Prospero; he would enslave himself to his drunken god, Stephano; he would be "free"; and finally he would "find himself" in the recognition of Prospero's true mastery:

> I'll be wise hereafter,
> And seek for grace.

Caliban provides, perhaps even more than Antonio does, the extreme opportunity for Prospero to exert his own control: "The rarer action is/ In virtue than in vengeance."

Epilogue

Rosalind says at the end of *As You Like It*, " 'tis true that a good play needs no epilogue." Although many additional scenes and characters could elaborate the point that Shakespeare and his contemporaries assumed analogical principles in the construction of their plays—differentiated only by the skill and effectiveness with which the analogies are drawn—the function of the principle is constant throughout the plays. I have been concerned primarily with the occurrence of scenes in which comic form has been imposed on serious matter as a particular instance of Shakespeare's employment of the analogical scene. On watching the Royal Shakespeare Company's production of *The Merchant of Venice*, directed by John Barton, in July 1981, I was impressed again with the powerful effect of this combination. Shylock has long been a problem because his character presents both tragic and comic potentialities. Productions of the play, such as Laurence Olivier's, tend to emphasize either one or the other possibility in order to achieve coherence of character. Yet Shakespeare's strategy seems to insist on having both sides simultaneously apparent in an unremitting balance that defies easy resolution. Especially in the scene with Tubal (III.i), who reports alternately the news of Antonio's argosy's destruction and Jessica's squandering of Shylock's wealth, the insistent comic form creates a hiatus in the play's progress, what some might be tempted to call "comic relief." But far from releasing tension, this scene builds it. We want to laugh at Shylock for equating his love of his daughter with his possession of wealth, and yet the ostensibly funny line, "I would not have given it [Leah's ring] for a wilderness of monkeys" (III.i.108–9), is almost heart-rending in the sympathetic understanding that it can evoke from an audience. No quantitative evaluation may be placed on love tokens, and yet to limit the exchange rate at even a "wilderness of monkeys" reminds us that Shylock is basically numerative in his evaluation of love. We have seen him and heard of him as a calculating equator in "my daughter and my ducats" and shall see him so again in "Is it so nominated in the bond?" That Shylock should be caught by his own exact equation of monetary value with human *being* is fitting, yet pitiful. We know that it must happen, but the condign punishment is almost overwhelming for comic purposes (as when Volpone is sentenced to imprisonment in a hospital to become the invalid he has pretended to be). Nonetheless, this emotional position of close *and* distant is exactly where Shakespeare insists that we be with Shylock. It is not a casual matter of toying with our emotions, as I see it, but a firm commitment to encourage us to accept both the "ayes" and "nays" of human personality, and by extension, of human existence. "Odi et amo," Catullus says, and so we do with many of Shakespeare's characters, but when it comes to a particularly difficult cliché of apprehension, such as Shylock's Jewishness or Othello's blackness, the audience is asked to recognize its own ambivalence about such issues through the complexities of tragicomic form.

Instances of Shakespeare's use of the analogical scene confront us at almost every turn, but the use of parody so conjoined seems often to elude critical apprehensions of Shakespeare's intent as well as of effects. What I have tried to suggest in this study is that "parody" is a term that deserves a place in Shakespearean criticism, despite the problems that may accompany it. Not every parallel is a parody, and not every ironic parallel is a parody, as I have indicated in the first chapter's discussion of the Gloucester plot in *King Lear* and the Polonius plot in *Hamlet*. Nevertheless, the concept of parody as an imitation that both delimits and heightens by contrast is a useful one and should not be avoided because there are dangers of overlapping definitions of terms. The Shylock scene to which I have referred, for example, might not be viewed as a parodic scene, but if we look at it as the initial instance of the "ring plot," placing quantitative value on love tokens, we can recognize that the play's ending is a replay of just such reckoning. The scene at Belmont, so far removed from Venice, is linked to it by the parallels in valuing or not valuing the ring. Comic in itself as a farcical routine, Shylock's sense of loss when he hears of Jessica's exchange of her mother's ring for a monkey suggests proleptically the kinds of limits and irrelevancies that attend Portia's and Nerissa's extortion of their husbands' rings. Conversely, when Portia and Nerissa finally move beyond the "letter" of their "ring vows" and forgive their husbands for violating those vows, we remember Shylock and his inability to get beyond the letter of the bond and its material measure.

The scenes I have examined here—simplifications through reduction, literalization, exaggeration, or allegorization—produce an immediate other way to look at central issues and allow the audience to refocus on the complex dimensions that the play explores. It is less informative and less understandable to witness Caesar's assassination without Cinna the Poet's mutilation, or to see Macbeth as an isolated vulnerability given up to wickedness, or to look only at Hamlet without Polonius. We can move through any play without these special, puzzling, and often obtrusive scenes and characters, but need we?

In a sentence, the way its parts are put together—its syntax—makes it a vehicle for communication. In a play, the little scene that makes ideas physical in delimited terms—be they parodic or emblematic—forms part of a structural syntax. Whereas in a sentence we *require* only a subject and a verb, the richness of its power to communicate is enhanced by the addition of modifiers, phrases, and clauses. So too in a play, we *require* only the characters and the narrative action to understand the story. To grasp the fullness of the play's exploration of the human psyche at work in the world, however, we need as well the little scene that shows us by analogy aspects of thought and action only partially realized in the play's major scenes.

Notes

Chapter 1

1. Both these scenes are discussed in detail below, in chapters 2 and 4.

2. See, for example, John Florio, *A Worlde of Wordes 1598* (facsimile reprint, Hidesheim and New York: Georg Olms, 1972); Robert Cawdrey, *A Tale Alphabetical of Hard Usual English Words* [*1604*] (Gainesville, Fl.: Scholars' Facsimiles & Reprints, 1966). For later repetition and elaboration of the definition, see Thomas Blount, *Glossographia* [*1656*] (Menston, England: The Scolar Press, 1969); and Edward Phillips, *The New World of English Words* [1658] (Menston, England: The Scolar Press, 1969).

3. *Bacon's Advancement of Learning and The New Atlantis* [Preface by Thomas Case] (London: Oxford University Press, 1906), p. 108 [Second Book, VIII, 3]. My italics.

4. Francis Fergusson, *The Idea of a Theater* (Princeton, N.J.: Princeton University Press, 1949), Appendix: "The Notion of Analogy," pp. 234–36.

5. Dean Frye, "The Question of Shakespearean 'Parody'," *Essays in Criticism* 15 (1965): 22–26; Richard Levin, "Elizabethan 'Clown' Subplots," *Essays in Criticism* 16 (1966): 84–91 (restated in chapter 4 in *The Multiple Plot in Renaissance Drama* [Chicago: University of Chicago Press, 1971]).

6. Leo Salingar, *Shakespeare and the Traditions of Comedy* (London: Cambridge University Press, 1974), p. 97.

7. John Florio, *Queen Anna's New World of Words* [1611] (Menston, England: The Scolar Press, 1968).

8. Samuel Johnson, *A Dictionary of the English Language* [1755] (New York: AMS Press, 1968).

9. Pierre Legouis, in his revised (third) edition of H. M. Margoliouth's edition of *The Poems and Letters of Andrew Marvell* (Oxford: Clarendon Press, 1971), vol. 1, p. 238, adds a note to the poem *"Ad Regem Carolum Parodia"* based on his correspondence with Hilton Kelliher: "In view of the fact that the *O.E.D.* denies the word 'parody' any meaning that does not contain the idea of ridicule . . . it should be noted that a purely neutral meaning is found in Johnson's dictionary, where Pope is quoted in support." He also refers to T. W. Baldwin's *William Shakespere's Smalle Latine & Lesse Greeke* (Urbana: University of Illinois Press, 1944) to support the idea that the writing of "parody" was a common literary exercise in the earlier seventeenth century. Baldwin says, vol. I, pp. 395–97, that the curriculum of the Merchant Taylors' school required "parodiae, or imitacons of Latine verses . . . [and] also . . . some parodiae, or imitations of Greeke verses" of the fifth form in the afternoons. For a linguistic history of the word, see Fred W. Householder, Jr., "ΠΑΡΩΙΔΙΑ," *Classical Philology* 39 (1944): 1–9.

10. An example of "burlesque" is Richard Armour's *Twisted Tales from Shakespeare* (New York: McGraw-Hill Book Co., 1957). It is burlesque, rather than parody, because it refuses to take either the original or itself seriously and because the author understands the process of literalization to be a "gag" or "joke." In parody, however, the imitation accepts the potential of meaning in its cross-references. The burlesque insists on the reader's attention being detained in the frivolous mockery that is its own end, whereas parody allows the reader to return to the original and rethink its meaning. To illustrate scrupulous avoidance of using the term "parody" where it would be more appropriate than "burlesque" or "travesty," see Jonas A. Barish's essay "The Double Plot in *Volpone*," *Modern Philology* 51 (1953): 83–92. Also see G. K. Hunter's comments on parody, Arden edition, *All's Well That Ends Well* (London: Methuen & Co., 1959; reprt. 1966), p. xxxv, n. 1.

11. For discussion of the "obvious fiction" of Gloucester's "fall" at Dover's cliffs, see Alan C. Dessen, *Elizabethan Drama and the Viewer's Eye* (Chapel Hill: University of North Carolina Press, 1977), pp. 119–25. Alvin B. Kernan, *The Playwright as Magician* (New Haven: Yale University Press, 1979), pp. 121–28, sees the scene as a "brief morality play," a "shabby theatrical device" that exposes the "illusory quality of all theater." John Reibetanz, *The "Lear" World: A Study of "King Lear" in Its Dramatic Context* (Toronto: University of Toronto Press, 1977; reprt.

1979), pp. 40, 43, 97–98, suggests the emblematic resonances of the scene. For a fuller discussion of Polonius, see below, chapter 7.

12. Cf. Judith H. Anderson's comment, "Redcrosse and the Descent into Hell," *ELH* 36 (1969): 482: "The result is parody, but of a deadly serious sort."

13. See Eric Rothstein, "Structure as Meaning in *The Jew of Malta*," *The Journal of English and Germanic Philology* 65 (1966): 260–73.

14. Bruce R. Smith, "Perspectives on Shakespeare's Pageants-within-the-Play," a paper delivered at the Southeastern Renaissance Conference in April 1982, noted that the gardeners "are declaiming the verses of one of the most popular Renaissance emblems for the right governing of a commonwealth" and used emblem #41 from Guillaume de la Perrière, *La Morosophie* (Lyon, 1553 et seq.) to illustrate this point.

15. Helpful essays on the scene are David J. Houser, "Armor and Motive in *Troilus and Cressida*," in *Renaissance Drama*, n.s. IV, eds. S. Schoenbaum and Alan C. Dessen (Evanston: Northwestern University Press, 1971), pp. 121–34; and Alice Shalvi, " 'Honor' in *Troilus and Cressida*," *Studies in English Literature* 5 (1965): 283–302.

16. See below, chapter 2, for fuller discussion of this scene (III.iv). For a review of the long-running critical debate over Desdemona's innocence, see W. D. Adamson, "Unpinned or Undone?: Desdemona's Critics and the Problem of Sexual Innocence," *Shakespeare Studies* 13 (1980): 169–86.

17. A similar effect is created in Marlowe's *The Jew of Malta*, which begins with an apparent attempt to move beyond typical biased views about Barabas as a stage type only to validate them by the conclusion.

18. See Hereward T. Price, "Mirror Scenes in Shakespeare," in *Joseph Quincy Adams Memorial Studies*, eds. James G. McManaway et al. (Washington, D.C.: Folger Shakespeare Library, 1948), pp. 101–13, who considers these "apparently loose detachable scenes" under the category of "mirror scenes."

Chapter 2

1. Algernon de Vivier Tassin, "Julius Caesar," in *Shaksperian Studies,* eds. Brander Matthews and A. H. Thorndike (New York: Columbia University Press, 1916), p. 278.

2. Paul Stapfer, p. 188, n. 29, and F. Kreyssig, p. 188, n. 31, in Horace Howard Furness, Jr., ed., New Variorum edition, *The Tragedie of IVLIVS CAESAR* (Philadelphia and London: J. B. Lippincott Co., 1913).

3. M. M. Mahood, *Shakespeare's Wordplay* (London: Methuen & Co., 1957), p. 131, in discussing the loss of the meaning of the "word" and the "name," observes: "The odd episode of Cinna the poet being lynched in error for Cinna the conspirator seems irrelevant, but in fact sums up a main theme of the play. There is everything in a name—for the ignorant and irrational." Norman N. Holland, "The 'Cinna' and 'Cynicke' Episodes in *Julius Caesar*," *Shakespeare Quarterly* 11 (1960): 439–44, relates the scene point-by-point to the assassination of Caesar, which precedes it, and also to the brief intrusion of the Cynic poet on Brutus and Cassius, who are quarreling, in Act IV. Nicholas Brooke, *Shakespeare's Early Tragedies* (London: Methuen & Co., 1968), p. 158, remarks: "A final emblem is provided in the brutal little farce of the lynching of Cinna the poet." John W. Velz, " 'If I Were Brutus Now . . . ': Role-Playing in *Julius Caesar*," *Shakespeare Studies* 4 (1968/1969): 153, calls it a "pathetic microcosm of the assassination"; and Marjorie Garber, *Dream in Shakespeare* (New Haven: Yale University Press, 1974), p. 57, says: "The scene of Cinna the poet is in many ways the most symbolically instructive of the whole play. . . . [It] may be seen as a kind of emblem for the entire meaning of *Julius Caesar*."

4. Hereward T. Price, *Construction in Shakespeare* (Ann Arbor: University of Michigan Press, 1951), p. 21, says that this kind of scene is Shakespeare's "typical" scene. See also Mark Rose, *Shakespearean Design* (Cambridge, Mass.: Harvard University Press, 1972), and James E. Hirsh, *The Structure of Shakespearean Scenes* (New Haven: Yale University Press, 1981).

5. Plutarch, *Lives of the Noble Grecians and Romanes,* trans. Thomas North [1579] (London: David Nutt, 1896), vol. 5, pp. 69–70.

6. Ibid., vol. 6, p. 201.

7. Ibid., vol. 5, p. 70.

8. Ibid., vol. 6, p. 201.

9. Leo Salingar, *Shakespeare and the Traditions of Comedy,* pp. 246–47.

10. Desiderius Erasmus, *The Praise of Folly,* trans. Leonard F. Dean (New York: Hendricks House, 1969), p. 49.

11. These situations are exemplified in Chaucer's "The Miller's Tale," by January and May in "The Merchant's Tale," and by his expert on the subject, the Wife of Bath. See also Giacomo Oreglia, *The Commedia dell' Arte,* trans. Lovett F. Edwards (New York: Hill and Wang, 1968; first published in Italian in 1961).

12. See glossaries of Eric Partridge, *Shakespeare's Bawdy* (New York: E. P. Dutton & Co., 1960; first published in 1948); E. A. M. Colman, *The*

Dramatic Use of Bawdy in Shakespeare (London: Longman Group, 1974); James T. Henke, *Renaissance Dramatic Bawdy (Exclusive of Shakespeare)*, 2 vols. (Salzburg: Institut Für Englische Sprache Und Literatur, 1974); and Thomas W. Ross, *Chaucer's Bawdy* (New York: E. P. Dutton & Co., 1972).

13. Eric Partridge, *A Dictionary of Slang and Unconventional English* (London: Routledge & Kegan Paul, 1961), vol. 1, p. 305.

14. Such as in the banter between Claudio and Benedick in *Much Ado About Nothing*, I.i.175–240.

15. My students have suggested that the Second Plebeian's remark could be interpreted as a homosexual joke. That, too, is possible.

16. As described by Sister Miriam Joseph, *Shakespeare's Use of the Arts of Language* (New York: Columbia University Press, 1947), who draws on Puttenham and Wilson.

17. Kreyssig, in the Furness *Variorum*, says that the notion of killing a man for his bad verses is "manifestly English in its humour," p. 188, n. 31.

18. Mahood, *Shakespeare's Wordplay*, pp. 179–81, observes that "the dramatic conflict of that play [*Julius Caesar*] is above all a conflict of linguistic attitudes" that reflects Shakespeare's own dilemma between linguistic scepticism and faith in the power of words. The Cinna-the-poet scene epitomizes the discovery that words are "arbitrary signs and not right names," a discovery she sees as central for all of Shakespeare's tragic heroes.

19. Holland, "The 'Cinna' and 'Cynicke' Episodes in *Julius Caesar*," pp. 441–43, compares the two poets and their bits of scenes because "both are said to be bad poets, both are witty, . . . and both are associated with Caesar's spirit." Whereas the "Cinna episode, as a miniature of Caesar's death, identifies Brutus's motives with those of the mob and establishes the attitude of the play toward the assassination," the "Cynicke episode underscores the theme of separation between Brutus the idealist and Cassius the realist that is their joint tragedy."

20. T. S. Dorsch, Arden edition, *Julius Caesar* (London: Methuen & Co., 1955), pp. xliii–xliv, observes that Shakespeare's presentation of Brutus differs from "the common Renaissance view of him as the great liberator and patriot" because Shakespeare "accentuates any weaknesses or errors for which there is the slightest warrant in Plutarch, and gives him what is in many respects a disagreeable personality. . . . On the other hand, he makes him act from an entirely sincere belief that he is serving his country by killing Caesar."

21. Lawrence J. Ross, *The Shakespearean Othello. A Critical Exposition*

on Historical Evidence, 3 vols., University Microfilm of Dissertation, Princeton, 1955, pp. 714–17, 825–28, and 839–44, discusses the mutual participation in "lying" in this scene as well as Bianca's function in the play.

22. Cf. Mahood, *Shakespeare's Wordplay,* pp. 182–83.

23. Colman, *The Dramatic Use of Bawdy,* p. 123.

24. Emrys Jones, *Scenic Form in Shakespeare* (Oxford: Oxford University Press, 1971), p. 63, attempts to set this controversy to rest: "The conclusion we are drawn to is that the action of *Othello,* like that of its narrative source, Cinthio's *novella,* extends through a considerable, though unspecified, period of time, and consequently that there is no need to resort to a double-time theory to account for features of the play which in any case do not exist for an audience at a performance."

25. In Bianca's "reckoning" a pun begins with the word "score," meaning both "twenty" and a "tally" or "account" kept by cutting notches in a stick. When Cassio promises "in a more continuate time/ [to] Strike off this score of absence," he makes the pun clearer, adding a sexual innuendo. In the next scene, when Othello "encaves" himself in order to watch Cassio's conduct as orchestrated by Iago, he is convinced because of Cassio's laughter that Cassio has cuckolded him and exclaims, "Have you scored me?" C. T. Onions, *A Shakespeare Glossary,* 2nd edition, revised (Oxford: Oxford University Press, 1980), p. 190, notes this line and equates it with "made my reckoning; branded me." "To score" in modern slang means to have succeeded sexually with a partner. The potential for this meaning seems latent in these two scenes of *Othello* as well as in other Shakespearean instances, notably Mercutio's taunting song about the Nurse:

> But a hare that is hoar
> Is too much for a score
> When it hoars ere it be spent.
> (*Romeo and Juliet,* II.iv.129–31)

As clear an association appears in Chaucer's "Shipman's Tale" when the sexually active wife suggests a way for her husband to regain a loan: "And, if so be I faille,/ I am your wyf; score it upon my taille,/ And I shal paye, as soone as ever I may." As Thomas W. Ross points out in *Chaucer's Bawdy,* pp. 218–19, the spelling of "taille" encouraged puns on "tail"—meaning sexual intercourse—and "tally"—the keeping of accounts, with the idea of marital debt implicit.

26. Jones, *Scenic Form in Shakespeare,* p. 149, notes that in the quarto version of Ben Jonson's *Every Man in His Humour* the jealous husband,

later called Kitely, is called Thorello and Thorello's wife's name is Bianca.

27. In rhetorical terms, substitution is the transference of "adjuncts" to another subject, and this transference changes more than the "subject" to which these adjuncts are transferred—the shift of "adjuncts" also changes others. See Joseph, *Shakespeare's Use of the Arts of Language,* pp. 119–20.

28. See J. W. Lever's notes in support of this reading, Arden edition, *Measure for Measure* (London: Methuen & Co., 1965), p. 27. Also see Mahood's comments on garden images in the play, *Shakespeare's Wordplay,* pp. 17–18.

29. The italicized line in the First Folio indicates that these are sententiae.

30. In the 1820 edition of *The Family Shakespeare,* vol. 2 (London: Longman, Hurst, Rees, Orme, and Brown, 1820), Thomas Bowdler excludes not only Escalus's lines but the entire section of the scene involving Elbow, Pompey, and Froth. Bowdler says, p. 3, that he is following Mr. Kemble's text as performed at the Theatre Royal, Covent Garden. See Hilda Hulme, *Explorations in Shakespeare's Language* (London: Longmans, Green and Co., 1962), p. 93. Hulme's discussion of the "brakes of ice" passage suggests the association of "ice" with chastity, and her reference to *The Revenger's Tragedy* (IV.iv), together with Anne Barton's citations of lines from *As You Like It,* III.iv.18, and *Hamlet,* III.i.140, in *The Riverside Shakespeare,* gen. ed. G. Blakemore Evans (Boston: Houghton Mifflin Co., 1974), make John P. Collier's emendation of "breaks" for "brakes" very tempting.

31. Mistress Overdone's response to the news that all the brothels shall be pulled down—"Why, here's a change indeed in the commonwealth!" (I.ii.105)—supports James T. Henke's gloss on the pun: wealth got by "common" means, prostitution, *Renaissance Dramatic Bawdy.* Eric Partridge, *Shakespeare's Bawdy,* notes Elbow's line as a reference for common houses–brothels. Partridge, Henke, and Colman, *The Dramatic Use of Bawdy,* all gloss "use" as sexual enjoyment or the act of copulation. Partridge notes that "abuses" refer to the making of a cuckold or to the seduction of someone's wife, in general, to wrong by infidelity. Colman discusses the various possibilities for "nothing" in *The Dramatic Use of Bawdy,* pp. 15–18.

32. Sir Philip Sidney's criticism occurs in the *Defence of Poesie,* ed. Albert Feuillerat (Cambridge: Cambridge University Press, 1923), vol.3, p. 39. Mary Lascelles, *Shakespeare's Measure for Measure* (London: The

Athlone Press, 1953), p. 63, advocates flexibility toward the idea that Shakespeare's comedy had to flush "such muddy channels."

33. Sidney Musgrove, "Some Composite Scenes in *Measure for Measure*," *Shakespeare Quarterly* 15 (1964): 67–74. Ernest Schanzer, *The Problem Plays of Shakespeare* (New York: Schocken Books, 1963), p. 116.

34. Note the similarity to Claudius's tag at the end of the prayer scene in *Hamlet* (III.iii.97–98), where the couplet points out the irony of Hamlet's mistaken perception. See discussion below, chapter 7.

35. Josephine Waters Bennett, *Measure for Measure as Royal Entertainment* (New York: Columbia University Press, 1966), p. 31.

36. Lever, Arden edition, *Measure for Measure*, p. 33, n. 134–36.

37. Rosalind Miles, *The Problem of 'Measure for Measure'* (New York: Barnes & Noble, 1976), p. 256.

38. Hulme, *Explorations in Shakespeare's Language*, p. 113.

39. Gordon Ross Smith, "Isabella and Elbow in Varying Contexts of Interpretation," *Journal of General Education* 17 (1965): 75–76.

40. Partridge, *Shakespeare's Bawdy*, glosses "do=to copulate with," and Henke, *Renaissance Dramatic Bawdy*, cites an instance of the past tense "done" that carries the same meaning.

41. Less obvious as a substitution is Pompey's taking over Escalus's role in the interrogation of Froth, a point made by Miles, *The Problem of 'Measure for Measure'*, p. 272. When Escalus agrees to Pompey's false syllogism that concludes this reversal of roles—if Froth's face is the worst thing about him, then he could not harm the constable's wife—we might doubt Escalus's sufficiency as a judge.

42. In the sense that "virtú" in the Renaissance, especially after Machiavelli, implied a power gained from the ability to manipulate people and circumstances to the practical good of the state, rather than a simply good=virtuous ruler such as Angelo thought he was at the play's opening.

Chapter 3

1. See Kenneth Muir, ed., Arden edition, *Macbeth* (London: Methuen & Co., 1951), pp. xiv–xv, xxvi–xxvii.

2. Muir, Arden edition, discusses J. Dover Wilson's 1947 editorial suggestions on pp. xxii–xxiii as well as on pp. xii–xiii.

3. Thomas De Quincey, "On the Knocking at the Gate in *Macbeth*," *The London Magazine* (October 1823), reprinted in *The Collected Writings of Thomas De Quincey*, ed. David Masson (Edinburgh: Adam and Charles

Black, 1890), vol. 10. Also see Jay L. Halio, ed., *Approaches to Macbeth* (Belmont, Ca.: Wadsworth Publishing Co., 1966).

4. See Muir, Arden edition, *Macbeth,* p. xxx, for Father Garnet, and pp. xvii–xxi for a discussion of interconnections between his trial and the play.

5. Muir notes, p. xxi, that "we cannot assume that the Porter's allusion refers to any particular year," and, for purposes of dating the play, I would agree. Perennially thwarted expectations in agriculture, however, make my point. See Edward A. Armstrong, *Shakespeare's Imagination* (Lincoln: University of Nebraska Press, 1963), p. 135, on "Mr. Farmer" as an alias for Garnet.

6. See John B. Harcourt, "I Pray You Remember the Porter," *Shakespeare Quarterly* 12 (1961): 398.

7. Hilda Hulme, *Explorations in Shakespeare's Language,* pp. 99–102. E. A. M. Colman, *The Dramatic Use of Bawdy in Shakespeare,* p. 217, finds this value for the word unlikely, however, because of the lack of non-Shakespearean parallels.

8. On "goose," see Armstrong, *Shakespeare's Imagination,* pp. 57–65, 201–2. That syphilitic pox, the result of lechery, is a national characteristic of the French is a favorite English slur that Shakespeare often employs.

9. On Shakespeare's use of proverbs, see especially F. P. Wilson, *Shakespearian and Other Studies,* ed. Helen Gardner (Oxford: Oxford University Press, 1969), chapter 5, "The Proverbial Wisdom of Shakespeare," pp. 143–75.

10. *Julius Caesar,* III.i.265–69.

11. A. P. Paton's observation appears in the New Variorum *Macbeth,* ed. Horace Howard Furness, Jr. (Philadelphia: J. B. Lippincott Co., 1903), p. 88, n. 9; and Marvin Rosenberg, *The Masks of Macbeth* (Berkeley: University of California Press, 1978), p. 244.

12. *The Merchant of Venice,* II.ix.22–29.

13. Joan Ozark Holmer, "Loving Wisely and the Casket Test: Symbolic and Structural Unity in *The Merchant of Venice,*" *Shakespeare Studies* 11 (1978); 54–57, compares Shakespeare's changes from his sources in the silver casket's motto.

14. The "martlet" or "marlet" in Shakespeare's usage was apparently the same as the "house-martin," whose nesting habits are the subject of Shakespeare's interest in both passages. Caroline F. E. Spurgeon, *Shakespeare's Imagery and What It Tells Us* (Cambridge, Eng.: Cambridge University Press, 1952; first edition, 1935), pp. 188–89, points out that the

name "martin" had the slang value of "dupe" in the sixteenth and seventeenth centuries, and this potential pun may be operative in both plays since the guest is about to be deceived. Peter M. Daly, "Of Macbeth, Martlets and other 'Fowles of Heauen'," *Mosaic* 12 (1978): 25, objects both to the equation of martin and martlet and to the transference of the sense of martlet in *The Merchant of Venice* to *Macbeth*. See also Jay Halio, "Bird Imagery in *Macbeth*," *Shakespeare Newsletter* 13 (1963): 7.

15. *As You Like It*, III.ii.185–86. See Leo Salingar, *Shakespeare and the Traditions of Comedy*, pp. 297–98, for his discussion of Rosalind's disguise, especially his comment that "in the background action of the play, 'feigning' corrupts a humane society; Rosalind's 'counterfeiting' restores it."

16. Phyllis Gorfain, "Riddles and Tragic Structure in *Macbeth*," *Mississippi Folklore Register* 10 (1976): 201, makes a similar observation: "She then uses disguise to serve deception through lies rather than to serve discovery through indirection; . . . Their conspiracy travesties all those forms of re-creation which comedic riddlers release when they expand the scope of language and love through imagination."

17. Cleanth Brooks, *The Well Wrought Urn* (New York: Harcourt, Brace & World, 1947), p. 35.

18. In training a horse to use the unnatural gait of "the amble," two legs on one side are "trammeled" so that he will not follow his natural alternating movement. The idea of containment is clear, but the punning context has several possibilities, for which see Hulme, *Explorations in Shakespeare's Language*, pp. 21–22.

19. Frank Kermode, ed., *Macbeth, The Riverside Shakespeare*, gen. ed. G. Blakemore Evans (Boston: Houghton Mifflin Company, 1974), p. 1320, n. 35–36.

20. *Othello*, III.iv.11–13.

21. See M. M. Mahood, *Shakespeare's Wordplay*, p. 39; Armstrong, *Shakespeare's Imagination*, pp. 201–2; and Harcourt, "I Pray You Remember the Porter," pp. 393–402.

22. Allan Park Paton, *Notes and Queries* (11 Sept. 13, Nov. 1869), opened the debate over whether Macbeth himself was meant to be the Third Murderer. See the Revised New Variorum edition, Horace Howard Furness, Jr., ed. (Philadelphia & London: J. B. Lippincott Co., 1915), pp. 200–3, for a summary of the debate over Paton's suggestion by earlier critics. F. A. Libby countered with the theory that Ross is the third murderer (see p. 24, n. 53). Muir, Arden edition, p. 90, discounts these theories as "fantastic": "Macbeth's agitation in III.iv. when he hears that

Fleance has escaped is proof that he cannot have been present at the murder of Banquo."

23. Other examples of role-shifting are Launcelot Gobbo with his Father in *The Merchant of Venice,* II.ii, and Feste's alternation between Sir Topas and Feste for Malvolio's benefit in *Twelfth Night,* IV.ii.

24. I have quoted the Holinshed edition of 1587 from the Appendix to the Revised New Variorum edition, *Macbeth,* pp. 390–92.

25. Paul Jorgensen, *Our Naked Frailties: Sensational Art and Meaning in "Macbeth"* (Berkeley: University of California Press, 1971), p. 106.

26. Wilbur Sanders, *The Dramatist and the Received Idea* (London: Cambridge University Press, 1968), pp. 258–62.

27. It does not matter if James I was in the audience or not. The description of King Edward's practice in curing his subjects fits perfectly with the rest of the scene's design.

28. *Antony and Cleopatra,* II.v.31–33. Muir notes this echo in the Arden edition of *Macbeth,* p. 137, and quotes Hardin Craig's citation of Heywood, "Faire Maid of the West": "Why well . . . He's well in heaven, for mistresse, he is dead." See also *Romeo and Juliet,* V.i.16–17.

29. Jorgensen, *Our Naked Frailties,* pp. 215–16, calls it a condign punishment that shrinks Macbeth's ability to feel when he is the "tragic hero whose life as we see it has been the most persistently and intensely one of sensation."

Chapter 4

1. G. Wilson Knight, *Principles of Shakesperian Production* (New York: Macmillan, 1937), p. 56, remarks of a then recent production that "the Apothecary scene was given hurriedly as nothing more than a necessary action link." Several productions I have seen treated the scene perfunctorily. When the scene comes in for special recognition, it often appears more bizarre than Shakespeare could have meant it to seem. For example, in Thad Taylor's production, West Hollywood, Ca., 1977, the Apothecary appeared in a nightgown and nightcap, the inner curtain having been drawn on him counting his coins. His extraordinarily thin appearance was appropriate for Romeo's descriptions, but the scrawny legs beneath the short nightgown evoked laughter.

2. John Russell Brown, *Shakespeare's Plays in Performance* (London: Edward Arnold Publishers, 1966; reprt. Baltimore, Md.: Penguin Books, 1969), pp. 172, 174.

3. Knight, *Principles,* p. 122.

4. Brown, *Shakespeare's Plays in Performance,* pp. 188–89.

5. Clifford Leech, "The Moral Tragedy of *Romeo and Juliet,*" in *English Renaissance Drama,* eds. Standish Henning et al. (Carbondale: Southern Illinois University Press, 1976), p. 67.

6. Julius Cserwinka, "Die Apothekerscene in 'Romeo und Julia,'" *Shakespeare-Jahrbuch* 37 (1901): 165–75; and Ralph Waterbury Condee, "The Apothecary's Holiday," *Shakespeare Quarterly* 3 (1952): 282.

7. See G. K. Hunter, "Were There Act-Pauses on Shakespeare's Stage?" in *English Renaissance Drama,* eds. Standish Henning et al., pp. 15–35; and Bernard Beckerman, "Shakespeare and the Life of the Scene," in *English Renaissance Drama,* pp. 36–45. Emrys Jones, *Scenic Form in Shakespeare* (Oxford: Clarendon Press, 1971), argues convincingly for continuous performance: see esp. chapter 3, "The Two-Part Structure."

8. Representations of Despair appear in emblem books and other pictorial art, such as in Cesare Ripa, *Iconologia; or, Moral Emblems,* ed. Peirce Tempest (London: Benj. Motte, 1709), p. 2, fig. 5; Geffrey Whitney, *A Choice of Emblemes and Other Devises* (Leyden, 1586), facsimile reprint (Amsterdam and New York: De Capo Press, 1969), p. 30; Giotto's fresco in the Scrovegni Chapel in Padua; the "Temptation to Despair," from *Ars moriendi,* 4th ed. (Augsburg, 1465), p. 7 [reproduced in John Doebler, *Shakespeare's Speaking Pictures: Studies in Iconic Imagery* (Albuquerque: University of New Mexico Press, 1974), between pp. 82–83]. See also Susan Snyder, "The Left Hand of God: Despair in Medieval and Renaissance Tradition," in *Studies in the Renaissance* 12 (New York: The Renaissance Society of America, 1965): 18–59. *The Works of Edmund Spenser,* a variorum edition, eds. Edwin Greenlaw, Charles G. Osgood, and Frederick Morgan Padelford (Baltimore: The Johns Hopkins Press, 1932), vol. 1, pp. 268–81, describes other episodes in earlier and in contemporary literature and art that resemble Spenser's despair.

9. J. C. Smith, ed., *Spenser's Faerie Queene,* vol. 1 (Oxford: Clarendon Press, 1909), Bk. I, canto ix, stanzas xxi–liv [pp. 113–21]. I have used this text for all quotations from Spenser.

10. See Katherine Koller, "Art, Rhetoric, and Holy Dying in the *Faerie Queene* with Special Reference to the Despair Canto," *Studies in Philology* 61 (1964): 128–39.

11. Harry R. Hoppe, *The Bad Quarto of "Romeo and Juliet"* (Ithaca, N.Y.: Cornell University Press, 1948), p. 87. Richard Hosley, ed., *The Tragedy of Romeo and Juliet* (New Haven: Yale University Press, 1954), p. 79, notes that in the modern theater the Friar usually performs the

action, but most texts include the Q1 stage direction. Hosley also warns, p. 164, that "while most of them [Q1 stage directions] probably indicate the action and stage business of Shakespeare's company, some of them may have originated with another group of players." Brian Gibbons, ed., Arden edition, *Romeo and Juliet* (London: Methuen & Co., 1980), p. 180, n. 107, explains his omission of the stage direction: "There is nothing in the dialogue (or the characterization of the Nurse generally) to prepare for or to support this intervention by the Nurse." I disagree.

12. *The Taming of the Shrew*, IV.v.1–22.

13. M. Andreas Laurentius, *A Discourse of the Preservation of the Sight: of Melancholike Diseases; of Rheumes, and of Old Age*, trans. Richard Surphlet, 1599, Shakespeare Association Facsimiles, No. 15 (London: Oxford University Press, 1938), p. 64. Franklin M. Dickey, *Not Wisely But Too Well* (San Marino, Ca.: The Huntington Library, 1957), p. 29, points out another possibility of association, although not specifically with this scene in mind: Francis Bacon (as did Ficino, Burton, and others) affirmed the commonplace opinion that *"Much Use* of *Venus* doth *Dimme* the *Sight"* because of "the Expence of Spirits": *Sylva Sylvarum* (London, 1628), sec. 693.

14. Cf. Lawrence Babb, *The Elizabethan Malady: A Study of Melancholia in English Literature from 1580 to 1642* (East Lansing: Michigan State College Press, 1951), p. 103.

15. The approach to the Cave of Despair in *The Faerie Queene* emphasizes the charnel-house appearance of the place: "Darke, dolefull, drearie, like a greedie graue,/ That still for carrion carcases doth craue." The "carcases" of many desperate "wretches" who have hanged themselves lie "scattered on the greene,/ And throwne about the cliffs" (Bk. I, canto ix, stanzas xxiii–xxiv). Juliet envisions the "bones/ Of all my buried ancestors" as well as the sight of Tybalt's "festering" corpse being there to frighten her if she wakes before Romeo comes. She anticipates the "loathsome smells" and "shrieking" night spirits that may drive her mad. In *The Faerie Queene*, "the ghastly Owle" shrieks "his baleful note" and "all about it wandering ghosts did waile and howle."

16. See discussions of this staging and editorial problem in George W. Williams's critical edition of *The Most Excellent and Lamentable Tragedie of Romeo and Juliet* (Durham, N.C.: Duke University Press, 1964), pp. 147–48; Richard Hosley, "The Use of the Upper Stage in *Romeo and Juliet*," *Shakespeare Quarterly* 5 (1954): 377–78; and H. Granville-Barker, *Prefaces to Shakespeare* (Princeton, N.J.: Princeton University Press, 1947), vol. 2, pp. 318–19.

17. S. L. Bethell, *Shakespeare and the Popular Dramatic Tradition* (London: P. S. King and Staples, 1944), pp. 110–12.

18. Peter J. Seng, *The Vocal Songs in the Plays of Shakespeare* (Cambridge, Mass.: Harvard University Press, 1967), pp. 69, 225. John H. Long, *Shakespeare's Use of Music: The Histories and Tragedies* (Gainesville: University of Florida Press, 1971), pp. 45–48, has a useful summary of the critical positions about this section of the scene. Long agrees with F. W. Sternfeld that "this can only be an artificial woe for a feigned death. . . . I believe that the musicians continue to play offstage through the clamorous lamenting until Friar Lawrence ends the burlesque." Edward Dowden, ed., Arden edition, *The Tragedy of Romeo and Juliet* (London: Methuen Press, 1900; reprt. 1935), p. 152, n. 49, quotes Grant White's suggestion that the artificial rhetoric of all the mourners was meant to parody a recently published (1581) translation of Seneca's *Tragedies*. See also Charles B. Lower, "*Romeo and Juliet,* IV.v: A Stage Direction and Purposeful Comedy," *Shakespeare Studies* 8 (1975): 177–94; and Susan Snyder, *The Comic Matrix of Shakespeare's Tragedies* (Princeton, N.J.: Princeton University Press, 1979), pp. 68–69.

19. See Thomas P. Harrison, "*Romeo and Juliet, A Midsummer Night's Dream:* Companion Plays," *Texas Studies in Literature and Language* 13 (1971): 209–13.

20. As Bethell points out, *Shakespeare and the Popular Dramatic Tradition,* pp. 111–12, Capulet's description—"Death lies on her like an untimely frost/ Upon the sweetest flower of all the field" (IV.iv.28–29)—might easily have come from Romeo's speech in the tomb. Compare: "Death, that hath sucked the honey of thy breath,/ Hath had no power yet upon thy beauty" (V.iii.92–93). For further discussion of preparative parody, see chapter 7, on Polonius, and chapter 1. Josephine Waters Bennett makes a similar point in "New Techniques of Comedy in *All's Well That Ends Well,*" *Shakespeare Quarterly* 17 (1967): 348. Nicholas Brooke, *Shakespeare's Early Tragedies* (London: Methuen & Co., 1968), p. 96, comments that Mercutio's bawdy wit that preceeds the garden scene "is a case of the parody coming *before* the thing parodied."

21. Robert O. Evans's chapter "Oxymoron as Key to Structure," in *The Osier Cage: Rhetorical Devices in "Romeo and Juliet"* (Lexington, Ky.: University of Kentucky Press, 1966), pp. 18–24, does not discuss the oxymorons in the lamentation passage, but I agree that, even though the term *oxymoron* "does not appear in the English rhetoric books of the time," it "dominates the rhetoric of the play" and is "an important clue to theme and structure of the play" (p. 40).

22. *Twelfth Night,* I.v.52–69.

23. James C. Bryant, "The Problematic Friar in *Romeo and Juliet,*" *English Studies* 55 (1974): 340–50, cites this action to support his view that the Friar "adopts a Machiavellian policy to employ wrong means to engender a good end." Bryant sees the "disparity between the cleric's holy commitment and his actual behavior in the drama" to be "problematic," possibly a subtle reflection of Shakespeare's anti-Catholic views. Rosalind Miles, *The Problem of 'Measure for Measure',* pp. 167–78, discusses the "friar disguise" on the Renaissance stage as having roots in the "folk memory of comic and contemptible friars."

24. John Parkinson, *Paradisi in Sole Paradisus Terrestris* (London: printed by Humfrey Lownes and Robert Young, 1629), p. 426. I have modernized the "u," "v," and "s" in this and in the following quotation.

25. John Parkinson, *Theatrum Botanicum, The Theater of Plantes* (London: printed by Tho: Cotes, 1640), p. 76.

26. Peter [Pierre] de la Primaudaye, *The Third Volume of the French Academie,* trans. Richard Dolman (London: George Bishop, 1601), p. 344. *The French Academie* was first published in French in 1577, and was translated by Thomas Bowes for its London publication in 1586. See Madalene Shindler, *The Vogue and Impact of Pierre de la Primaudaye's "The French Academie" on Elizabethan and Jacobean Literature,* Ph.D. dissertation, The University of Texas, 1960.

27. *Hamlet,* IV.v.174. Bridget Gellert Lyons, *Voices of Melancholy, Studies in Literary Treatments of Melancholy in Renaissance England* (London: Routledge & Kegan Paul, 1971), p. 111, says that many of Ophelia's flowers, "rosemary, rue, fennel and violets, aside from the meanings that are usually assigned to them, were associated with melancholy cures," and she cites La Primaudaye as one authority.

28. *Hamlet,* V.i.232–33. Philip Williams, "The Rosemary Theme in *Romeo and Juliet,*" *Modern Language Notes* 68 (1953): 400–3.

29. Richard Levin, " 'Littera Canina' in 'Romeo and Juliet' and 'Michaelmas Term'," *Notes & Queries* 207 (1962): 333–34, suggests that the Nurse breaks off in her association, "R is for the—" because it sounds to her like "ar," the first letters of "arse."

30. Laurentius, *A Discourse of the Preservation of Sight,* etc.: "The Second Discourse," p. 197.

31. Timothy Bright, *A Treatise of Melancholie (1586),* facsimile reprint (Amsterdam: De Capo Press, 1969), p. 247.

32. F. W. Sternfeld, *Music in Shakespearean Tragedy* (London: Routledge & Kegan Paul, 1963), p. 102. In other words, what Peter requests to

comfort him is an oxymoron, a song that is like Quince's play, both "merry and tragical" (*A Midsummer Night's Dream*, V.i.58).

33. Kenneth Muir informs me that in the many productions of *Romeo and Juliet* that he has seen, none omitted the segment with Peter and the Musicians. On the other hand, I have never seen a production that did not omit at least part of the scene. Cedric Messina's BBC/PBS production of the 1977 season included the first part but omitted the banter with the Musicians, leaving a heavily melancholy effect, with Peter in tears.

34. See Richard Hosley, "A Stage Direction in *Romeo and Juliet*," *The Times Literary Supplement*, June 13, 1952, p. 391, and his further comment in his Yale edition of the play, p. 153, n. 123 S.D.

35. See Eric Partridge, *Shakespeare's Bawdy*, pp. 84–85. He supports his gloss of "case=pudend . . . because it sheathes a sword" with citations from *Merry Wives*, IV.i.49–54 and *All's Well*, I.ii.21–23. Sternfeld, *Music in Shakespearean Tragedy*, p. 101, calls it a feeble pun. Barry Gaines suggested to me that there may also be a pun on the sense of "case" as "disguise," in that Juliet is now disguised as dead.

36. See glossary in Partridge, *Shakespeare's Bawdy*, and in E. A. M. Colman, *The Dramatic Use of Bawdy in Shakespeare*.

37. Colman, *The Dramatic Use of Bawdy*, p. 73.

38. Vincentio Saviolo, *His Practise, in two bookes* (London: John Wolfe, 1595); facsimile reprint in *Three Elizabethan Fencing Manuals*, ed. James L. Jackson (Delmar, N.Y.: Scholars' Facsimile and Reprints, 1972). In the Furness Variorum of *As You Like It*, see the lengthy note on pp. 274–76 that discusses this manual as source for Touchstone's "seven kinds of lies" speech. Egerton Castle, *Schools and Masters of Fence* (London: George Bell & Sons, 1892), pp. 127–28, quotes Mercutio as an example of the Elizabethan's awareness of rules of fence and the controversy between George Silver and foreign masters over styles of fence.

39. S. P. Zitner, "Hamlet, Duellist," *University of Toronto Quarterly* 39 (1969): 4–5.

40. Castle, *Schools and Masters of Fence*, p. 123. See also A. L. Soens, "Cudgels and Rapiers: The Staging of the Edgar-Oswald Fight in Lear," *Shakespeare Studies* 5 ([1969] 1970): 149–58, esp. p. 153 and notes. Zitner, "Hamlet, Duellist," p. 3, notes that William Bas issued a book actually entitled "Sword and Buckler, or Serving Mans Defence."

41. The title of Saviolo's second book in *His Practise* is "Of Honor and Honorable Quarrels." According to Jackson, *Three Elizabethan Fencing Manuals*, p. vi, the second book is for the most part "an adaptation of the authoritative Italian book on the duello, Girolamo Muzio's *Il Duello*,

Venice 1551." See also Ruth Kelso, "Saviolo and His *Practise*," *Modern Language Notes* 39 (1924): 33–35.

42. Hoppe, *The Bad Quarto*, p. 153, notes the similarity of Peter's response to the Nurse as having much in common with the dialogue between Sampson and Gregory that opens I.i. He further suggests that the actor of Peter might also have taken the part of Sampson or of Gregory, and, if that is so, "the indecent reference to *tool* in Q1, II.iv echoes a bit of gag by this actor for the entertainment of the groundlings." In Q2 and in my quotation, *tool* changes to *weapon*.

43. Saviolo, *His Practise*, p. 381.

44. James Black, "The Visual Artistry of *Romeo and Juliet*," *Studies in English Literature* 15 (1975): 245–56, discusses several sets of scenes that reduplicate the "stage picture" with the effect of intensifying by parallel the "progressively tragic . . . pageant of death." Black does not discuss these particular scenes, but his general thesis applies here.

45. See Sternfeld, *Music in Shakespearean Tragedy*, Appendix I, pp. 119–22, for his discussion of the song's attribution to Richard Edwards (and transcriptions of the music) and his argument that Peter probably sings it acappella.

46. See important discussions of these ideas in Lawrence J. Ross, "Shakespeare's 'Dull Clown' and Symbolic Music," *Shakespeare Quarterly* 17 (1966): 107–28; S. K. Heninger, Jr., *Touches of Sweet Harmony: Pythagorean Cosmology and Renaissance Poetics* (San Marino, Ca.: The Huntington Library, 1974); and Sternfeld's remarks on "Pan's Pipes versus Apollo's Strings," *Music in Shakespearean Tragedy*, pp. 226–33.

47. Sternfeld notes the resemblance, *Music in Shakespearean Tragedy*, p. 101, n. 1, as does Harry Levin, "Form and Formality in *Romeo and Juliet*," *Shakespeare Quarterly* 11 (1960): 11.

48. Both Levin, "Form and Formality," p. 11, and Vincent F. Petronella, "The Musicians' Scene in 'Romeo and Juliet'," *Humanities Association Bulletin* 23 (1972): 55, make similar points.

49. William Hugh Jansen, "Riddles: 'Do-It-Yourself Oracles'," *American Folklore*, ed. Tristram Coffin, III (Washington, D.C.: Voice of America Forum Lectures, March 1968), pp. 231–32, defines the riddle as "a question, direct or indirect, complete or incomplete, in traditional form whereby the questioner challenges a listener to recognize and identify the accuracy, the unity, the truth, in a statement that usually seems implausible, or self-contradictory, but that is in its own peculiar light always true. . . . Many cultures or mythologies have considered divine both the power to deceive and, naturally, the power to recognize and

frustrate deceit. . . . To man's awe for this limited wisdom must be attributed the trickster gods in many of the world's mythologies." Jansen also notes that "in certain cultures . . . riddling has now or has had in the past various religious connotations as an appropriate activity during the harvest, or *funerals,* or other rituals" (p. 235; my italics). That Peter is playing the trickster with the Musicians seems clear enough, and his riddling answer that "musicians have no gold for sounding" may have a thematic connection to Romeo's moral chastisement of the Apothecary in the next scene.

50. That Peter has an overbearing attitude might be inferred from the servant who tells Capulet, in the earlier part of the scene, that he has a head to find logs without asking Peter.

51. Hunter, "Were There Act-Pauses on Shakespeare's Stage?", pp. 29–31. Granville-Barker, *Prefaces to Shakespeare,* vol. 2, pp. 326–27. Hunter's argument assumes "that the function of the act-pause may be compared with the function of pause in musical performance. . . . Its existence allows the skillful performers to play the formal structure against the informally expressive material" (p. 35).

52. Marjorie B. Garber, *Dream in Shakespeare: From Metaphor to Metamorphosis* (New Haven: Yale University Press, 1974), pp. 45–47, may go too far with "the transposition of Romeo's dream thoughts from the literal to the metaphorical plane, from the predictive almost to the mythic," but her analysis of dream-lore background and its relationship to this passage is worthwhile.

53. Michael Goldman, *Shakespeare and the Energies of Drama* (Princeton, N.J.: Princeton University Press, 1972), p. 37.

54. Contrast Ross's report to Macduff about his wife and children in *Macbeth,* IV.ii.177 (discussed above, chapter 3). In that case, Macduff hears Ross's words that his wife is "well" literally.

55. See my comments earlier in this chapter on how the audience is persuaded to approve of disguised emotions and role-playing where at first it laughed at them.

56. Arthur Brooke, *Romeus and Iuliet,* ed. P. A. Daniels, The New Shakespeare Society, Ser. III, No. 1 (London: N. Trübner & Co., 1875). These are lines 2561–68, p. 77.

57. *The Faerie Queene,* I.ix.35–36.

58. See Snyder, "The Left Hand of God," pp. 18–59. Two studies that compare Shakespeare's and Spenser's use of similar material do not consider this scene: W. B. C. Watkins, *Shakespeare and Spenser* (Princeton, N.J.: Princeton University Press, 1950); and Abbie Findlay Potts, *Shake-*

speare & "The Faerie Queene" (Ithaca, N.Y.: Cornell University Press, 1958). Potts, for instance, says, p. 9, that there is a "complete absence of analogies with *The Faerie Queene* in . . . *Romeo and Juliet.*"

59. Robert Burton, *Anatomy of Melancholy,* ed. A. R. Shilleto (London: George Bell and Sons, 1896), 3 vols. Quotation is from Part 3, Section 4, Member 2, Subsection 3, p. 453.

60. Laurentius, *A Discourse of the Preservation of Sight,* etc., "The Second Discourse," p. 82.

61. Bright, *A Treatise of Melancholie,* p. 123. I have regularized spelling by the addition of "n"s.

62. Raymond Klibansky, Erwin Panofsky, and Fritz Saxl, *Saturn and Melancholy: Studies in the History of Natural Philosophy, Religion and Art* (London: Thomas Nelson & Sons, 1964), p. 284.

63. Plates 1 and 2 (Cesare Ripa's "Melancholia" and Henry Peacham's "Melancholia").

64. Plates 3 and 4 (Geffrey Whitney's emblems "In auaros" and "Saepius in auro bibitur venenum").

65. Rosemary Freeman, *English Emblem Books* (London: Chatto & Windus, 1948), p. 63, n. 3, points out that although it is likely Shakespeare knew Whitney, "to maintain that there was necessarily always direct influence is to make peculiar to the emblem writers themes and images which were the common property of the age." Lawrence J. Ross, "Art and the Study of Early English Drama," *Renaissance Drama: A Report on Research Opportunities* 6 (1963): 40, cites Freeman, and adds: "the common property of the age is what we need to repossess. . . . How a dramatist came by his material generally is very unsafe to assert and not always necessarily important to inquire. What is essential is that we become aware of a rich hoard of potentially dramatic 'vocabulary' available to the Renaissance English playwright—a 'vocabulary' to which visual and related traditions can provide a key." Robert J. Clements, *Picta Poesis* (Rome, 1960), p. 182, comments that "since both the emblematists and their creative contemporaries were borrowing from the same antique sources, it becomes more difficult to establish when these two categories of Renaissance writers were borrowing from one another." See also Dieter Mehl's essay, "Emblems in English Renaissance Drama," *Renaissance Drama,* ed. S. Schoenbaum, New Series II (1969), pp. 39–57.

66. *The Works of Geoffrey Chaucer,* ed. F. N. Robinson, 2nd edition (Boston: Houghton Mifflin Company, 1957), p. 153.

67. Klibansky, Panofsky, and Saxl, *Saturn and Melancholy,* pp. 10–11.

See also Babb's note on "the melancholic character of old age," *The Elizabethan Malady*, p. 11.

68. John Reibetanz, "Theatrical Emblems in *King Lear*," in *Some Facets of King Lear: Essays in Prismatic Criticism*, eds. Rosalie L. Colie and F. T. Flahiff (Toronto: University of Toronto Press, 1974), p. 49, observes: "A series of incidents, all involving Edgar, counterpoints abstract statements with theatrical tableau that negate rather than fulfil the statements: in each case, the emblem contradicts its motto." Reibetanz argues that this technique of "pitting an emblem against its motto" is the result of adopting a "private-theatre convention," p. 50. My analysis of this scene in *Romeo and Juliet* indicates that the technique developed earlier. Reibetanz incorporates this argument into his later book, *The "Lear" World: A study of "King Lear" in its dramatic context* (Toronto: University of Toronto Press, 1977), pp. 112ff. On p. 114 of that book, he comments that "none of the other tragedies tantalizes us with even the possibility of hope," and by omitting it he makes clear that he does not consider *Romeo and Juliet* to be in this category.

69. Williams, "The Rosemary Theme," p. 401, disagrees with Thomas P. Harrison's identification of the Friar's flower as "aconite" in "Hange Up Philosophy," *Shakespeare Association Bulletin* 22 (1947), 203–9, because Williams prefers to see the flower's ambiguous properties suited to rosemary. Henry N. Ellacombe, *The Plant-Lore and Garden-Craft of Shakespeare* (London: Edward Arnold, 1896), p. 1, identifies Romeo's description of the kind of poison he wishes to purchase (V.i. 64–65) as "aconite" (Ellacombe uses John Parkinson—Apothecary of London in the early seventeenth century—as his major source).

70. Raymond Chapman, "Double Time in *Romeo and Juliet*," *Modern Language Review* 44 (1949): 374, commenting on the elongation of the time Romeo has spent in Mantua, says that "the suggestions of a more prolonged action modify the breathless pace of events and make them more credible."

71. The Q2 stage direction, "Enter Romeo and Peter," has raised a question as to whether the actor, Will Kemp, who plays Peter earlier in the play, is now doubling as Balthasar. If so, he certainly was a busy actor, since he is also thought to have doubled as the illiterate Capulet servant in I.ii.34–83. The Q1 stage direction reads "Enter Romeo and Balthasar." To explain this discrepancy, George Williams suggests that it "is another indication of Shakespeare's indifference to the names of the minor characters in the retinues of the feuding families," p. 149. I am inclined to think that Shakespeare was at this point following Arthur

Brooke's poem closely, and simply transferred the name of Romeo's servant, there named Peter, without thought for the other Peter who served the Capulet household.

72. Zeffirelli seems determined to simplify the emotional value of the play's conflicting pulls when he omits Paris at the tomb in his 1968 film. It is perhaps worth nothing that Arthur Brooke has no Paris at the tomb in his poem.

73. Thomas Walkington, *The Optick Glasse of Humors* (London: Imprinted by John Windet for Martin Clerke, 1607), p. 64 (chapter 7).

74. See Mahood, *Shakespeare's Wordplay,* p. 72, for comments on the puns "true" and "quick." For symbolic associations of the pilot metaphor, see Lawrence J. Ross, ed., *The Tragedy of Othello the Moor of Venice* (Indianapolis: Bobbs-Merrill Company, Inc., 1974), p. xvii, and illustration, p. xi; and Douglas L. Peterson, *"Romeo and Juliet* and the Art of Moral Navigation," in *Pacific Coast Studies in Shakespeare,* eds. Thelma Greenfield and Waldo F. McNeir (Eugene, Oregon: University of Oregon, 1966), pp. 33–46.

75. Both Clifford Leech, *Shakespeare's Tragic Fiction,* Annual Shakespeare Lecture of the British Academy 1973, vol. 59 (London: Oxford University Press, 1973), p. 7, and Jill L. Levenson, "The Fox and the Fable: Shakespeare's Treatment of Legend in *Romeo and Juliet,"* in a paper delivered before the Shakespeare Association of America meeting in April 1977, have commented on the ironic juxtaposition of Romeo's harsh remarks about gold in V.i and the families' proposed acts of repentance in erecting the two golden statues. Arthur Brooke, in his poem, says that the monuments were to be made of marble.

Chapter 5

1. E. K. Chambers, ed., *King Richard the Second,* Falcon Series, 1891, quoted in the New Variorum edition, *The Life and Death of King Richard the Second,* ed. Matthew W. Black (Philadelphia: J. B. Lippincott Company, 1955), pp. 294–95: "As they stand, these scenes approach the verge of the grotesque: they would have passed it, had the Duchess' zeal for Aumerle lacked the excuse of motherhood. . . . In the latter part of it [V.ii] we cannot but see and acknowledge again the dramatic immaturity of the poet. . . . Style and metre are rough, loose, and weak: the dotage of York becomes lunacy." On V.iii, the New Variorum, p. 308, n. 1, quotes Henry Hallam (*Introduction to the Literature of Europe,* 1873): "The scene is ill conceived and worse executed throughout"; and Henry Irv-

ing (ed., *Works,* 1888), p. 316, n. 79ff.: "I believe that the whole of the latter part of this scene is taken, almost entirely, from some old play, and contains scarcely a line written by Shakespeare; or, if his, it must be some of his very earliest work." John Russell Brown, *Shakespeare's Plays in Performance* (New York: St. Martin's Press, 1967), p. 127, notes that "almost invariably the scenes are cut from modern productions."

2. See Waldo F. McNeir, "The Comic Scenes in *Richard II,*" *Neuphilologische Mitteilungen* 73 (1972): 815–22. McNeir summarizes the few recognitions of this scene's humor by the critics on p. 816. See also Robert Ornstein, *A Kingdom for A Stage* (Cambridge, Mass.: Harvard University Press, 1972), pp. 122–24, who finds the "tone . . . uncertain"; and Michael F. Kelly, "The Function of York in *Richard II,*" *Southern Humanities Review* 6 (1972): 257–67.

3. [Edward] *Hall's Chronicle . . .* collated with the editions of 1548 and 1550 (London: G. Woodfall, Printer, 1809), pp. 17–18.

4. Raphael Holinshed, *The Chronicles of England,* 2nd edition, 1587, vol. 3: quoted from the New Variorum edition, *The Life and Death of King Richard the Second,* p. 441. [Extracts from Holinshed note variants between the 1577 and 1587 editions.]

5. See, for example, M. P. Taylor, "A Father Pleads for the Death of His Son," *The International Journal of Psycho-Analysis* 8 (1927): 53–55.

6. Samuel Daniel, *The Civil Wars,* ed. Laurence Michel (New Haven: Yale University Press, 1958), p. 117.

7. Compare the description in the anonymous play *Woodstock: A Moral History,* ed. A. P. Rossiter (London: Chatto and Windus, 1946), p. 153 (V.i.91–95), spoken by Edward III's Ghost about Richard II's destruction of his kingdom:

> [Richard] racks my subjects
> That spent their lives with me in conquering France,
> Beheld me ride in state through London streets
> And at my stirrup lowly footing by
> Four captive kings to grace my victory.

Rossiter thinks that *Woodstock* is a probable source for Shakespeare's play, and both Daniel's and Shakespeare's descriptions treat Henry's leading of Richard II into London as a "triumph" over what is usually a foreign king.

8. Matthew W. Black, ed., the New Variorum edition, *The Life and Death of King Richard the Second,* has compiled some useful sources: the two mentioned here are on p. 465 and pp. 469–70.

9. To pair the beggar and the king is a commonplace with proverb writers, for which see Morris Palmer Tilley, *A Dictionary of Proverbs in England in the Sixteenth and Seventeenth Centuries* (Ann Arbor: University of Michigan Press, 1950), p. 39, B 232: "Every *Beggar* is descended from some king and every king is descended from some beggar"; p. 356, K 67: "A King or a beggar"; and with a more specialized reference, p. 358, K 93: "King Harry [Henry VIII] robbed the church and died a beggar." Linking the two opposed roles often accompanies mention of the leveling operation of Fortune in men's lives. An early combination of the pairing, with the simile of Fortune as playwright, according to Leo Salingar, *Shakespeare and the Traditions of Comedy*, p. 144, appears in a third-century B.C. sermon by the preacher Teles, explaining Cynic moral doctrine:

> Fortune is like a playwright, who designs a number of parts— the shipwrecked man, the poor man, the exile, the king, the beggar. What the good man has to do is to play well any part with which Fortune may invest him.

In *King John,* the Bastard's soliloquy at the end of Act II compiles a list of opposites to suggest that no one is safe from "that daily break-vow, he that wins of all,/ Of kings, of beggars, of old men, young men, maids. . . . " The coincidence of just such a listing of roles with the moral doctrine of Cynic and Stoic philosophers and their use of the "world is a stage" metaphor appears again in James Sanford's 1567 translation of Epictetus' *Encyridion,* Facsimile Reprint of *The Manuell of Epictetus* (Amsterdam: Theatrum Orbis Terrarum, 1977), chapter 22:

> Thou must remember that thou arte one of the players in an enterlude, and must plaie a parte, which the authour thereof shall appoint, thou must play be it lo[n]g, be it shorte. If he appoint thee to play the beggar, a Creple, a Prince, or the private person, do it well and wittilie, for it lieth in thee to play that part, wherunto thou art appointed, and in an other to choose and appoint thee.

10. See Anne Righter, *Shakespeare and the Idea of the Play* (London: Chatto & Windus, 1962), pp. 113–28; James Winny, *The Player King: A Theme in Shakespeare's Histories* (London: Chatto & Windus, 1968); Thomas F. Van Laan, *Role-playing in Shakespeare* (Toronto: University of Toronto Press, 1978); and Eileen Jorge Allman, *Player-King and Adversary: Two Faces of Play in Shakespeare* (Baton Rouge: Louisiana State

University Press, 1980). For two quite different views of this scene's effects, see McNeir, "The Comic Scenes in *Richard II*," p. 821, and Warren J. MacIsaac, "The Three Cousins in *Richard II*," *Shakespeare Quarterly* 22 (1971): 144–45.

11. Dorothy C. Hockey, "A World of Rhetoric in *Richard II*," *Shakespeare Quarterly* 15 (1964): 186, notes that anaphora "is used by almost the complete *dramatis personae*."

12. McNeir, "The Comic Scenes in *Richard II*," p. 822.

13. Lawrence J. Ross, "Wingless Victory: Michaelangelo, Shakespeare, and the 'Old Man'," *Literary Monographs,* vol. 2, eds. Eric Rothstein and Richard N. Ringler (Madison: The University of Wisconsin Press, 1969), p. 27.

14. See Salingar, *Shakespeare and the Traditions of Comedy,* pp. 283ff.; and Peter Hyland, *Disguise and Role-Playing in Ben Jonson's Drama* (Salzburg: Salzburg Studies in English Literature, 1977), pp. 22–25.

15. *The Workes of Lvcius Annaevs Seneca, Both Morrall and Natural,* trans. Thomas Lodge (London: William Stansby, 1614), Epistle CXX, pp. 480–81.

16. See Mahood, *Shakespeare's Wordplay,* pp. 73–88; and Terence Hawkes, "The Word Against the Word: The Role of Language in *Richard II*," *Language and Style* 2 (1969): 318. McNeir, "The Comic Scenes in *Richard II*," p. 819, observes that "Aumerle's penitential gesture begins in earnest what becomes visually ludicrous through repetition, just as the word 'pardon' later becomes verbally comic through its iteration sixteen times by the Duchess, York, and Bolingbroke within the space of twenty-four lines."

17. See Peter Ure, Arden edition, *King Richard II* (London: Methuen & Co., 1966), p. 170, n. 15–17, for a summary of the second biblical text: camel="cable-rope," postern="city-gate," etc. The New Variorum edition's comments provide, as usual, resistances to Shakespeare's reiteration of the same "word against word" line in V.iii.130 and V.iv.13–14, e.g., "[Edmund] Chambers (ed. 1891): It is hard to see why Shakespeare should repeat a line in such a carefully written play"; and "[J. Dover] Wilson (ed. 1939): The repetition betokens careless haste on Shakespeare's part. He seems to have unconsciously transferred the phrase from V.iii[130], where he found it in the old play."

18. See Louis L. Martz, *The Poetry of Meditation: A Study in English Religious Literature of the Seventeenth Century* (New Haven: Yale University Press, 1954), for a discussion of the form of meditation commonly employed and the background of its use in the Renaissance. Joseph Hall,

The Arte of Divine Meditation (London: Imprinted by Humfrey Lownes, for Samuel Macham, and Matthew Cooke, 1605[?]/1606), defines the required "Circumstances of Meditation" in chapter 9 as "Secrecy, Silence, Rest: whereof the first excludeth company, the second noise, the third motion," p. 53. Richard's circumstances in Pomfret prison fit all three requisites.

19. Sister Mary Catharine O'Connor, *The Art of Dying Well: "The Development of the Ars Moriendi"* (New York: Columbia University Press, 1942); Nancy Lee Beaty, *The Craft of Dying: A Study in the Literary Tradition of the "Ars Moriendi" in England* (New Haven: Yale University Press, 1970).

20. *Henry V,* III.vii.30–35. For a fuller study of the many references, see the master's thesis by Charles Blake McClelland, "The Equestrian Element in Shakespeare's Plays and Poems," University of Tennessee at Knoxville, June 1961.

21. *Measure for Measure,* I.ii.152–60. The word "staggers" in Claudio's speech and in Richard II's words to Exton, who has struck him down, may contain a potential pun, in that "staggers" is a disease common to horses. See Thomas Blundeville, *The Order of Curing Horse Dyseases* (London: William Seres, 1566), chapter 21 [fol. 16, p. 1].

22. Sir Philip Sidney, *The Complete Works,* ed. Albert Feuillerat (Cambridge, England: Cambridge University Press, 1923), vol. 3, p. 3.

23. Ibid., p. 133.

24. Roger Ascham, *The Schoolmaster (1570),* ed. Lawrence V. Ryan (Ithaca: Cornell University Press, 1967), p. 33. See also Ruth Kelso, "The Doctrine of the English Gentleman in the Sixteenth Century," *University of Illinois Studies in Language and Literature* 14 (1929): 154–56.

25. Count Baldassare Castiglione, *The Book of the Courtier* [1561], trans. Sir Thomas Hoby, introduction by Walter Raleigh (London: David Nutt, 1900), p. 54.

26. The earliest equine monuments still extant are the four bronze horses that adorn the Basilica in the Piazza San Marco in Venice, which date from the first century A.D. These ancient horses and the Marcus Aurelius statue in Rome, from the second century A.D., are the classical models for the Italian Renaissance versions of equestrian monuments. According to art historian H. W. Janson, "The Equestrian Monument from Congrade della Scala to Peter the Great," in *Aspects of the Renaissance,* ed. Archibald R. Lewis (Austin: University of Texas Press, 1967), pp. 73–85, the equestrian monument's power to symbolize greatness did not begin until a millenium after the horse was introduced into Western

civilization, which was a thousand years before the birth of Christ. The Greeks apparently were the first to endow the rider with an aura of heroism, but their statues survive only in fragments from the sixth century B.C. The Romans established the equestrian monument as the privilege of the aristocrat in the later days of the Republic, but during the Empire the privilege of such representation, Janson says, "was restricted to the emperor alone, as the most monumental and awe-inspiring visible expression of his authority." The statue of the Marcus Aurelius is the only surviving specimen. The Middle Ages produced no monuments of their own, and the first bronze equestrian monument of the Italian Renaissance was destroyed in the eighteenth century, so the first major extant equestrian monument after the hiatus is Donatello's Gattemelata of 1448–1453. Donatello chose a heavier breed than the somewhat slight horse that Marcus Aurelius rides, which creates an impression that the rider not only dominates his mount by sheer physical force but also by intellectual superiority. Frederick Hartt, *History of Italian Renaissance Art* (New York: H. N. Abrams, 1969), p. 204, describes it: "The horse, with its swelling veins, open jaws, and flaring eyes and nostrils, seems an extension of this overpowering personality," a personality that holds all tensions, emotional and physical, in control while he views his troops in the vast space outside Saint Anthony's Basilica in Padua. The historical Richard II was much interested in horsemanship, and his request in 1395 for the ashes of an English condottiere who became a hero to the Florentines, Sir John Hawkwood, relieved the city fathers of erecting a proposed monument to their English champion. Instead, Paolo Uccello was commissioned to create a fresco after the proposed monument to Hawkwood, which still may be viewed on the wall of the Cathedral at Florence. Commissioned thirty years after the Gattamelata, Verrocchio's statue of Colleoni, a nobleman as well as a financially successful military leader, stands in the Campo Ss. Giovanni e Paolo in Venice. Leonardo da Vinci's colossal clay model of a horse, twenty-four feet tall, was exhibited in Milan in 1493 but was never cast in bronze. The clay model was later destroyed when the French invaded Milan, but Giorgio Vasari, *The Lives of the Painters, Sculptors and Architects,* ed. William Gaunt, trans. A. B. Hinds, vol. 2 (London: J. M. Dent & Sons, 1963), p. 162, records that "in truth, those who have seen Lionardo's large clay model aver that they never beheld anything finer or more superb." All these fifteenth-century equestrian figures are bound together by a similar emphasis on virtú, the prowess of the individual hero. According to Janson, p. 83, "From the mid-sixteenth century on, with the growth of the idea of absolute monarchy, the equestrian monument assumes a different flavor and a different purpose: in conscious imitation of Roman imperial practice, it becomes a public assertion of dynastic authority."

A century lapsed before the statue of Cosimo I by Giovanni Bologna was unveiled in 1595 (a date contemporaneous with Shakespeare's play *Richard II*). John Pope-Hennessy, *Italian High Renaissance and Baroque Sculpture,* Vol. 1 (London: Phaidon Press Ltd., 1963), pp. 103–4, observes that "the purpose of the statue was to immortalise the virtue and wisdom of the first of the Medici Grand-Dukes, and in its setting in the Piazza della Signoria [in Florence] it has a moral significance that is recognisably related to that of the statue on the Capitol [the Marcus Aurelius in Rome]." What effect the preparation of the statue and its unveiling would have had in England is difficult to assess, but it seems possible that renewed interest in the equestrian monument to commemorate dynastic power and its imitation of classical models would have filtered into the cultural ambience of Elizabethan England. In any case, the ideas that these sculptures demonstrate appear in Shakespeare's treatment of the horse in *Richard II:* the horse is perceived as beast, willful but governable; the rider as master of the potentially savage and uncontrollable in nature.

For further illustrations and discussion of equestrian sculpture, see Francis Haskell and Nicholas Penny, *Taste and the Antique: The Lure of Classical Sculpture 1500–1900* (New Haven: Yale University Press, 1981), pp. 136–256.

27. Nicholas Morgan, *The Perfection of Horse-manship* (London: Edward White, 1609), sig. B3. Stephen Booth has pointed out another Renaissance tribute to horses and horsemanship in George Chapman's lines from *Byron's Conspiracy,* II.ii.71–81, in T. M. Parrott's edition of *Chapman's Tragedies* (London: George Routledge & Sons, 1910), p. 173:

> And being consider'd in their site together,
> They do the best present the state of man
> In his first royalty ruling, and of beasts
> In their first loyalty serving (one commanding,
> And no way being mov'd; the other serving,
> And no way being compell'd) of all the sights
> That ever my eyes witness'd; and they make
> A doctrinal and witty hieroglyphic
> Of a blest kingdom: to express and teach

Kings to command as they could serve, and subjects
To serve as if they had power to command.

28. See Ernst H. Kantorowicz, *The King's Two Bodies* (Princeton, N.J.: Princeton University Press, 1957) for definition and discussion of the two bodies as a common concept in medieval political theology. Kantorowicz devotes chapter 2 to *Richard II*. See also Marie Axton, *The Queen's Two Bodies: Drama and the Elizabethan Succession* (London: Royal Historical Society, 1977), for an extension of Kantorowicz's discussion.

29. *1 Henry IV*, IV.i.104–10.

30. Richard's final words to Exton may be a consummation of the equestrian imagery in puns:

> That hand shall burn in never-quenching fire
> That *staggers* thus my person. Exton, thy fierce hand
> Hath with the king's blood stained the king's own land.
> *Mount, mount,* my soul! thy *seat* is up on high:
> Whilst my gross flesh sinks downward, here to die.
> (V.v.108–12; my italics)

Parker Tyler, "Phaethon: The Metaphysical Tension between the Ego and the Universe in English Poetry," *Accent* 16 (1956): 35, suggests also the recognition of the "mount-seat" pun. Allman, *Player-King and Adversary,* p. 52, observes also that "Richard's death, tragic in the sense of wasted possibility and squandered wisdom, is yet glorious and strange, unprecedented by the character of the king who was not himself."

31. See Philip C. McGuire, "Choreography and Language in *Richard II*," in *Shakespeare: The Theatrical Dimension,* eds. Philip C. McGuire and David A. Samuelson (New York: AMS Press, 1979), pp. 77–79, for his discussion of the metaphoric function of the many gage-throwings. McGuire notes, p. 78, that "theater audiences frequently laugh as the gages rain down during this scene, but far from being a problem for a director to overcome, such laughter, if it occurs, is an appropriate response to the futility, at this moment, of trying to clarify the past by means of ritualistic gestures."

32. Georges A. Bonnard, "The Actor in *Richard II*," *Shakespeare-Jahrbuch* 87/88 (1952): 90.

Chapter 6

1. Cf. Leo Salingar's remark in "The Design of *Twelfth Night*," *Shakespeare Quarterly* 9 (1958): 132: "The sub-plot action reproduces the main

action like a comic mirror-image, and the two of them are joined to form a single symmetrical pattern of errors in criss-cross."

2. Others such as Sir Toby and Fabian participate in the gulling of Malvolio. Fabian has a vengeful motive because, as he says to Sir Toby, Malvolio has at some previous time "brought me out o' favor with my lady about a bear-baiting here" (II.v.4–7), yet Fabian indicates that all was done in the spirit of "sportful malice" meant to "pluck on laughter than revenge" when their plot is revealed (V.i.355–56); and Sir Toby gives up on the entire plot after his painful battle with Sebastian. Only Feste persists in the "will" to have Malvolio acknowledge his, as well as time's, revenge.

3. Viola's Captain calls this power "chance" (I.ii.6, 8); Viola submits herself to "time" (I.ii.60; II.ii.39); Olivia and Sebastian refer to "fate" (I.v.296; II.i.4); Malvolio speaks of Jove's control (II.v.158, 164; III.iv.68–77); and the forged letter names "the stars," "the Fates," and "Fortune" (II.v.131–46). Olivia discovers that her will (to have her love for Cesario flourish) must be circumvented in order for her to achieve happiness. Inversely, Duke Orsino's intention to replace Olivia's brother in her "debt of love" becomes a literal reality, despite his intended romantic meaning, when he is about to become her brother-in-law at the play's end.

4. Notice the similarity between Feste's description of events and Iago's prediction as he encourages Roderigo to join him in his revenge against Othello: "There are many events in the womb of time which will be delivered" (I.iii.366). Iago implies that he is merely an agent bringing about time's inevitable retributions.

5. Rosalind Miles, *The Problem of "Measure for Measure,"* p. 163, finds Feste's disguise as Sir Topas "inescapably cruel." Thad Jenkins Logan, *"Twelfth Night:* The Limits of Festivity," *Studies in English Literature* 22 (1982): 223–38, sees the negativity of the subplot as informing the main plot rather than as balancing it or providing a parody of it, and that " 'what we will' is potentially dark and dangerous."

6. Maria indicates her "foreknowledge" of Malvolio's certain response (II.iii.137–40), and Malvolio's comments fulfill her prediction (II.v.110–12, 150–52).

7. Paul Mueschke and Jeannette Fleisher, "Jonsonian Elements in the Comic Underplot of *Twelfth Night,*" *PMLA* 48 (1933): 722–40, discuss Sir Andrew's similarity to Master Stephen in *Every Man in His Humour:* "Shakespeare's treatment of Andrew exemplifies to the fullest extent the Jonsonian conception and treatment of the gull and his relationship to his victimizer."

8. A sexual pun on the word "cut" is likely, as well as its meaning "a horse with a docked tail": see p. 54, n. 187, Arden edition, *Twelfth Night*, eds. J. M. Lothian and T. W. Craik (London: Methuen & Co., 1975). Malvolio too will not have Olivia in the end, so "cut" is appropriate in a denigrative way.

9. The editors of the Arden edition, p. 78, n. 74, call Sir Andrew's ability to understand French in III.i a "contrast" to I.iii.

10. Olivia has drawn a similar conclusion about herself in the opening lines of this scene: "I am as mad as he,/ If sad and merry madness equal be" (III.iv.13–14). Because Olivia concurs with Maria in classifying Malvolio's peculiar behavior as "madness," she inadvertently begets the subplotters' plan for imprisoning Malvolio. We have Rosalind's word for it in *As You Like It* that the typical treatment for lunatics in the sixteenth century was imprisonment:

> Love is merely a madness, and I tell you, deserves as well a dark house and a whip as madmen do; and the reason why they are not so punished and cured is that the lunacy is so ordinary that the whippers are in love too. (III.ii.376–80)

11. S. L. Bethell, *Shakespeare and the Popular Dramatic Tradition* (London: Staples Press, 1944, reprt. 1948), p. 34. Bethell attempts to defuse the Victorian misreading of Malvolio's plight as a tragic one while he calls attention to the breaking of illusion in Shakespeare's craft as a repeated technique.

12. Sir William Segar, *The Booke of Honor and Armes* (London: printed by Ihones, 1590); and Vincentio Saviolo, *His Practise* (1595), in *Three Elizabethan Fencing Manuals*, ed. James L. Jackson (New York: Scholars' Facsimiles & Reprints, 1972).

13. Saviolo, *His Practise*, Bk. 2, pp. 353–54.

14. Cf. Julian Markels, "Shakespeare's Confluence of Tragedy and Comedy: *Twelfth Night* and *King Lear*," in *Shakespeare 400*, ed. James G. McManaway (New York: Holt, Rinehart, and Winston, 1964), pp. 85–86, for a similar observation. Feste makes evident his assumption that Malvolio is "possessed" by associating carnal sexual interests with Malvolio's request that Sir Topas "go to my lady" (cf. Leslie Hotson, *The First Night of Twelfth Night* [New York: Macmillan, 1954], pp. 108–9). Feste replies: "Out, hyperbolical fiend! How vexest thou this man! Talkest thou nothing but of ladies?" (IV.ii.25–26). Obsessive interest in sexual lust seems to have been a kind of shorthand to indicate madness for

Renaissance dramatists: for examples, see Ophelia's mad songs in *Hamlet* (IV.v), Edgar's speech to King Lear as poor Tom o' Bedlam (III.iv), and the masque of madmen in *The Duchess of Malfi* (IV.ii).

15. Compare the opposite pulls between literal action and emblematic values in the Apothecary scene, *Romeo and Juliet,* discussed in chapter 4.

16. The problem of whether to sympathize with or to reject and ridicule Malvolio is an old one. Charles Lamb probably opened this Pandora's box when he praised Malvolio as what Lamb thought he should have been—"brave, honourable, accomplished": from "On Some of the Old Actors," *The London Magazine,* 1822, reprinted in *Shakespeare's Twelfth Night,* ed. Leonard F. Dean and James A. S. McPeek (Boston: Allyn and Bacon, 1965), p. 150. Many arguments have been advanced against Malvolio's "humanity" as realized in the play. Two of the more interesting are by Bethell, *Shakespeare and the Popular Dramatic Tradition,* pp. 77–78, and Barbara K. Lewalski, "Thematic Patterns in *Twelfth Night,*" *Shakespeare Studies* 1 (1965): 168–81.

17. Markels, "Shakespeare's Confluence of Tragedy and Comedy," p. 84, and Lewalski, "Thematic Patterns," discuss the regenerative potentials of madness. Both discussions are pertinent to the emblematic values presented in this scene.

18. Cf. Harold Jenkins, "Shakespeare's *Twelfth Night,*" in *Shakespeare: The Comedies,* ed. Kenneth Muir (Englewood Cliffs, N.J.: Prentice-Hall, 1965), p. 76.

19. Salingar discusses some of the other parodic functions of the subplot, "The Design of *Twelfth Night,*" pp. 119–39.

20. Joseph H. Summers makes a similar point, "The Masks of *Twelfth Night,*" *The University of Kansas City Review* 22 (1955): 31. In contrast, the song becomes an appropriate description of the play's world in *King Lear* (III.ii.64–77).

21. I disagree with John A. Hart's opinion that Feste's song "is not hard to fathom": "Foolery Shines Everywhere: The Fool's Function in the Romantic Comedies," *Starre of Poets,* Carnegie Series in English 10 (Pittsburg: Carnegie Institute of Technology, 1966), p. 47. Hart's own reading of the song's "general meaning" differs in several major points from other readings. One of the most generally held readings is by John Weiss, *Wit, Humour, and Shakespeare* (Boston, 1876), p. 204. It is impossible to list every variant, but worth noting by contrast is Leslie Hotson, *The First Night of Twelfth Night,* pp. 168–71, who centers his discussion of the song on the sexual innuendoes that proceed from reading "thing" as male genitalia.

22. Hotson, ibid., p. 171, n. 2, points out that this line "recalls the Elizabethan euphemism for coition, 'To dance The Beginning of the World!' " Without discounting that allusion, I suggest that a much more general pattern of action is implied.

Chapter 7

1. T. S. Eliot, *The Complete Poems and Plays 1909–1950* (New York: Harcourt, Brace and Company, 1960), p. 7.

2. For a discussion of this aspect of Polonius's characterization, see Lily Bess Campbell, "Polonius: The Tyrant's Ears," in *Joseph Quincy Adams Memorial Studies,* eds. James G. McManaway, et al. (Washington, D. C.: The Folger Shakespeare Library, 1948), pp. 295–313.

3. See Niccolò Machiavelli, *The Prince,* trans. Edward Dacres, in *Three Renaissance Classics* (New York: Charles Scribner's Sons, 1953). The attitude is pervasive, but see especially chapters 18, "In What Manner Princes Ought to Keep Their Words," and 23, "That Flatterers Are to Bee Avoyded." Polonius's speech has been the source of much critical debate, for which see: Josephine W. Bennett, "Characterization in Polonius' Advice to Laertes," *Shakespeare Quarterly* 4 (1953): 3–9; R. H. Bowers, "Polonius: Another Postscript," *Shakespeare Quarterly* 4 (1953): 362–64; Elkin C. Wilson, "Polonius in the Round," *Shakespeare Quarterly* 9 (1958): 83–85; O. B. Davis, "A Note on the Function of Polonius' Advice," *Shakespeare Quarterly* 9 (1958): 85–86; Doris V. Falk, "Proverbs and the Polonius Destiny," *Shakespeare Quarterly* 18 (1967): 23–36.

4. Francis Fergusson, " 'Hamlet, Prince of Denmark': The Analogy of Action," in *The Idea of a Theater* (Princeton, N.J.: Princeton University Press, 1949), pp. 108–9, discusses briefly the "alternation of the Polonius story and the Hamlet story in Acts I and II." He, however, considers the sequence to end with Reynaldo's departure and Ophelia's entrance in II.i.

5. This is another instance of Shakespeare's frequent use of images from equestrian practice as metaphor for rhetoric. Polonius does, of course, run his horse—the word "tender"—too hard and breaks its wind.

6. On the variation of Hamlet's "roles," see Peter Ure's excellent essay, "Character and Role from *Richard III* to *Hamlet,*" *Stratford-Upon-Avon Studies 5* (London, 1963), pp. 9–28. For the historical tradition of Vice's foolery in Hamlet's assumption of the "antic disposition," see Sidney Thomas, *The Antic Hamlet and Richard III* (New York: King's Crown Press, 1943).

7. The shakiness of this "proof" becomes evident if we step beyond

the play's dictates to consider the possibility (not the probability) that Claudius, even though he were innocent of murder, might for other reasons (such as concern for Gertrude) react with shock to the play. William A. Ringler, Jr., "Hamlet's Defence of the Players," in *Essays on Shakespeare and Elizabethan Drama in Honor of Hardin Craig*, ed. Richard Hosley (Columbia, Mo.: University of Missouri Press, 1962), p. 211, argues that "Shakespeare knew that he would have to work upon the psychology of his audience in a way that would lead them to expect, and render them willing to accept, Claudius's reaction." Dieter Mehl, *The Elizabethan Dumb Show* (London: Methuen & Co., 1965), p. 114, points out that "it seems certain that for most Elizabethans the stage was a kind of moral institution and the drama was expected to produce visible results." See also, Anne Righter, *Shakespeare and the Idea of the Play* (London: Chatto & Windus, 1964), p. 162. Despite the possibility that the Elizabethan audience viewed the "play" as a moral barometer, Hamlet's "proof" is an assumption rather than a fact.

8. Hamlet interprets the Ghost's first command to "revenge his foul and most unnatural murder" to mean "murder Claudius." But as Fredson Bowers points out, "*Revenge* need not be equated exactly with *blood-revenge*. . . . That Hamlet cannot see how else to take revenge on Claudius, given the secrecy of the murder, is another matter": "Hamlet's Fifth Soliloquy, 3.2.406–17," in *Essays on Shakespeare and Elizabethan Drama in Honor of Hardin Craig*, p. 217, n. 3. The possible discrepancy between the Ghost's intent and Hamlet's interpretation would not change my point about the "limitations of a man-made code of vengeance," but it would provide another instance in which Hamlet's interpretation of circumstances may not be as accurate as he thinks.

9. Kittredge makes a similar comment in his note on the caution to the First Player. He says that this is "another indication of Hamlet's courtesy. He himself can poke fun at Polonius, for his mockery will pass as madness and is therefore not an insult. But it would be quite another thing for the players to make sport of the old nobleman, and Hamlet is alive to the temptation they might feel to follow his own example, especially since they may not have heard of his supposed madness": *The Tragedy of Hamlet, Prince of Denmark*, ed. George Lyman Kittredge, revised by Irving Ribner (Waltham, Mass.: Blaisdell Publishing Company, 1967), n. 529–30, II.ii.

10. See, for example, J. Dover Wilson, *What Happens in Hamlet* (Cambridge, Eng.: Cambridge University Press, 1962), p. 180; and Anne Righter, *Shakespeare and the Idea of the Play*, p. 163.

11. John Payne Collier, *Memoirs of the Principal Actors in the Plays of Shakespeare* (London: Printed for the Shakespeare Society, 1846), pp. 52–55, quotes in full "A Funeral Elegy on the Death of the Famous Actor Richard Burbadge," which enumerates Burbadge's various roles. Using the elegy as principal evidence, Collier infers, pp. 21, 24, that the actor played both Brutus and Hamlet. T. W. Baldwin, *The Organization and Personnel of the Shakespearean Company* (Princeton, N.J.: Princeton University Press, 1927), charts II and III, between pp. 228–29, lists Richard Burbadge as Brutus and John Heminges as Caesar in the winter 1599 production of *Julius Caesar,* and lists Burbadge as Hamlet and Heminges as Polonius in the summer 1603 production of *Hamlet.* E. A. J. Honigmann, "The Date of *Hamlet,*" *Shakespeare Survey* 9 (1956): 29–30, cites the same passage from *Hamlet* to support his 1601 dating of that play and says: "The two actors who played the original Hamlet and Polonius—almost certainly Burbage and Heminges—must have taken Brutus and Caesar in *Julius Caesar.*"

12. Ernst H. Kantorowicz, *The King's Two Bodies* (Princeton, N.J.: Princeton University Press, 1957), pp. 13 and 7.

13. Jerah Johnson, "The Concept of the 'King's Two Bodies' in *Hamlet,*" *Shakespeare Quarterly* 18 (1967): 430–34, develops this idea with a different interpretation.

14. The reduction of all ranks to the same common denominator in the proverbial linkage between the beggar and the king is obviously in Hamlet's mind when he speaks here and also when he speaks about death with the Gravedigger and Horatio in V.i. See further discussion of the "beggar and the king" in chapter 5, above.

15. See similar observations in O. B. Hardison, Jr., "The Dramatic Triad in *Hamlet,*" *Studies in Philology* 57 (1960): 144–64; and in Mark Rose, "*Hamlet* and the Shape of Revenge," *English Literary Renaissance* 1 (1971): 132–43.

Chapter 8

1. See my discussion of Autolycus's parodic role in *Shakespeare's Tragicomic Vision* (Baton Rouge: Louisiana State University Press, 1972), pp. 117–32; and in "Cloten, Autolycus, and Caliban: Bearers of Parodic Burdens," in *Shakespeare's Romances Reconsidered,* eds. Carol McGinnis Kay and Henry E. Jacobs (Lincoln: University of Nebraska Press, 1978), pp. 98–101.

Notes to Pages 163–78

2. See Giambattista Guarini, *Il compendio della poesia tragicomica*, trans. Allan H. Gilbert, in *Literary Criticism: Plato to Dryden* (Detroit: Wayne State University Press, 1962), pp. 505–33; and John Fletcher's Preface to the First Quarto of *The Faithful Shepherdess* in *The Works of Beaumont and Fletcher*, ed. Alexander Dyce, vol. 2 (London, 1843), p. 17.

3. Cf. Harry Zuger, "Shakespeare's Posthumus and the Wager: From Delusion to Enlightenment," *Shakespeare-Jahrbuch* 112 (Weimar, 1976): 138: "It is the identity Cloten assumes when he dons Posthumus' clothing and which could be said to die with Cloten because when Posthumus later reappears he is a changed man."

4. *Samuel Johnson on Shakespeare*, ed. W. K. Wimsatt, Jr. (New York: Hill and Wang, 1960), p. 108.

5. See my discussion of the Orpheus parody in *Shakespeare's Tragicomic Vision*, pp. 78–80. Joan Carr, "*Cymbeline* and the Validity of Myth," *Studies in Philology* 75 (1978): 316–30, recognizes the parallel between Cloten's and Orpheus's beheading, but applies a psychoanalytical-folkloristic approach to reach quite different conclusions.

6. Gretchen Ludke Finney, *Musical Backgrounds for English Literature: 1580–1650* (New Brunswick, N.J.: Rutgers University Press, 1961), pp. 259–60, n. 55, comments that Cloten's attempt to win Imogen by music combines "(with bawdy implications) the idea referred to by Buoni, that lovers 'delight in morning Musicke,' with Ficino's suggestion of music's power to penetrate." For further discussion of music's symbolic powers, see Finney's chapters 1, 2, and 4; Lawrence J. Ross, "Shakespeare's 'Dull Clown' and Symbolic Music," *Shakespeare Quarterly* 17 (1966): 107–28; and S. K. Heninger, Jr., *Touches of Sweet Harmony: Pythagorean Cosmology and Renaissance Poetics* (San Marino, Ca.: Huntington Library, 1974).

7. The spoken dirge has occupied many critical minds. See Fernand Corin, "A Note on the Dirge in *Cymbeline*," *English Studies* 40 (1959): 173–79. For a general critical review, see Peter J. Seng, *The Vocal Songs in the Plays of Shakespeare: A Critical History* (Cambridge, Mass.: Harvard University Press, 1967), pp. 219–25.

8. The bawdiness of Cloten's speech is aggressively insistent. Colman, *The Dramatic Use of Bawdy in Shakespeare*, p. 137, says of these lines: "The peculiar vileness of Cloten's *double entendres* comes from their being delivered as monologues rather than in the course of any conversational cut and thrust. Shared between two or more speakers his innuendos would pass as harmless chatter. Flowing uninterruptedly from the black

229

holes of a single mind, they acquire a quality of sniggering gaucheness."
For the bawdy quibbles on "penetrate," "fingering," "try with tongue,"
and "unpaved eunuch," see Colman's glossary.

9. Warren D. Smith, "Cloten with Caius Lucius," *Studies in Philology*
49 (1952): 191, makes a similar remark and adds: "All of the speeches of
Cloten to Caius Lucius . . . fall far below the ideal of modesty in the
courtier set by Renaissance authorities whose conviction on the subject
Shakespeare normally seems to have shared."

10. It is difficult to ignore the echoes of Lady Macbeth's dying distur-
bance, also announced by the doctor at the moment of Macbeth's military crisis—a kind of intra-canon parody that seems particularly preva-
lent in *Cymbeline*.

11. See my fuller discussion of the various denouements in the scene in
Shakespeare's Tragicomic Vision, pp. 100–3. As Guarini points out, the
comic order is of primary importance at the end of a tragicomedy.

12. For a fine discussion of Falstaff's parodic function, see John Shaw,
"The Staging of Parody and Parallels in '1 Henry IV'," *Shakespeare Survey*
20 (1967): 61–73.

13. Harley Granville-Barker, *Prefaces to Shakespeare,* vol. 2, p. 140, calls
Cloten a "civilized Caliban." He finds Caliban to be "a more picturesque
and far more pardonable monster."

14. Allan H. Gilbert makes a similar point in *"The Tempest:* Parallelism
in Characters and Situations," *Journal of English and Germanic Philology*
14 (1915): 73.

15. William Rockett, "Labor and Virtue in *The Tempest,*" *Shakespeare
Quarterly* 24 (1973): 81–83, draws an interesting contrast between Ferdinand's "ability to serve for the sake of service itself" and "Ariel's service
[which] is payment for his freedom" and "Caliban [who] serves Prospero with a view to avoiding punishment." Rockett's argument employs
as authorities classical treatises on the nature of happiness, Christian
exegetes, and Shakespeare's contemporaries to support the idea that labor is not only valuable but virtuous.

16. For an elaboration of these ideas, see my *Shakespeare's Tragicomic
Vision,* pp. 162–64.

17. Reuben A. Brower, "The Mirror of Analogy: 'The Tempest'," in
The Fields of Light (New York: Oxford University Press, 1951), pp. 95–96,
points out that with the word "delicate" Stephano "is parodying Prospero when he rebukes Ariel as 'a spirit too delicate/ To act her [Syco-
rax's] earthy and abhorr'd commands' and when he says,

delicate Ariel,
      I'll set thee free for this!"

Robert Ralston Cawley, "Shakspere's Use of the Voyagers in *The Tempest*," *Publications of the Modern Language Association* 41 (1926), 688–726, makes interesting correlations between verbal echoes and attitudes expressed in the play and contemporary travel literature. See especially pp. 720–21 about the common practice of carrying Indians from the New World back to London in order to display them for money.

18. See Joseph H. Summers, "The Anger of Prospero," *Michigan Quarterly Review* 12 (1973): 116–35.

19. Raymond A. Urban's intriguing note, "Why Caliban Worships the Man in the Moon," *Shakespeare Quarterly* 27 (1976): 203–5, suggests that Shakespeare had in mind for the relationship of Caliban and Stephano and Trinculo the "burlesque religion [of] vagabond clerics of medieval Europe" transferred into sixteenth-century England as a "comic Bacchanalian sect that took the man in the moon as its god and the liquor bottle as its Bible."

20. I am tempted to use Joseph Summer's phrase, "ventriloquist manipulation of the trio"—"The Anger of Prospero," p. 125—to describe Ariel's action in this scene, but that is not what Ariel is about, literally speaking. The audience can see Ariel, but the others cannot, so Ariel moves about the stage, placing his voice where it seems to come from one of the visible characters. Thus no apparently silent projection of voice occurs for the audience, but a visible stage farce is produced.

21. Seng, *Vocal Songs,* p. 264. Lawrence J. Ross, in an unpublished lecture delivered in April 1964, " 'A Most Majestic Vision': A Lecture on Shakespeare and *The Tempest*," discussed these scenes as analogous action that is used for analysis in a comic key. In a discussion more complex than I can indicate in a note, he demonstrated that the comic analogue enacts the essential absurdity of the kind of moral choice made by all of the usurpers in the play.

Index

Holland, Norman N., 198 n. 3, 199 n. 19

Holmer, Joan Ozark, 203 n. 13

Honigmann, E. A. J., 228 n. 11

Hoppe, Harry R., 73, 206 n. 11, 211 n. 42

Horace, 5

Horse imagery: in *Richard II*, 116–17, 127–31, 134, 219 nn. 20–21, 219–21 n. 26; in *Macbeth*, 204 n. 18; in *Hamlet*, 226 n. 5

Hosley, Richard, 206–7 n. 11, 207 n. 16, 210 n. 34

Householder, Fred W., Jr., 196 n. 9

Hotson, Leslie, 225 n. 21, 226 n. 22

Houser, David J., 197 n. 15

Hulme, Hilda, 35, 38–39, 45, 201 n. 30, 202 n. 38, 203 n. 7, 204 n. 18

Humoral psychology, 75, 97–104, 187

Hunter, G. K., 91, 196 n. 10, 206 n. 7, 212 n. 51

Hyland, Peter, 218 n. 14

Icons: narrative in *Richard II*, 116; descriptive in *Henry V*, 130; in imagery, 206 n. 8

Imitation, 5, 6, 18, 25, 29, 31, 37, 54, 58, 77, 88, 134, 196 n. 10

Incremental repetition, 74, 152

Inversion, 20, 31, 37, 47, 63, 104

Irony, 14, 28, 30, 38, 45, 48, 51, 58, 64, 76, 77, 79, 80, 83, 90, 91, 104, 120, 121, 122, 132, 159, 162, 168, 192, 202 n. 34, 215 n. 75

Irving, Henry, 215–16 n. 1

Jackson, James L., 210 nn. 38, 41

James I, 82, 205 n. 27

Jansen, William Hugh, 211–12 n. 49

Janson, H. W., 219–21 n. 26

Jenkins, Harold, 225 n. 18

Jew of Malta, The, 8, 197 nn. 13, 17

Johnson, Jerah, 228 n. 13

Johnson, Samuel, 5, 175, 196 n. 8, 229 n. 4

Jones, Emrys, 200 n. 24, 200–201 n. 26, 206 n. 7

Jonson, Ben: *Volpone*, 192, 196 n. 10; *Every Man in His Humour*, 200–201 n. 26, 223 n. 7

Jorgensen, Paul, 61, 205 nn. 25, 29

Joseph, Sister Miriam, 22, 199 n. 16, 201 n. 27

Kantorowicz, Ernst H., 166, 222 n. 28, 228 n. 12

Kelly, Michael F., 216 n. 2

Kelso, Ruth, 211 n. 41, 219 n. 24

Kemp, Will, 84, 214 n. 71

Kermode, Frank, 204 n. 19

Kernan, Alvin B., 196 n. 11

Kittredge, George Lyman, 227 n. 9

Klibansky, Raymond: *Saturn and Melancholy*, 97, 98, 103, 213 nn. 62, 67

Knight, G. Wilson, 69, 205 nn. 1, 3

Koller, Katherine, 206 n. 10

Kreyssig, F., 17, 197 n. 2, 199 n. 17

Lamb, Charles, 225 n. 16

Lascelles, Mary, 201–202 n. 32

Library of Congress Cataloging in Publication Data

Hartwig, Joan.
Shakespeare's analogical scene.

Includes bibliographical references and index.
1. Shakespeare, William, 1564–1616—Technique.
2. Parody. 3. Shakespeare, William, 1564–1616—Humor,
satire, etc. 4. Analogy in literature. I. Title.
PR2997.P37H3   1984   822.3'3   83-6845
ISBN 0-8032-2324-2